The Fifth Bullet

A M MANTHORPE

Copyright © 2019 A M Manthorpe
All rights reserved.
ISBN-13: 978-0-9925318-5-0

ACKNOWLEDGMENTS

My most heartfelt thanks to my fellow Critters, Diane Hester, Kathy Blacker and Mary Gudzenovs, the three other members of my critiquing group. Without their encouragement I probably would have given up writing years ago. They have helped me both with my writing and with my plots.

To Diane in particular I owe a great debt, for her determination and enthusiasm make the glue that has kept us together for nearly twenty years.

Thanks also to all members of Eyre Writers for their continued support, and in particular to those who, many years ago, shared their writing with me and enticed me out of the closet: Margaret Vivian, Aileen Pluker, and Dionie McNair.

1

Two years after she left — left the farm, left her husband — Agatha Benson returned. She alighted from the Melbourne Express at the Kularook railway station in the middle of one hot January night in 1931 with a large suitcase in one hand and a baby, wrapped in a white knitted shawl, cradled in her other arm.

Mounted Constable William Brown, propped half asleep against the shelter-shed in the middle of the platform, had woken only when the Pacific engine, clanking like St George and breathing fire like the dragon, rolled past him. The couplings creaked. The carriages came to a smooth stop. Away to his left the engine hissed steam into the profound country silence. He heaved his shoulders away from the corrugated-iron wall and opened his eyes.

In the light from the carriage windows he caught sight of Agatha Benson. Intrigued, he would have stopped to see who was meeting her but a small man in a navy uniform was leaning from the door of the next carriage making hurry-up gestures.

Duty first. MC Brown, more commonly known as Bowler, was there to take an obstreperous passenger off the train. According to the message from further up the line the man was a heavyweight and fighting drunk, and as the train thundered south he had been holding several sleeping-car attendants at bay with a lump of wood wrenched from the arm of a seat.

As he boarded the train Bowler nearly tripped over another uniformed figure huddled on the floor, who was rocking himself and nursing a wrist dented to an odd shape. He stepped over the man.

The senior guard who had beckoned waved a hand. 'He's all yours.'

In the central aisle of the second class carriage, between the two rows of double seats, a hulking figure in shabby clothes filled most of the space. Half crouching, his head thrust forward on a thick bull neck, he was snarling obscenities and sweeping his improvised waddy in wild scything swings at two more guards, who kept backing and advancing in front of him. The carriage was otherwise empty.

'What set him off?'

'We threatened to put him off the train at Branden Corner and he quietened down for a bit. But he's got a bottle of whisky in his coat and he's been getting worse, abusing the other passengers, offending the women, offering to fight anyone who tried to shut him up. Then he went berserk when we tried to nick his bottle.'

'Anyway, you've got the other passengers out of the way. Makes it easier.'

'They got themselves, as soon as we had him bailed up.'

Bowler edged past the guard. 'G'day, sport. What's your problem?'

'Fight the lotta you,' the drunk yelled. He swiped his waddy across and back. 'Thieving bastards!'

Bowler was younger, fitter, and sober; he judged his moment. He blocked, forearm to forearm, a blow aimed at his head. Then he moved inside the man's reach, clamped a hand on his wrist, and while he was still off balance yanked him round until he could shove the arm up his back. The man doubled over, roaring.

The guards looked almost as surprised as the drunk at the speed of events. Bowler smiled on them complacently, exchanged names and details with the senior guard, and told his prisoner to shut up and behave himself.

'I don't play Queensberry rules either,' he said with cheerful menace. He glanced down at the injured man. 'Better take him on to Edgerton,' he advised the others. 'No doctor here.'

Duty done, he pushed his prisoner onto the platform, grabbed the other wrist, and clicked on handcuffs. The man reeled, seeming all at once to be much more drunken. Bowler gripped his arm and held him upright.

Agatha Benson, as though to make herself more easily seen, now stood in the lighted circle under the hurricane lantern that hung inside the shelter shed.

'Stay there,' Bowler told his prisoner, and turned to speak to her.

The drunk took a few unsteady steps in the other direction. Bowler stuck out his foot and watched with detachment as the man crashed forward and lay winded on the gravel.

'Told you,' he said. He walked back to Mrs Benson.

He couldn't imagine what extraordinary turn in her fortunes had brought her back. After her scandalous departure with Monty Whatsit nobody in Kularook had expected to see her again. Was she actually returning to her lawful husband?

But Bowler always had a soft spot for long-legged independent girls — after all, he'd married one — so he raised his hand to tip his hat, remembered he was bareheaded, and smiled instead. 'Mrs Benson? Is someone meeting you?'

She turned from watching the drunk's unavailing efforts to sit up and studied Bowler in the uncertain light from the lantern. 'Mr Brown, is it?'

'I haven't seen Lew anywhere about tonight,' he said.

The carriages began to move past them; the engine huffs gathered speed and dwindled into the south.

'He was supposed to meet the day train, but I missed it.' She sounded angry.

He wasn't certain whether her anger was against herself or her husband, to whom, it seemed, she was returning. Did she ask Lew or did Lew ask her?

Bowler took a sardonic interest in the excesses of those he referred to as his 'parishioners', and so was well aware of the stir this would cause among the district's numerous wowsers. Scandalised when she left, they wouldn't forgive her now, poor girl. That baby was none of Lew's getting.

All the same, he counted himself on her side. 'What are you going to do now?' he said.

She glanced into the shelter shed. 'Wait until daylight, I suppose, and then find someone to take me out to the farm.' She smiled, a quick softening of her taut, tired face. 'Don't worry, we'll be all right. It's a warm night.'

'You can't do that. I'll take you to the pub, wake Trotter Musgrave, get him to find you a bed. My car's just over there.'

'Sorry. I have no money.'

'Dammit, Lew can pay. Think of your baby.' Though if the child wasn't Lew's he might not be too complaisant about money spent on its welfare: he had a reputation as a mean bugger. Anyway, even if he didn't pay it wouldn't make any difference to the Musgraves, who would take her in for nothing if Bowler asked them. Em Musgrave must be the softest touch this side of the Dog Fence.

Agatha turned her face and rubbed her cheek against the baby's head; then she shrugged. 'All right. He won't like it but he can't kill me, after all.'

Bowler lifted the suitcase, using his other hand to haul his drunk to his feet. 'Sorry about this,' he said to Agatha. 'He has to come too. But he's harmless. Aren't you, sport?'

The man was hunched over, snivelling quietly, and made no answer; Bowler pushed him into the back seat of his Chrysler tourer. When he trod on the self-starter the stationmaster's dog at the nearest railway cottage started a frenzied barking, and set off most of the other dogs in the town.

The dogs had fallen quiet and silence blanketed the sleeping town when Bowler put his thumb on the night bell and heard a tinny ring somewhere deep inside the pub. He opened the never-locked front door. The pitch-dark hall smelled of old carpets and cigarette smoke, with a yeasty overlay of beer. A glow appeared in a passage to the left.

Not Trotter Musgrave but his wife Em trudged into view, a tall thin woman carrying a lighted candle and yawning to crack her jaws. Her feet were bare but otherwise she was fully dressed. Her iron-grey curls stuck up like a cocky's crest.

Bowler closed the door behind Agatha. 'Hullo, Em. Trotter poling on you, is he?'

She lifted her candle to see them better. 'Bowler? What the devil do you want at this time of night? And keep your damn voice down. Customers are sleeping.'

'Sorry. Em, can you rustle up a bed for Mrs Benson?'

'Come down to the kitchen.'

They followed her candle down a passage towards the back of the building. Shadows swirled in the big kitchen, still overheated from a day's cooking although the fire in the stove was out. A ticking clock on the mantelpiece underlined the silence.

Em turned. 'I was on my way to bed — a heavy night,' she said, and yawned again. 'I've been at Thompsons', Jeannette had her baby. Don't know why bloody babies can't keep office hours.'

Bowler said, 'Lew was expecting Mrs Benson on the day train, but she missed it and it seems he's gone home. She needs somewhere to sleep.'

'Yes of course, Mrs Benson,' Em said, as though she'd been trying to remember. 'Lew and his brother were in the bar around lunchtime. Looked a bit sour.' She studied the young woman with open curiosity.

'They would be,' Agatha said.

She stood parade-ground straight, both arms round her sleeping baby as though to protect it from their gaze. She must know Em's reputation as one of Kularook's most dedicated gossips. Bowler saw her strained expression, her attempted mask of indifference, and admired her fortitude.

Em smiled with a warmth that lifted Bowler's spirits too. 'Welcome back. There's a room over here,' she said, and crossed the passage to open a door on the other side.

'Thank you, Mrs Musgrave.' Agatha sounded stiff rather than grateful, as though she resented having to accept favours. 'I wouldn't be here if I had anywhere else to go.'

Bowler wondered whether she meant anywhere else that would give her a bed for the night, or anywhere else but back in Kularook, waiting for her lawful husband.

When Em came back she shoved aside the plates stacked ready for breakfast to make room on the table for the candle, then took a small spirit stove from a cupboard and put on a kettle. The smell of burning meths flooded over the odours of cooked mutton and wood ashes.

Bowler stood for a moment where the candle created a small island of light in the shadowed room, watching her make tea. 'No, none for me,' he said. 'Em, if Lew doesn't turn up tell Mrs Benson I'll run her out after breakfast. Thanks for taking her in.'

'What were you doing, meeting the express in the middle of the night?'

'Collecting a drunk. He's sleeping it off in the lockup.'

'Blasted drunks,' Em said, with the tolerance of a woman who earned part of her income selling intoxicating liquors. She glanced at the open door and lowered her voice. 'Do you suppose Lew knows about the baby? It can't be his.'

'No idea.'

'She looks at the end of her tether, poor girl.' When Bowler merely grunted she continued, 'She's pretty brave to come back.'

'Yes.'

'I was never surprised that she left, mind you. Those Bensons are a strange lot. I can't imagine why she married Lew in the first place.'

Bowler wasn't about to speculate on the workings of the female heart. Nor was he going to stand around gossiping with Em Musgrave in the middle of the night.

'See you tomorrow,' he said. He let himself out the back door and crossed the side street to his house.

2

The sun had risen while Bowler was feeding the two horses he kept in the police station paddocks. When he'd been transferred from the city he'd bought a pair of strong young horses, the same type as the Walers who had carried him and his fellow light-horsemen so faithfully through the desert campaign; they were half-brothers, both bay, both a little over fifteen hands. His wife Joan's Isma was better-mannered and more affectionate. Imshy, hard-mouthed and wilful, he had kept for himself.

Magpies raised their wild song in the trees in the railway yards. A hot day coming, probably over the century again. He pushed Isma's nose aside, slapped Imshy on his muscular rump, and ducked through the five-wire fence. He'd better check that his prisoner hadn't died in the night, although he didn't anticipate such a happy outcome. His prisoner, who rated a very poor second to his horses, would be far less nuisance to him as a corpse.

The lock-up was a square corrugated-iron box, rather like an overgrown dunny, in the middle of his back fence between the real dunny and the iron shed that housed his car. He unbolted the door, checked on his bleary-eyed prisoner, and offered a breakfast choice of eggs or cereal. The man, lying groaning on the bunk, wanted neither.

Bowler slapped the door shut. He was impatient to get rid of the man. He'd have to ring around for a local JP who could sit in judgement sometime that day. With luck, once fined the ex-drunk could be booted out — but he wasn't optimistic. The Railways would probably want their pound of flesh for the damage the man had done, which would take more time, more organising, and more paperwork. Under his breath he damned the lot of them.

An enamel bowl of scummy water stood on a wooden kerosene case beside his back door. Bowler stirred this with one finger, then went along the veranda and rapped with his knuckles down the ridged side of the rainwater tank at the end. The level was uncomfortably low for this time of midsummer. He swore, and went to wash his hands one more time in the stale water.

When he finished his telephoning he walked down the passage to the small kitchen, heated to tropic intensity by a brisk fire in the wood stove, where his wife was serving breakfast to their two children — Tom, aged twelve, and Rose, nine. Joan Brown was a tall, fair woman in her early thirties. She put a plate of bacon and eggs in front of Bowler as soon as he sat down.

'Eat up,' she said. 'You wouldn't want to keep Mrs Benson waiting.' Her precise diction, with its English upper-class vowels, made her words sound condescending.

Bowler glanced at her. Accustomed to her accent, he'd heard not condescension but sarcasm. When he'd been telling her of his adventures in the night had he sounded too enthusiastic about his promise to drive the runaway wife home? Too sympathetic towards her?

He said, 'She looked exhausted, poor woman, about a hundred and ten. She's aged.'

Joan raised an eyebrow, probably to show that she saw through this attempt to reassure her. She said, 'I remember Agatha Benson. She's the brainy one with a medical degree.'

Perhaps he was supposed to feel abashed, him with his lesser learning. Why was she having a go at him this morning? 'I've heard that yarn and it's a bit of a myth they reckon. Probably she went nursing, something like that.'

His wife shook her head. 'No myth.'

'No? How do you know?'

'John Shapcott told me.'

'Did he by God.' In spite of himself, Bowler was impressed. Shapcott was the doctor at Edgerton forty miles away, the only one for many more miles than that, and therefore the GP for Kularook whether he liked it or not; and if anyone knew the truth about a fellow medico, he would.

Mentally Bowler reassessed his view of the erring Mrs Benson, and his wife saw him doing it. To his profound irritation, she smiled.

The children, pleased to find their parents preoccupied, had been shovelling in their breakfasts at a speed normally not permitted. Now they folded their hands, sat back and gabbled in unison, 'Please may we leave the table.'

Joan nodded. 'Yes, run along,' she said, and they disappeared down the passage. The wire door banged and their voices receded.

Bowler wouldn't hurry. He finished his eggs, took another slice of toast, and pushed his cup across for more tea.

Then, hoping to appease his wife, he asked, 'Did you get any good shots yesterday?'

'Only of a couple of magpies.' Joan's tone suggested she was surprised he had bothered to ask.

'Any good?'

'I haven't developed the film yet.'

Bowler gave up. 'I'll be back by lunchtime. Got a couple of JPs lined up for one thirty to decide about the joker in the lockup.' He dragged out his handkerchief to mop his sweating neck and noticed his wife's flushed face, the sheen of perspiration on her forehead. 'Let the fire go out,' he said. 'We'll have a cold tea.' When she appeared about to protest he added impatiently, 'Open a tin of camp pie or something. It won't kill us for once.'

He got up and stretched. Then he grinned like an urchin, walked round the table and pulled his wife from her chair into his arms.

The kiss went on and on. She melted against him until finally he stepped back, his hands on her shoulders, and said gruffly, 'Steady on! I've got work to do.'

'So have I,' she muttered. 'Damn you, Bill.'

He smiled, dabbed another quick kiss on her mouth, and walked whistling up the passage to his office at the front of the house.

3

Bowler drove his car round to the pub's front door. The northerly wind was lifting puffs of dust from the white metalled road; the street elms rattled their branches overhead. Apart from two cars parked outside the general store further along, the street was empty.

He waved to the Musgraves' two teenage daughters, home from boarding-school for the summer holidays, who were pegging bedsheets to a clothesline in the paddock next door.

Agatha Benson must have heard his car. She came across the pub's front veranda tilted sideways by the weight of her suitcase in one hand; the other supported her baby, clinging to her neck like a little koala.

Bowler leapt to take the case from her.

In daylight he could see more clearly the changes in her since she left. She had always been a slender girl but now she looked mere bone and sinew, far too thin for a woman still under thirty. Though she carried herself as she always had: her head with its coronet of dark plaits erect, her shoulders squared. And gauntness could not change the bones shaping her face. She was still a good-looking young woman.

The same could not be said for her clothes. Her print dress was faded and fraying at the collar, and couldn't have been anything to write home about when it was new; and her shoes, tan leather with a single strap, plain as a child's school shoes, had been patched several times by an inexpert bootmaker.

'It's very kind of you to drive us, Mr Brown,' Agatha said. 'Because I can't pay you, you know.'

'Why on earth should you? I'm not a ruddy taxi.' Bowler heaved her case onto the back seat and opened the front door for her.

She made a savage grimace intended for a smile. 'Just so there's no mistake. I —'

The line of sheets blew out in a sudden gust; one cracked like a stockwhip, startling a horse and rider rounding the corner by the bakery. With a clatter of hoofs they plunged away.

Unruffled, the rider brought his trembling mount to a standstill; he leant and stroked its neck as the sheets subsided. He was impeccably dressed in polished tan riding boots, breeches and tweed hacking jacket. When he saw Bowler he urged his horse towards the car.

He reined in, touched his crop to the brim of his felt hat in salute to Agatha, and said, 'Good morning, Brown. I was coming to see you.'

Bowler had to admit the bugger could ride, in spite of his poncy clothes. 'Morning, Venables. What can I do for you?' He paused with the car door open, then turned to Agatha. 'Aubrey Venables,' he said. 'Mrs Benson.'

Venables bent his head and bowed from the saddle. 'Mrs Benson.' His gaze lingered. Then he turned to Bowler and said, 'Bub Gregory brought back our garden tools and the axe yesterday. Said he found them in the railway yards.'

'He did not. I found them, and nowhere near the railway yards. On his aunt's back veranda they were. Amazed when I pointed them out, but he agreed quite willingly to bring them back.'

'Was he the one who stole them?'

'Just the messenger. I know who did but I can't prove it, so I sent Bub as a warning to the rest of that sticky-fingered mob.' He ran his hand in a caress down the satin nose of the elegant bay mare; she was sweating lightly, still tense from her fright. 'I can't take it any further, much as I'd like to.'

'No, no, I understand. But you'd better warn the thief my sister says she'll shoot the next one who takes anything from our yard.'

Bowler laughed. 'No need for extremes.'

'No, no, of course not. Wouldn't put it past her, mind you — she's an excellent shot. Well, thank you for your trouble. Good morning.' He smiled at Agatha again, turned his horse, and trotted away down the road.

Agatha looked after him. 'He's new since I left. What's he do?'

'Our Aub? He's bought a scrub block out beyond Davidsons', but he's got a manager there.' Bowler trod on the self-starter. Luckily the battery was up and he wouldn't have to swing the starting handle.

'Yes, he looked a bit proud to dirty his hands.'

'Not proud, exactly. Men with money just see things differently.'

'Rich people are always proud.'

The baby was awake this morning. A serious, round-faced infant with a dusting of dark hair on its crown, it lay on Agatha's lap propped within her arm and made passes at a string of crystal beads she dangled from her free hand.

He smiled at the child, and was surprised at the instant response of a wide, gummy grin and a friendly squeal, rather like a bird's call.

'How old is your baby, Mrs Benson?' he asked. Then he thought perhaps she would think he was prying, not merely making conversation. 'I mean, I wasn't —' There didn't seem any openings that might not offend her in one way or another.

She wasn't offended. 'She's nine months old, Mr Brown. I —'

'Bowler. Call me Bowler. Everybody does.'

'All right, Bowler. And I'm Agatha, as you probably know. Well, Bowler, let's get it straight from the outset that I am not trying to hide anything. Everybody in Kularook can do simple arithmetic, and seeing that I left Lew two years ago they must know Cordelia is Monty Parmenter's daughter. And, although he might be trying to hush her up, I am not.' She bent forward and kissed the top of the baby's head. 'Well, how could I?'

'I wasn't thinking that.'

'I know you weren't. But you were afraid I might think so. Don't be so careful, Mr Brown. These days I'm pretty tough. I'm well aware most people won't even see me if I meet them in the street.'

He heard her take a breath of the hot, desiccating air. After the winter he'd removed the side-curtains from the car; the dusty wind was blowing through unimpeded, ruffling their hair and drying their skin.

On either side of the three-chain road lay paddocks of ripe wheat. A tractor crawled like an ant in the distance in the paddocks on the left, and on the right a team of ten Clydesdales, their great heads nodding, hauled a harvester along the edge of uncut grain. Clouds of cocky-chaff shook from the back of the machine and swirled round the driver, perched in front with his hands full of reins.

By the fence, where a collection of full bags stood upright propped together, a youth paused in sewing up the top of one. He raised his head and waved.

Bowler hadn't expected Agatha to wave back with such enthusiasm.

She explained, 'That's Alan. His mother was a good friend to me.'

He nodded. He too knew the boy — him and his two brothers. There were several good reasons why the law knew the Pedler brothers.

The baby was watching him. He reached and tickled her fat middle with a forefinger, and was rewarded with a gurgling laugh.

He said. 'She's a friendly soul.'

'I expect she'll learn.'

With one hand Agatha smoothed her hair where a few strands had blown loose from the plaits round her head. He heard the bitterness in her voice and felt uneasy for her.

The closer they came to the Benson farm the more withdrawn she became. She stared silently ahead through the windscreen, though Bowler doubted if she saw anything. Indeed, for the last two miles, jolting along a dirt track worn through mallee scrub so dense that occasional branches slapped the windscreen, she had her eyes closed. He could see her left hand — she still wore her wedding ring — clenched hard on the baby's shawl.

After a long silence she muttered, 'Cordelia must eat, and I will do anything to ensure that.' Her voice was low. Bowler, glancing at her, thought she probably didn't realise she had spoken aloud.

Through the last gate they drove into cleared paddocks. A couple of border collies, barking furiously, raced to meet them and attacked the front tyres. For Bowler the undisciplined brutes could take their chances, so without slowing he charged the slope to the house and stopped at the side, beside the rainwater tank.

Plain as a shoe-box, the house stood on a rise not much more than a ripple in the plains that reached to the dark horizon where the scrub began. Apart from a thicket of mallee at the far corner it was unprotected from any winds that blew. A windmill and three sheds of unpainted corrugated iron stood a couple of hundred yards off, on the flat in front.

You couldn't really call it a house, Bowler thought. It was merely another corrugated iron shed, long, flat-roofed. More sheets of iron had partitioned it into rooms and closed it along the front, where a kind of veranda had been added to act as a passage connecting the rooms. This was netted in with flywire and rendered partly weatherproof along its lower half by old wheat-bags stitched together and whitewashed.

At the sound of the car the Benson brothers, who had been working together on a harvester parked outside one of the sheds, started walking up towards them. Bowler heard Agatha draw in her breath sharply, saw her square her shoulders, before she opened the car door and walked to meet them, holding her baby tightly in her arms. He thought she looked both gallant and vulnerable beside the two solid barrel-chested men in their working clothes.

Bowler didn't know them as well as he knew most of his 'parishioners'. Because they lived nine miles out, and their ancient Ford not only lacked a hood and a windscreen but was held together mainly by faith and fencing wire, they came in to the township rarely.

The brothers Benson had a reputation for being disobliging and bad-tempered: a watchful, silent pair. Lew was what, about thirty? And Rupe, the unmarried brother, a few years more. The rest of the community tended to avoid them, and in this semi-isolation it seemed that they had come to regard anybody outside their family with strong suspicion.

'Hello, Lew,' Agatha said.

'Where the hell've you been?' Lew Benson's expression as his wife approached him was an unpleasant mixture of anger and gloating satisfaction.

'I missed the train. Not my fault — an accident on the suburban line so my train was late.'

Bowler lifted out the case and carried it over. He heard Lew, in a hissing undertone, say, 'You stood me up this time, you bitch, I'd've made you sorry. You won't make a monkey of me a second time.'

All three turned as Bowler set down the case; he saw Agatha's white face, her rigid stance; he thought, so much for a happy family re-union. But she had asked him to bring her, there had been no coercion that he could see, and so presumably she knew what she was doing. It was none of his business to interfere between husband and wife however much he might wish he had the right.

All the same, he hesitated. He glanced at Rupe; a more craggy version of his younger brother, he was watching the pair with all the animation of a fence post. Bowler turned back to his car. Agatha was on her own now. There was nothing he could do here to help her.

4

Almost in a dream Agatha stumbled through the veranda, hung with the same collection of old coats, ropes, and harness; cluttered with the same empty tins, kero cases filled with assorted nuts and bolts and other metal junk; piles of empty wheat-bags, the same three peeling paper bags of cement, the heap of rusting rabbit traps. She stopped in the kitchen door and looked around.

Nothing had changed there either, in the two years she had been away. A wood stove against the back wall, a cupboard, chairs, a table covered in green-patterned oilcloth standing on a beaten earth floor. The one uncurtained window showed a view of a bare stubble paddock with the flat dark line of scrub beyond.

Her first response was pure panic, a return to the desperate need to get away from the place and from Lew that had driven her out last time. Though there was one change: in her absence Lew's mother Vida had married for the third time. As Agatha entered, this new husband jumped from his seat at the table and held out his hand with a smile.

'You must be Agatha. Welcome home.'

'Thank you.' To Agatha even one friendly face in the household was an improvement.

'Figgy Higgins.' His smile was almost conspiratorial, as though seeing her, another outsider, as a possible ally. Still holding her hand he added, 'Short for Figaro. Yes I know it's weird, and before you ask, I don't sing.'

She managed to smile back. Of average height, stocky, with greying wavy hair and a small moustache, he was wearing working clothes that were newer and neater than those of his large untidy step-sons. But his wife, sitting at the head of the table, was watching this exchange with freezing disapproval.

Agatha disengaged her hand. 'Hullo, Vida.'

'So you've come back,' Vida said.

She was a short and strongly built woman, with peroxided golden hair and an aggressive manner towards all comers, including her sons, who treated her with a deference they accorded no one else. Agatha wondered what charms Vida possessed, hidden from female eyes, that had enabled her to achieve three husbands.

Heat, flies, the smell of grease and fried mutton — the iron room was full of all three. As it had been before. As it would be always.

Agatha choked, wanting to scream; she was nearly screaming, and knew exactly what she would sound like if she did; she could hear the horror and desperation in her voice as clearly as if she had let her pent-up feelings go in one long shriek of despair.

Vida got to her feet and ostentatiously turned her back.

Obviously, her daughter-in-law was beyond forgiveness. Why had she bothered to come back, Agatha wondered. Starvation couldn't feel much worse.

At the window, where the white cylindrical waterbag hung to catch the breeze, Vida unhooked the snake-like canvas spout and filled an enamel pannikin; she drank thirstily, then walked from the room, brushing past so closely that Agatha felt the tepid air eddy against her arm. After hesitating a moment, Figgy shrugged, smiled at Agatha, and went after her. Cordelia began to whimper.

Lew said, 'Me mother can't forgive you, what you did to me. You shouldn't be surprised.'

'I'm not. She has every right. But I must give Cordelia a drink and put her down for a sleep.'

Expressionless, his gaze flicked over the child then swerved away, as though he couldn't bear to look longer.

'I've borrowed a cot.'

'Thank you. And then we must talk, I suppose.'

'There's nothin to say.'

'I think there is. I want to explain —'

'Nothin to explain. Behaved like a slut, now you're back. I've said you can stay, you and your bastard. What else is there to say?'

'Lew, let me at least say I'm grateful for somewhere to live.'

'You're me wife. Should have been here all along. Come on, room's the same one.'

He picked up her case and led the way along the enclosed veranda to the eastern end; he held aside the curtains. She recognised them, the same curtains she had hung over the empty doorway in the early days of her marriage, now grey with dust and frayed at the hem.

'Not much bloody space with a cot in it.' He dropped the curtain and she heard his heavy tread returning to the kitchen. Then the rumble of voices.

The room was stifling, and smelt of sweat-stained sheets and Lew's working clothes. The floor, like that in the kitchen, was of hard-packed earth, with two empty wheat-bags split open and laid as mats. The cot stood against one wall, the double bed opposite, a chest of drawers under the two-foot-square window. This had been closed against the heat but now served only to keep heated air trapped inside. Like a brooding presence, Lew's one suit hung on a coat-hanger high against the back wall.

Cordelia must be protected from this breathless atmosphere. Wet sheets, Agatha thought, she'd have to hang up wet sheets; full marks to whatever benign god had prompted her to bring a few cot sheets with her. She couldn't use precious rainwater to damp them, though.

She went out to beg the use of a bucket to fetch bore water from the tank at the bottom of the hill.

Dressed only in her nap, lying on one bare sheet with another wet one draped around the iron cot to cool the air, Cordelia fell into a restless doze.

Agatha stripped to her petticoat and lay on the bed, fighting the bubble of desperation that swelled inside her, pushing it down as though squeezing it with her two hands, forcing it small; because she knew if she ever let it expand, let it grow to full size, it would rise from her chest and balloon into her skull, growing and swelling until it burst the top of her head off into madness.

She must have dozed. She woke and saw late sunlight slanting past the window. Her skin was wet, the pillow beneath her head soaked. She would have sat up but Lew, sitting on the side of the bed to pull off his boots, pressed her back with one hand. He pulled off his shirt and unbuckled his belt.

Agatha struggled against his hand. 'Lew! No! It's too hot.'

He took no notice. He stepped out of his trousers.

'Lew! Please! Not now.'

'You're my wife,' he said.

'Yes I know, of course I will be a wife to you. But please Lew, later.'

'You can't expect favours,' he said, and climbed on the bed. 'You've been gone a long time.'

Agatha closed her eyes. She had braced herself to face this, knowing she'd find these obligations hard to accept with anything like resignation but grimly determined to go through with them without a fuss. Fusses excited Lew, and then everything was very much worse.

The touch of Lew's breath on her face was enough to send shock-waves of revulsion through her. Not so soon, she thought, she hadn't expected him to move on her so soon.

She remembered his brutal impatience, and sat up to remove her petticoat before he tore it off her.

5

By the time she had gone halfway Agatha wished she had not begun the four mile trip. The trap had no canopy to keep off the sun, and the horse Socks, never the most energetic performer between the shafts, could barely raise a trot in the near-century heat. Dust spun up by the wheels stuck to her skin. Mallees crowding the track flavoured the dry air with eucalyptus.

She bent to check on Cordelia, lying in a nest of pillows under the seat and shaded by a wet towel. Poor baby, she looked hot and uncomfortable. But they might as well go on: the way back was just as far, and at least they could rest for a while at Pedlers' farmhouse which, being of stone, would be much cooler than the sunstruck tin box that was home.

Unless Miriam Pedler turned her away from the door. What if Miriam judged her as she believed most local women would, as a pariah, as one who had put herself outside the bounds of normal society — what if Miriam didn't want to see her? It was one thing to tell Bowler Brown she was prepared for rebuffs; it would be something else if she discovered she had no friend left in the world.

Miriam had befriended her during the first disastrous months of her marriage to Lew; not a close friend to whom she could unburden her heart but still a comfort in that lonely time. Now, when Agatha needed to get away from the spite and the empty hours at home, Miriam was the only person she wanted to see.

She'd asked Lew for the trap because she was afraid if she didn't escape she would start screaming insults at Lew's mother Vida, who would only scream worse ones back. Relations between them were becoming so bad Agatha doubted they could ever be mended. But there was no way out for either of them, and Vida didn't try to contain her rage at being forced to share her house with a woman she hated.

They had managed better when Lew first brought Agatha to the farm. Vida herself had not long moved back to Kularook after living in town for years with her second husband. When he died she had returned to keep house for her bachelor sons, and by the time Figgy Higgins had followed her to woo and win her, Agatha had left with Monty Parmenter.

Figgy made quite a romantic story of it, though it was difficult to associate hard-headed Vida with romance. He told Agatha that he had been a friend to the second husband, and after his death had helped the widow through some difficulties with death duties; their affections had developed from there. Now in an extraordinary twist Vida seemed to believe Agatha had designs on him, as if middle-aged, portly Figgy, for all his pleasant ways — such a contrast to Lew and Rupe's sullen taciturnity — was the stuff for which she'd break her marriage vows a second time.

She had to get away. She hoped Miriam would see her; she needed help to find her sense of perspective again.

At the sheds behind Pedlers' farmhouse she nodded to the man backing a couple of Clydesdales up to a binder. She was a little afraid of Miriam's husband Jack, reputed to be both bad-tempered and violent, so was pleased to see the teenage boy who came pelting down the slope from the house, scattering black hens as he ran, to hold her horse's bridle while she lifted down the baby.

'Thank you, Alan. I saw you sewing bags the other day.'

'Yeah. I told Mum you were back.' He was puffing, a thin towheaded youth with an attractive grin. 'Leave the horse with me, Mrs Benson. No trouble, I'll put him in the yards. Mum's inside.'

Reassured, Agatha propped her baby against her shoulder and walked up the sandy rise, past the woodheap and the wormwood hedge, to the stone house squatting under the pines at the top.

And Miriam, her friend Miriam, was waiting for her at the back door. Agatha saw her face, smiling and full of concern — saw for the first time a mother-figure, kind and welcoming, and despite herself ran to meet her.

If Miriam was surprised she didn't show it; she put her arms round Agatha, a little crookedly to avoid crushing Cordelia, and said, 'I didn't expect to see you here again, stranger.'

'Neither did I.' Agatha felt tears prick her eyelids, and stooped her head into her friend's shoulder. 'Neither did I,' she repeated, her voice muffled.

'What went wrong?'

'Everything,' Agatha said, and wept openly.

Later, when Cordelia had been put to sleep on one of the boys' beds and they were together in the kitchen, Miriam set the kettle over a spirit burner on top of the cold stove and said, 'Ever since I heard you were back I've been hoping you'd call in.'

'I've been wanting to, but Lew wouldn't let me have the trap until today. He seems to think I might run off again, though God knows where he imagines I'd run to.'

This kitchen was set out in the same way as Bensons', and far from luxurious, yet this was a proper house, not a tin shed; and even a working space, Agatha thought, could be made pleasant without much effort. The floor was covered in blue linoleum, there were curtains at the window, a row of brightly-painted canisters on the mantelpiece above the stove, coloured prints cut from magazines — a Vermeer interior and Streeton's 'Purple noon' — pinned up beside the calendar on the painted walls.

A few tentative piano notes sounded from the front room.

'Melissa,' Miriam said, sitting at the table and selecting a fresh sock from her mending basket. 'She nagged me into starting her off and now she's at the piano every chance she gets, whenever —' She hesitated, then said, 'Agatha, what's been happening to you? We haven't heard a whisper since you left. I asked Lew once, but he couldn't tell me anything.'

'He should have — I've always let him know where I was. After leaving him like that it was the least I could do. I expected him to want a divorce.'

'What happened to Monty? Wasn't he supposed to take care of you?'

Take care of her, Agatha thought. He'd sworn to her that if she left Lew, if she would only entrust her future to him, he would devote his life to making her happy. His only purpose would be to love and cherish her for the rest of her days. Even taken with a grain of salt, those had been sweet words.

She said, 'I'm not much good at picking men, am I?'

'Seems not,' Miram said, matter-of-fact. 'Was Monty violent too?' She laid down the sock and brought two cups from a cupboard. 'I thought —'

'No, nothing like that. We were happy — well, I thought we were — and for a while it looked as though we'd be all right. But he just disappeared when he couldn't ignore my pregnancy any more. Really disappeared. I haven't seen him since and I have no idea where he is.' Agatha stared down at her hands. 'He refused to believe it at first, though heaven only knows why it was such a shock to him — he'd done nothing to prevent it and he'd kept me so short of cash I couldn't afford anything. Now his mother won't tell me where he's gone because she believes I'm hell-bent on ruining his life. As though it was my idea we went off together; as though the pregnancy was my fault.'

Miriam said, 'He didn't last long, did he. So what on earth did you do?' She carried the teapot from the hob and filled the cups.

'Oh, this and that. You don't want to hear the whole gory story. But I didn't choose to come back.'

'I do want to hear the whole gory story. You've been away two years, and I've had no news of you whatsoever.'

Agatha said, 'I should have written to you. I imagined you'd forget about me once I'd gone. After all, I was only here six months. Six months of marriage,' she repeated. 'You've been married — what? Twenty something years?'

'Twenty-five.'

'My god, twenty-five years of Lew! I hope I can find some way to support myself inside twenty-five years.'

'Then don't have any more children,' Miriam said. 'Children are the anchors that keep you fixed.'

And she would know, thought Agatha. Her pianist daughter Melissa was five years old, ten years younger than the next child, Alan. And, although this was undoubtedly good advice, it might be a bit late. 'Not so easy to arrange,' she said.

Miriam nodded. 'Agatha, what did you do after Monty abandoned you?'

'Abandoned is a good word. That's what I felt like, a bit of rubbish he'd discarded and left to rot. The bastard. I can't even think of him without —' She took a breath. 'I did think he might get in touch after Cordelia was born, but never a word.'

'Lear,' Miriam said. 'He repudiated a daughter too, didn't he.'

'I've regretted saddling her with the name ever since. At the time I believed I was thinking of her, not Monty.'

'Don't regret it. It's a pretty name, and it wasn't her fault either, Shakespeare's Cordelia. She was brave and honest — you can't want more than that.'

They sat in silence for a while, elbows on the table, sipping their tea. Miriam said, 'So what did you do?'

'I couldn't stay in the house because he stopped paying the rent, so I took a job housekeeping and baby-minding. She was sort of a friend — we'd been students together — though she couldn't pay more than a few bob. But we did get a room and our keep.'

'Why did you come back?'

Agatha shrugged. 'Her slimy husband tried to put the hard word on me. I couldn't stay. I've tried for dozens of other positions, but nobody wants a runaway wife with a bastard under her arm. I thought as a divorcee I might have better chances, but Lew won't divorce me. So when he offered to send me the price of a train ticket it was that or starve.'

Miriam said, 'I'm glad you're back, anyway. Nobody else ever visits me.'

Agatha wished she had more of her friend's stoicism. Her husband Jack never let Miriam take the car to go anywhere; she wasn't allowed to go visiting, only to drive in for stores. At least Agatha could get Socks and the trap sometimes. What a miserable bastard Jack was. Yet Miriam would never say a word against him.

'So Lew really wanted you back?' Miriam said.

'I suppose so, though he barely speaks to me,' Agatha said. 'Neither does Rupe. And Vida only if she's got something unpleasant to say. Figgy tries to be friendly, but Vida is so damn jealous that he can't even say good morning to me without putting her in a foul mood for the rest of the day. And none of them —'

'Mum, hey Mum!' Alan burst in at the back door. 'Dad says will you go into Kularook —' the wire door clashed behind him '— a couple of —'

'Alan!'

'Sorry Mum, sorry Mrs Benson, forgot, I didn't mean to interrupt.' Flushed with embarrassment, tense with urgency, he stood inside the door, his gaze fixed on his mother.

Miriam said, 'Well, what is it?' She sounded resigned.

'Dad's in a stink, busted a couple of bits on the binder, wants you to collect some rivets and chain and stuff from Bob Norman. He'll explain.'

'You mean now? Can't it wait?'

'No, Dad says. He has to get on with it straight away.'

'Why can't he go himself?'

Alan turned his head away. 'He just said to tell you.'

'All right, say I'll be there in a minute.' Alan vanished. Miriam said, 'Look, I'm dreadfully sorry, Agatha, but you know how it is. The men's work has to come first.'

'Yes of course.' Agatha, embarrassed by her friend's dog-like obedience to her demanding husband, was disappointed too. She had intended to stay for at least another hour, in the hopes that the afternoon would be cooler later. 'I'll come back another day.'

Miriam reached across the table and laid a hand on her arm. 'Please. I'll be expecting you.'

6

Heading for home, Socks leant into his collar with more enthusiasm than on the outward trip, and trotted steadily along without urging. Cordelia, hot and grumpy after being woken early, rolled about the floor of the trap and wouldn't stay still; she grizzled herself into a crying fit, so that her mother had to pick her up to comfort her, holding her awkwardly on her lap with the reins in the other hand.

There were six gates on the track. In thick mallee at the fourth gate, which marked the limit of Jack Pedler's back scrub, Agatha started the tedious ritual necessary for safety — pull on the wheel-brake, climb down from the trap, lift down the baby and put her beside the track, open the gate, take off the brake, lead the horse through, pull on the brake, bring the baby through, fasten the gate — but before she could then get herself and the child into the trap again Socks was dragging it forward with the wheel grinding against the brake-block.

She jogged after it and made a snatch at the reins, which were tied short round the metal arm of the seat. Cordelia's wriggling body in her other arm made her clumsy; she couldn't keep her hold on the reins and they slipped from her hasty knot and released the horse's head. She grabbed for the brake lever, yanking hard. Under the sudden jerk of pressure the old wooden block split and Socks, startled by the crack, bounded forward; he found his head free and no dragging weight behind him and kept going. Agatha was pulled against the side of the trap. She had to let go.

With murder in her heart she watched as the horse trotted briskly away from her along the track.

Agatha swore. She wasn't having much luck today. The next gate would stop the horse, but that was nearly a mile away, a long walk on the sandy track in the heat of the day.

Cordelia had no hat. Agatha put her own cotton tennis hat on the child's head, propped her on her hip, and trudged off in the wake of the runaway. It was only the heat bothered her; otherwise she was in no hurry to return to the house.

In that house there was nowhere to sit except the kitchen, and if she wanted to avoid Vida's company she had to keep to her room. That iron box had become more like a prison cell than a bedroom.

While the track ran through the mallees walking wasn't so bad: patches of shade lay here and there to temper the sun. Later she came to the end of the scrub and had to cross half a mile of open pasture where, although clumps of trees grew randomly, none were near enough to shade the road. She could see the line of the scrub ahead where the next gate lay, the gate which would stop Socks. It looked a long way off.

Her legs seemed ineffectual, making no appreciable reduction in the distance. She felt tiny, a midget, diminished by a huge sky, hard and high, where a kestrel hung almost motionless over the sunburnt grasses. She pointed it out to her daughter, but Cordelia wasn't interested; she was fretful, and grizzled most of the time.

Agatha transferred the child to her other hip and started singing to her, tunes without words in time to her steps. Then she found she didn't have enough breath to continue. Strange black holes began to appear in the afternoon. Her head buzzed.

When Agatha's head cleared she found herself lying on the ground while somebody swabbed her forehead with a wet cloth, a cool wet cloth that felt wonderful against her burning skin.

'Agatha!' said an urgent voice. 'Agatha! Are you all right?'

Trickles of water snaked down the side of her neck. She opened her eyes.

A strange man she had never seen before knelt beside her with a bunch of wet fabric in his hand. She saw bare shoulders, a broad expanse of navy singlet..

Her daughter was crying. She tried to sit up, exclaiming, 'Cordelia!'

'She's here, she's all right.'

Agatha fell back. Dried grass stems pricked her through her cotton dress. The man put one hand behind her head, lifting her into a half sitting position, and held the china spout of a waterbag to her mouth. 'Drink a bit. You'll feel better.'

She gulped a few times and the water hit her throat in delicious canvas-scented waves, washing away the dust and the dryness. She struggled to sit up. Cordelia, half lying against her, whimpered like a puppy; Agatha put an arm round her. The man was a blurred presence against the sun.

'Did I faint?' she asked; then, 'Who the devil are you?'

'I didn't know you were back,' he said. 'I was out at your place an hour ago and they didn't tell me you were back.' He studied her face, as though trying to read something there. 'Can you walk a few steps? There's a bit of shade under those trees behind you.' When he reached a hand to help her up she realised he had been shielding her from the sun, interposing his shoulders to shade her head; and then she was embarrassed to find that even with assistance her head spun and her legs gave way. She fell against him, felt an arm at her waist; another arm lifted her knees and she was carried to the shade, and set down with her back resting against the trunk of a sapling gum.

Cordelia was squalling, but subsided when he deposited her in her mother's arms.

Agatha's vision cleared. She sat in the shade of a clump of trees, her legs stretched out along the ground, her hot sticky baby clutched to her breast. She watched the man walk to the track for his waterbag, a tall man and still a stranger — but how did he know her name? He pulled on his wet shirt — it must have been his shirt he used to mop her face — then lifted the square waterbag and tilted his head to drink as he walked back. Ahead of him his blue shadow slid over the yellowed grass towards her.

'I don't know you,' Agatha said.

He folded down to sit on his heel before her and looked at her steadily, his head a little slanted, as though giving her a chance for further study of his features. But there wasn't anything there to trigger her memories. A young man's face, not bad looking but nothing special, sunburnt and dusty. A strong face, though, and a mouth accustomed to laughter.

He said, 'Yes you do. But it's a while ago. Franklin, Matt Franklin, from Edgerton.'

She squinted at him. 'I knew Robby Franklin, and Jack — Jack was in my grade at school. But I don't remember any Matt.'

The man half smiled. 'Try Snow.'

'My God!' Agatha stared, disbelieving. 'Snow Franklin! The terror of Grade Two!'

'Was not,' he said, grinning.

'Little Snowy! I'd forgotten you.'

He laughed, not pleased about something. Well, there was no reason he should feel like that; she couldn't be expected to recognise on sight all the little tackers in the school five years her junior. His appearance gave her no clue: the once flaxen hair had darkened, the snub freckled nose had developed into a respectable, evenly-tanned beak.

'You've grown,' she said. It seemed such a silly, obvious thing to say that she started to laugh. Then it wasn't funny, it was tragic — tragic how everything had changed and the girl who had raced round the playground of the Edgerton primary school had gone on from there to make such a disaster of her life. Her laughter got away from her, she couldn't stop, she was laughing and sobbing, catching her breath helplessly, remembering the child she once was, remembering this tall young man as a wild skinny little boy of six or seven, somehow grieving and crying for all she had lost and at the same time overwhelmed by her present despair.

'Oh! Oh! Oh!' she sobbed, her hands over her face.

Snow Franklin knelt beside her and pulled her head against his shirt, rocking her gently, hushing through his teeth as though she were a horse, stroking his hand over the thin cotton dress covering her back.

She got her breath under control and tried to pull away. For a split second his arms constrained her and then he let her go.

'It's all right,' he said, with a grunt of laughter. 'Only you've thrown me rather. I didn't know you were back.' He rubbed his hand over his mouth, looking at her as though checking for signs of change. He shook his head. 'But I'd like to know what the hell you thought you were doing when you married that Benson bastard.'

Agatha started to gape at him; she shut her mouth, swallowed.

Cordelia began to wail, struggling against her arm. Agatha realised she'd been holding the baby too tightly. 'Hush,' she said. 'Hush, little one.' She let the child crawl out of her lap.

The plaits she wore round her head were falling down; she fingered through her hair until she found some hairpins to re-fasten them. With her head bent she said, 'Sorry about that, Snow. I don't know what set me off.'

'Don't change the subject. Don't you remember dancing on the bike shed roof?'

'Dancing — No, what's that got to do with —' As she paused, not sure where these reminiscences were supposed to lead, the memory returned with surprising clarity. She said slowly, 'Yes, in fact I do.'

She'd been shouting and yelling and dancing, jeering at the other kids and stamping quite viciously on their fingers when they tried to climb up too, clattering her leather-soled shoes across the rattling corrugated iron, laughing and shrieking. And yes, she did recall the other child with her, a lunatic small boy all arms and long thin legs, screeching as loudly as she did, stamping with as much gusto on the fingers groping for a handhold.

That must have been Snow. She couldn't remember how they'd arrived there, or why, only the heady exhilaration of looking down on the others, of being on top of the others for a change, of somehow winning — but winning what?

Snow grinned. 'That's right. You and me against the rest.'

Well, he needn't imagine that a temporary alliance in a school yard donkey's years before, between a prickly twelve-year-old girl and a maniacal small boy, gave him any privileges now. What was the matter with him?

A little on the defensive, she said, 'You must have been about six when I went away to secondary school.'

'Seven. But you've seen me since then.'

'No I haven't.' He was still watching her too intently. In an attempt to get the situation back to a more normal level she said in a bright social voice, 'I was lucky you came along just now. Thank you so much for the drink. We'd better be going on our way.'

Snow stood, and flexed his shoulders. 'No hurry. It's too hot to be walking far today.'

'We weren't walking. The brake-block on the trap broke at the last gate and the horse took off. I'll catch him at the next gate.'

'That was your trap? I saw it in the distance but I didn't realise it was a runaway. I was cutting fence posts in the scrub over there.' He nodded towards the edge of the clearing, where a number of small eucalypts stood up above the banksias and mallees.

'That's Bruce Wilson's scrub.'

'Yeah, they're his posts. I'm just the bunny cutting them.'

'Don't you live at Edgerton any more? Your father had a farm, I think.'

He nodded. 'Still has. But what with Rob and Jack he doesn't need me. I'm between jobs, so I came up here to shoe a few horses and now I'm putting in a couple of weeks for Uncle Bruce. Then I'm off.'

'Bruce Wilson's your uncle?'

'Yeah. Mum was a Wilson.'

'Then you're cousin to —'

'I know, I know, half the ruddy district. Look, I'll go and round up your trap for you. My horse is just over there, in the shade of those trees.'

When he had fetched the horse, a sturdy brown mare, he dumped his gear on the ground beside her and swung into the saddle. 'You wait here. I'll be quick as I can.'

The hoof-beats faded. Cordelia rolled on her stomach and squirmed over to inspect the shining blade of his axe. Agatha moved the sharpened edge beyond her reach, then gazed abstractedly at his billy and the worn, rather grubby coat he had laid beside it. From one pocket protruded the top edges of a red book.

If it had been a railway timetable she'd still have read it, so starved was she for the printed word.

Manshy, she read, and opened the pages. 'Chapter one, Telling of the Herd. The mustering for drafting and branding was a distressing time for the cattle . . .'

Cordelia fell asleep in her lap. She turned a page without waking the baby.

'You can borrow it if you like,' Snow's voice said.

Engrossed in a red heifer's struggles for existence, her battles for freedom, Agatha hadn't heard his return in the trap. The sandy earth had muffled the sound of the horses' hoofs, but she was surprised she hadn't heard the rumbling wheels.

She laid the book on his coat. 'Sorry. I didn't mean to go ferreting through your pockets, but it was sticking out. I couldn't help myself. There's nothing to read in that house, not even an old newspaper.'

'I could bring you some more books.' He climbed down from the trap and turned to smile at her. He cuffed the horse Socks on the jaw as it swung its head sideways and tried to nip his arm.

Agatha imagined Lew's reaction if a personable young man arrived at the farm bearing gifts for her, even an ephemeral gift like the loan of a few books. 'No. I mean, thanks for offering, but I couldn't ask you to put yourself out like that.'

'Or I could leave them for you by the track,' he said, as though he had read her thoughts. Were her expressions so transparent? 'Somewhere not too far, so that you could walk down and collect them. It'd be no trouble. Take that one, anyway. I can finish it anytime.'

When he had helped her into the trap and handed up Cordelia, he untied his horse from the back of it and swung into the saddle. 'I'm coming with you. I'll open the gates this time.'

7

Agatha wasn't quite sure where she stood with Lew's sister Thelma. Once, when she'd been living there before, they had spent the best part of an afternoon together and had seemed to be moving towards a genuine friendship. The next time Thelma had visited she had come with her husband Dick, and had been in such a mood of fretful irritation with him, so impatient with her two young children, that she'd had no time to speak to Agatha.

This afternoon she had left Dick behind. Tense, her mouth set, she stalked into the kitchen where Vida sat at one end of the table sewing a button on a shirt and Agatha stood at the other, making up her baby's formula.

Thelma's children, a girl of six and a boy of eight, ran in after her and dropped to their knees to play with Cordelia, who was crawling round the table-legs clashing a spoon against a tin plate. She chirruped greetings to them.

Thelma glanced down. 'You can play with the baby later. Run along, I want to talk to Granny.' She seated herself at the table and helped herself to one of her mother's cigarettes. 'She's a pretty kid, Agatha. How's Lew managing?'

She didn't wait for an answer. She leaned on the table, smoking in quick puffs, while she complained at length to Vida about her husband

and her husband's employer. She was so abusive of both that Agatha couldn't tell which had angered her more.

'Mr Venables expects too much, Mum,' Thelma said. She took a brief drag on her cigarette. 'Stuck up bastard. We have to live out on the block in a humpy not fit for pigs while he swanks round Kularook on that twitchy little horse of his and calls himself a "gentleman farmer" — for god's sake, gentleman farmers went out with the ark.' She glanced at her mother as though to assess how much sympathy she was eliciting. 'Dick doesn't mind, says at least it's a job, but he never thinks how it is for me, stuck there in a dump of a place that's falling down round our ears, ten miles out and I can never get the car, he always needs it up the paddock or —'

'You've got it today,' Vida said.

Thelma dismissed this with a shake of her head. 'We're that far out the kids can't walk to school, and I'm not going to teach them, I got enough to do. Anyway, soon as the white ants finish off the rafters the roof will fall in and that'll be that.'

Unmoved, Vida asked, 'Is Dick working today?'

'Reaping. What there is of it. The harvester was on the other side of the paddock so I took the damn car. Why shouldn't I have it sometimes?' Thelma ground her cigarette into the dented-in lid of a tobacco tin that served as an ashtray. 'Dick sweated to increase the crops this year, but the ground's that new they're not worth taking off they're so damn spindly. They won't even pay for themselves. No doubt Mr Venables will make it an excuse to pay Dick less. He only gets a pittance anyway.' She took a deep breath and said in a rush, 'Mum, could you let me have a quid or two? Alf Birch left you something, couldn't you spare me a bit? You could afford it, and if I have to go on scrimping and saving and never having anything nice I'll go mad. Mum, really, I'm desperate.' She raised her eyes to her mother's face and added in a wheedling tone, 'I need a new dress and some stockings and I could do with another —'

'I lived on a pittance too, when I was your age,' Vida said. 'And I haven't got money to spare. I wish I did. Your father left nothing but debts, and you all exaggerate the few bob poor Alfie left me.'

'Well, what about the kids? They're that sick of bread and dripping they've damn nearly stopped eating. What about a few bob for them? Come on, Mum, they're your grandchildren. He left you quids.'

Vida shot her a scornful glance. 'You know nothing about it. He left no such thing. And I'll thank you not to discuss my private affairs.' She twisted in her chair. 'Agatha, when you've finished there could you make a pot of tea please?'

This was the most civil request Agatha had received from Vida since she had been back. 'Yes, of course,' she said, hoping it was an omen, that a thaw was setting in, that Vida would no longer either treat her and her child as invisible or address her in terms that would have been harsh to a clumsy servant; hoping that this meant she had heard the last of that loaded name, Aggie. She reached to the high mantelpiece and lifted down the tea caddy.

Thelma said, 'But Mum, you got *some* money when Alf Birch died. You're not suggesting that I should bump off Dick so that I can marry a well-off second husband, are you? Do better next time, like you did? Though it might be an idea,' she added, sinking into gloom. 'I couldn't very well do worse.'

Vida was wearing the stony expression brought on by any discussion of money. Her sons knew better than to ask her for any; only Thelma persisted. Agatha wondered why she continued such a futile exercise, since Vida consistently denied that she'd inherited anything from her second husband. And probably she didn't have much. Her mother-in-law was quite capable of spreading rumours of a fictitious fortune merely to provide herself with opportunities to be disobliging.

The children, who had been down at the yards watching the men drafting sheep, came racing inside, jostling in the doorway and both trying to speak at once. Beryl shouted, 'Granny, Granny, Uncle Rupe said — Les, stop pushing — Uncle Rupe said to tell you they'd be up in a minute for smoko. Go away, Les, I'm telling Granny.'

Her brother, who had been trying to out-shout her, fell silent and pinched her hard on the back of her arm when their mother wasn't looking. She roared.

'Shut up, Beryl.' Thelma gripped her hands together on the table in front of her. 'Mum, before the men get here, I was going to ask you, can we stay here tonight? Me and the kids?'

Vida's head jerked round. 'What have you been up to?'

'Nothing. It's bloody Dick's fault. Oh, one thing led to another and then we had a row about the car and then I took it anyway. He'll kill me if I go home tonight.'

'You should have thought of that before. Where do you imagine you'd sleep, now Lew's wife is home?'

'I'll sleep in the shed, I'll sleep on the ground,' declared Thelma, her voice cracking with passion. 'But I'm not going back to Dick. Never!'

'Thelma!' Vida started to say more, then bit off the words as they heard the men washing their hands in the enamel basin on the bench at the back door. Dusty, smelling strongly of sheep and Solvol soap, they clumped in.

Vida continued to look at her daughter for some moments before she recovered enough to set out cups and dispense tea and rock-buns. Then she turned a hard, speculative stare on Agatha, as though wondering whether one runaway wife had incited another to revolt.

Agatha picked up Cordelia and walked out. How long would she have to be a docile wife before her mother-in-law stopped suspecting her of planning further flight, or of subverting others? Heaven knew, she'd been submissive enough since her return.

At the other end of the narrow veranda she ran the last few steps to her room. She put the baby on the bed and stood mouthing silent oaths at the ceiling. Her nails bit into her palms so deeply they hurt.

She let her breath go. After a moment she took her book from where she'd hidden it under the baby's mattress, curled herself on the bed beside Cordelia, and tried to read.

She was over halfway through *The Old Curiosity Shop*, the second book Snow Franklin had lent her, and wished she could make it last longer. Little Nell rather gave her the pip — far too good to be true — but she was revelling in all the other strange characters who populated the pages.

All the same, she had liked the first book more; she'd read *Manshy* twice, to savour every last nuance of meaning in it, before she'd handed it back. The story of the wild red heifer she'd found both inspiring and depressing, and so close to her own experience it had made her wince: men made the rules, administered them, and if you wanted freedom to live by your own rules then you died, one way or another.

But *The Old Curiosity Shop* was fascinating in its own way. Unfortunately, she would finish it in another couple of days. Perhaps when she left it under the bush for Snow to collect there would be another book waiting. Last time she'd found it easy to carry the book with her when she took Cordelia for her afternoon walk.

She usually went out in the late afternoons, when Vida was busy clattering about in the kitchen preparing tea. After her first offers of help had been rudely rejected, Agatha had determined never again to be available. Bloody Vida was trying to have it both ways: she told Agatha to bugger off she was only in the way, and then told Lew within her hearing that she was a selfish bitch too lazy to lift a finger to help her hard-working mother-in-law. And that fixed it. After that, Agatha took her walks abroad with a clear conscience.

Another reason for getting out of the house was her need to keep her daughter out of everyone's way. All the family ignored the baby as far as possible, though Vida immediately complained if she grizzled, or woke in the night crying. They didn't speak to her, and apart from Figgy they rarely looked at her. Cordelia, to most of the Benson family, occupied an invisible space, which had so confused the child that her friendly smiles had turned tentative, or been replaced by puzzled frowns. She looked with suspicion on them all, including Figgy, who at least tried to be amiable.

Lew, who shared a bedroom with the baby, occasionally spoke to her but would never touch her. Agatha had pointed out to him once that he was the child's legal father, which had put him in a black mood for days; that was something he hadn't reckoned on when he'd refused her a divorce.

Cordelia, who had been dozing, awoke; Agatha kissed her and laid the book aside. They were in the middle of a noisy, laughing game of peekaboo and tickling when she heard a car drive up to the front of the house, and the sound of raised voices. She got off the bed, pulled aside the curtain in the doorway, and looked out.

Through the flywire along the veranda she could see Thelma with all the members of the household grouped together outside the back door, as though they had gone out in a body to confront the man glowering at them from three paces away. Agatha recognised Thelma's husband, big, florid Dick Thompson.

Whoever had driven Dick to the farm was now making a fast getaway before he could be involved in any family disputes; she could hear the car roaring and bouncing as it headed down the rough track from the house.

Thelma shrieked, 'Don't hit me! Don't hit me!'

Dick stumbled back a pace. 'I didn't, I —'

'I'm not coming home, you can't make me. Rupe, don't let him touch me, I won't, I can't, he's a beast.' Hysterical sobs choked her words.

Dick's shoulders rose and he glared at her. 'I never hit her,' he said loudly, clenching his fists in his rage. 'Never have, wouldn't. She's lying, she makes things up. She's got to come home, the kids need her. I dunno what's got into her.'

The two children Beryl and Les, white-faced, unsure whether to bawl or to listen, were standing irresolute half way to his tourer car. Dick said, 'Run along, kids, and get in the car. Be with you in a minute.'

Thelma cowered against her mother, clutching her arm as though trying to hide behind her. 'I wish I'd never married you,' she shouted.

'Thelma!' Dick was appalled.

'I won't go!' she cried. 'Mummy, Lew, don't make me. Please, let me stay!' Her sobs grew louder. To Agatha they sounded forced; she suspected Thelma was keeping half an eye on her furious husband.

Dick turned on Vida. 'You encourage her, you bitch,' he snarled, shaking a meaty fist in her face. 'You're as much to blame as she is. Give yourself airs — dunno what you've got to be so bloody stuck up about.'

'Well, of all the — You've got a nerve. Mob of crooks like you, you and your thieving family. Why should I care what a bastard —'

'At least we're not as miserable as you mongrels.'

Lew said, 'Now listen,' at the same time that Figgy started angrily, 'Watch what you're saying —'

Vida's strident voice rose above her daughter's histrionic weeping. 'Why should I care what a bastard like you thinks? Rupe, are you going to let that moron insult me?' She jutted her jaw at Dick. 'No wonder she cleared out, if that's the way you carry on.'

'You can't even support her, you lazy bugger,' Rupe shouted.

'Who supports that useless Figgy?' Dick yelled. 'Who keeps that bastard, eh?'

Hubbub broke out again. Her neck corded with fury, Vida screeched, 'Well at least he's never been inside.'

Figgy raised his hands in front of his smiling face and clapped gently where she could see him. 'That's my girlie. My word, that's telling him. Go it, girl.' To Dick he said, laughing, 'Put that in your pipe and smoke it, chum.'

Dick raised his fist to flatten Figgy. Vida was shouting abuse, Rupe roaring oaths. Thelma sobbed hysterically.

Fast as a pouncing cat Lew jumped. He gripped Dick's wrist and twisted his arm up his back, forcing him down, ignoring his yells and twisting brutally until he was on his knees, forcing him lower and lower until his cheek was in the dirt and his yells changed to agonised screams that rose above the shouts and abuse of the others.

Agatha, watching aghast, knew that if Lew twisted much further ligaments would rip and the shoulder would be wrenched from its socket. Should she intervene? She took a step. No. Any protest to Lew in this mood could drive him to greater excesses.

'SHUT UP!' Lew bellowed.

Silence fell, except for Dick's moans. Agatha was interested to see the others now turned to Lew, watching him expectantly.

'Shut up the lotta ya,' he said more mildly. He released Dick's wrist and kicked him away, a savage kick in the side with a heavy work-boot that sent him sprawling. The surgeon in Agatha winced again. That was hard enough to crack ribs, and possibly had. Dick lay folded tightly, clutching his side.

'You're gettin nowhere,' Lew said. 'Just listen.' He glanced around at his family as though searching for opposition, but there was none. 'All right. Thelma's goin to stop whingein and get in that car and if she won't walk I'll damn well carry her. Then Dick is goin to take her home. I won't help any bloody wife leave her husband.' He glared at his brother-in-law, who was struggling to his feet still holding his ribs, and snarled, 'All the same, I ever hear Dick's not treatin her right I'll knock his bloody block off. You hear me, y' bastard?'

'You got me wrong,' protested Dick, cowed and conciliatory after his previous sound and fury. But no matter how he tried to arrange his features into a semblance of amiability he couldn't hide his hatred when he looked at Lew.

Thelma whimpered, 'No, no, no,' in an exhausted voice. Lew took her shoulders and pushed her towards her husband, who wrapped an arm around her and tried to lead her towards the car. He seemed more protective than coercive. She looked up into his face.

For several seconds they stood face to face. Then the tension drained from her, and she allowed herself to be guided. It seemed to Agatha that Thelma had a satisfied air as though, now that she had made her fuss and achieved her aim of upsetting Dick, she would be content to let her marriage go on as before — until the next time.

The sound of the car's engine faded. Those left subsided, and turned to go indoors. They appeared suddenly smaller, like fighting cocks that had sleeked their ruffled feathers to reveal tame birds within.

As the three farm dogs trotted back panting from chasing Dick's car, Vida turned to her sons. Her aggression barely diminished, she demanded, 'When are you going to shoot that bloody dog? It had another go at one of my chooks yesterday.'

'I'll do it now,' Rupe said. 'Where's the ammo, Lew?'

'Beside the rifle, shelf by the back door.'

Agatha retreated, sickened. She didn't like the dog, a slinking, bad-tempered roo dog, but the casual way they decided on its death was somehow shocking. They had raised the brute from a pup; it had been part of the farm, even if it hadn't been much liked. Now it would be extinguished like a candle flame.

She shivered. She didn't like guns.

8

Two days later Agatha finished her book, and tucked it into the front of her dress when she set off along the track for her daily walk. The sun was dipping below the mallees beyond the mill; the leaves hung motionless in the cooling air. Cordelia, bobbing up and down astride her hip for the half-mile distance, chattered non-stop nonsense.

Agatha put one foot before the other along one of the two sandy gutters that the farm vehicles had worn through the scrub. Strings of exposed roots crossed the depression; lizard tracks marked the sand. The heat had drawn astringent scents from the thick bush that stretched away on either hand, broken here and there by clumps of mallee standing up from the rest. In one, a magpie was pouring out its evening song.

Ahead, she saw the barrel shaped banksia bush beside the first gate, where she would hide the book if Snow wasn't there. She didn't expect him to be; surely it was only coincidence that he had ridden up six days ago as she was stowing *Manshy* under the branches. Originally he'd wanted to leave several books at a time, but she'd explained she could only manage one unobtrusively when she had to carry Cordelia as well.

She'd had to fight a battle with her basically honest soul before she had agreed to this clandestine exchange. But the whole damn Benson family were treating her with so much arrogant contempt she was almost forced into rebellion to retain any self-respect. She didn't owe them any favours. Of course Lew would have stopped her, probably with violence, if he'd known; but what was so criminal about wanting a book to read?

She hesitated when she saw Snow waiting, sitting on his heel under his horse's nose with the reins through his arm. He stopped doodling in the sandy soil with his finger when he saw her, jumped up, threw the reins over a post, and walked over to lift Cordelia across the fence while her mother climbed between the wires. The baby squealed happily and grabbed at his hair.

Agatha regarded him with some suspicion. 'How did you know I would finish the book today?'

Once might be coincidence, but this time he'd been waiting. Had he been waiting every evening, or was he merely a good guesser?

'I'm only checking,' he said, as though she might have expected that. 'How are things with you?'

'I don't know what you think you're playing at.' Taking Cordelia from him, she sat the child on a bare patch of ground between two bulloaks and handed her a rusk.

She looked up. Snow was studying her so intently that she flushed. She half turned from him and knelt beside her child to adjust her floppy cotton bonnet. Over her shoulder she said, 'You haven't seen me for umpteen years — you don't even know me.'

'Sixteen years,' he said, moving round to a position where he could see her face and folding down in front of her. 'What you mean is, you don't know me.'

He must have counted the years, and such accuracy was unsettling. Sure of only one thing, that he had to be stopped before he became too involved in her unhappy life, she said, 'Snow, I'm grateful for the books, but you'd better not bring any more. I'm a marked woman, as any of my in-laws would tell you, not fit company for decent people now.'

'Give it a rest, for god's sake. I don't give a toss for any of that nonsense.'

'You might not, but everyone else within a radius of fifty miles does. Think of how your family would feel if your name got bandied about with mine.'

'What the hell has my family got to do with this? You might think I've been in Grade Two for the last sixteen years but my family knows better.' Snow propped his elbow on his knee, his cheek on his fist, and gazed at her all innocence. His mouth twitched, and she thought for a moment that he was laughing at her.

Surely not. She said, 'Yes, all right. Sorry. But not only am I a scarlet woman I am also married, and I don't like this secrecy. If Lew got wind of me meeting you, even only to borrow books, he'd raise the roof. You're acting as though I'm free to do as I like. I'm not.'

The sun was sliding behind the mallees, throwing long blue shadows across the scrub; the air was heavy with the scents of heated earth and eucalyptus. The mare stamped restlessly by the fence.

'"Scarlet woman!" What lurid Victorian novels were you brought up on?'

With controlled irritation she said, 'It's a damn sight quicker than saying "a woman who has disgraced herself by running away from her husband, living in sin with another man, and bearing a bastard child."'

'Yeah, true,' he conceded. 'But you're making too much of a production of this. You can't care tuppence for that oaf Benson.'

Who the hell did he think he was? 'That's none of your business, and you know it. Keep out of what doesn't concern you.'

'Of course it concerns me. Any friend would be concerned to see the god-awful mess you're making of your life. Have made. Continue to make.'

'And how could you change that?' she asked, in a tone close to jeering.

He smiled, a slow smile of conscious devilment. 'Give me the chance and I'll show you.'

'Snow, you don't know —'

'If you could forget for a minute that I am not as old as you, you'd soon find out that I've been around long enough to know the score. Then perhaps you'd stop patronising me.'

'I'm not patronising you.' Damn Snow. He hadn't outgrown his six-year-old effrontery.

'Agatha, Agatha, of course you are,' he said, laughing. 'And I know I'm not as brainy as you or as well educated as you, but neither am I the illiterate idiot you think I am.'

'I don't think that,' she protested.

And she couldn't forget the age difference, whatever he said. She felt about a hundred, four times his age, old and stale and exhausted, nothing like the girl she'd been once. She had nothing — no occupation, no thoughts, no friendly words — only the dreary round of her life from day to day. He was right, she'd made a thoroughgoing mess of her life, but she couldn't now do much about it. She didn't really believe that this cheerful young man was suggesting that she should now run off with him. And if she left Lew for a second time the mess would be fifty times worse, the scandal stupendous, and good-natured young men like Snow deserved better than that.

He was saying something, but her thoughts had returned to the farm where soon she too must return, bracing herself to endure the insults and the enmity because there was no other place for a self-made outcast like herself. She said, 'I've no place with ordinary people now.'

'Baloney. Stop dramatising yourself.' He grinned at her. She suspected that he was patronising her, now, but couldn't put her finger on exactly how. He said, 'But it's all right, I'll back off. So you can stop beating your breast about your mistakes and all that garbage. We went over that last time and it's high time you gave it a rest.'

'Back off?' She wasn't sure that she wanted that either. Though of course it would be better if he did. Certainly safer.

He rose to his feet as smoothly as well-oiled machinery. 'Yeah. You've been wasting your time — I'm off tomorrow. So I'm sorry, but there won't be any more books. I've put *The Mayor of Casterbridge* under the banksia. You can keep that one.'

'Going home?'

'Going home first, but in a week or so I'm heading north. I'll be back in three months — four months — I don't know. Maybe I'll see you around then.' He scooped up Cordelia, who was happily trying to stuff a fistful of earth and twigs into her mouth, and tossed her in the air; she crowed with delight. He kissed the child's cheek and dropped her into her mother's arms, then stepped to his horse. 'So you can forget about me and settle down to happy domesticity with Lew, if that's what you want. Good luck.'

Apparently he regretted his sarcasm: a moment later he grinned, leant from his saddle, and offered his hand. 'Don't run away,' he said, gripping her fingers a few seconds longer when she would have pulled her hand free. 'I'll be back.' He kicked his horse round towards the track. Agatha, Cordelia in one arm, lifted her hand.

She looked after him, a little disappointed after all to see him go; but still angry with him, she reminded herself. She watched his tall form in the saddle riding away from her. He didn't look back.

Then out of the bushes stepped Lew, and Rupe, and Figgy; shoulder to shoulder they formed a line across the track, ahead of Snow's horse.

9

Bowler said, 'I don't know what you expect me to do about it. If it's his land I can't stop him ploughing it.'

'If it is his land,' the young man said. 'The old goat can't produce the bloody deeds.'

He prowled restlessly on the other side of the counter that divided Bowler's front room, the Kularook Police Station, in half; a door at the end of the half veranda provided access to the public.

'Neither can the Council,' Bowler pointed out.

Graham Fielding said, 'All the same, when Dad rang the district clerk he seemed pretty sure old Spog had made the land over to them donkey's years ago, given them the deeds and everything. Only problem is, if he did they haven't a clue where they've put them. Dammit all, Bowler, it's been the town oval for as long as anyone can remember, and now the mad bastard says he never gave it away at all, it's still his paddock.'

Bowler leant an elbow on the counter and gazed out his front window. He knew the view by heart: the side of the single-storey Kularook Hotel, the dusty unsealed road, the dried weeds along the verges. Silhouetted against a glowing red sunset Durwin Harris, the pub handyman, was swinging up an axe on the woodheap in the pub's backyard. The kitchen chimney belched smoke as Em stirred up her cooking fire.

A peaceful scene. In an absent voice Bowler said, 'The footy boys shouldn't have mucked around with Spog's gig. That was the last straw.'

'He started it. Anyway, we — I mean they — were only celebrating. Who'd have expected Kularook to beat Edgerton in the finals?'

His gaze still averted Bowler cocked an eyebrow. 'We?'

Graham scowled. 'All right, I was one of them. But you knew that.'

'I know exactly which of you were there that time, and who was there the time before that, *and* the time before that. What do you think I am, asleep? I even know who nicked his chooks, and I'll bet you don't.'

'Why don't you arrest somebody, then?'

'Not so easy when they've eaten the evidence,' Bowler said. 'But I'll get there. Why don't you go away, young Graham, and annoy someone else?' He walked across and seated himself behind his desk, peered in his inkwell, picked up his fountain pen. 'I've got work to do.'

Rump jutting, Graham planted both elbows on the counter and propped his angry face in his fists. He stared moodily at the policeman. 'Can't you argue with Spog? Tell him we need the oval, it's for the good of the whole district?'

'Archie tried that and it didn't work.'

'Why the hell can't the bugger wait until the cricket is over? We could probably find somewhere else for the footy, but that's the only pitch we have. Come on Bowler, you play cricket, why don't you do something?'

'Sometimes I play cricket, you mean. If I've got some spare time I play cricket, but at the rate I'm going I won't see any spare time ever again. Go away.'

'I hope when he gets to the pitch the concrete stuffs up his plough. Why the devil can't he —'

'What was that?' Bowler's head jerked round; he pushed back his chair and went to the window.

'What was what? I didn't hear anything.'

Durwin was no longer on the pub woodheap. Bowler said, 'I thought I heard a shout.'

Then he saw Durwin, normally a slow-moving man who believed in conserving his energies, racing across the road towards the police station gate. Bowler leapt round the counter, shouldered Graham aside, and was at the gate to meet Durwin who, too winded to speak, waved an arm up the street.

An old Ford Model T without a hood was pulled up at the corner, beside the pub. Em Musgrave leaned into the car while beside her Rupe Benson, holding a struggling, screaming baby awkwardly in his large hands, tried to make his voice heard above the baby's squalling. Behind them, head bent, arms folded to grip his own shoulders as though to hold himself together, Figgy Higgins stood rocking himself from foot to foot.

Over his shoulder Bowler barked at Graham, 'Get my wife.' As he sprinted towards the group he saw half a dozen men emerge from the corner door of the bar and gather round the car.

Baby Cordelia was fighting and shrieking to escape from Rupe's inexpert hands. Her cries tore at Bowler's nerves, and without even thinking he snatched her into his own arms, not surprised that she clung like a monkey and subsided to hiccoughing sobs against his neck. He shouldered the men aside and leaned over Em Musgrave to peer into the car.

Across the back seat, legs trailing on the floor, lay a female figure drenched in blood, spattered and painted in blood, covered in bunched wet red clothing; blood dripped to the floor; to his horrified eyes it seemed that there was blood everywhere except in Agatha Benson's waxen face. She lay with her eyes half closed, so still that he couldn't see if she was dead or alive. A purplish bruise clouded her left cheek.

Em turned her head. 'Bowler, good. Have you got a knife? There's been a shooting.'

With his free hand he dug out his pocket knife and handed it over. 'Is she alive?'

'Just. We'll have to get her to John as fast as we can. I can't even see the damage yet.' Em, trained nurse, the highest medical expertise the district possessed, slit the bloodied cloth and peeled it gently back to expose the bullet wound in Agatha's chest.

Bowler said, 'That's an entry wound, it'll be worse in her back. That's where the blood's coming from.' He thought of the long forty miles of rough road to Doctor John Shapcott and the hospital in Edgerton. 'Can we move her? My Chrysler's bigger and faster.'

'We'll have to try, I think.' Em let the limp wrist drop and straightened out of the car. 'I'll come with you, look after her on the way. It's gone through her right lung. Could be worse, but I wish there was some way to stop the bleeding. Most of the damage is inside her chest.'

Bowler turned to Rupe Benson. 'What rifle? A three-o-three? Bloody hell, that's not mucking about. Was it an accident? Where's Lew?'

Then he heard his wife's voice saying, 'I can take the baby, Bill.'

'Good.' Thankfully he disengaged the small clutching hands and put the child into Joan's arms. He touched her cheek, this elegant, maddening woman who shared his board and his bed, thankful that at times like this he could rely on her utterly, knowing that her practical good sense would surface in any emergency. 'Ring John Shapcott, will you? Em can tell you what to say, he'll probably come out to meet us on the road.'

Joan nodded, conferred briefly with Em, and turned to go, cuddling the exhausted baby against her shoulder; then she stopped. 'Do you know her name, poor mite?'

'For God's sake, I can't remember it now. '

'Cordelia.' Em, bent over Agatha again, didn't turn her head.

'That's right, Cordelia.' He patted Joan's shoulder, remembered too late that she disliked what she saw as a patronising gesture, and was scowling as he beckoned to Graham Fielding, hovering in the middle distance. 'Graham, get my car out, will you? And bring it here. The rest of you get the hell out of the way. There's nothing to see.'

Shoving Splinter Thompson, Jockey Gallagher, and two gawping Pitcher boys aside, he grabbed Rupe Benson's arm and dragged him clear of the others. 'What the hell happened? Was it an accident?'

Rupe shook his head violently. He opened his mouth, his throat worked, but he uttered no words.

'Then who shot her, Benson? Where's Lew?' This had all the signs of marital conflict brought to a hideous climax and he hoped Lew was sitting quietly at home waiting to be arrested.

If he'd been asked, Bowler would have said that nothing could ruffle Rupe Benson's dour composure, but now his granite countenance was slack with shock, his square shoulders slumped, his eyes staring. For the first time he saw that the front of the man's shirt was also smeared with blood. Rupe said, 'Lew's dead.'

'*Lew* is?'

'Shot himself. And that's not —' Rupe's voice jammed; he couldn't finish his sentence.

'Jesus.' Bowler shook his head. 'That's bloody awful. Still, if he shot his wife I suppose he wanted a way out. In a way —'

'Shut up!' Rupe said almost hysterically, his voice high and shaking, an extraordinarily disconcerting sound from such a barrel chest. 'Let me finish, damn you. There's my mother and sister too — there's three fucking bodies out on the farm. Three of them! Came in from the paddock and found the fucking place like an abattoir.'

'Christ!' Bowler found he had no breath left for further speech. The captain had used much the same words as Rupe when they'd come on the scene of the ambush, and he was transported to the desert sands of Palestine gazing on khaki-clad bodies lying in tangles of dead horses. After a moment he said automatically, 'Watch your language.' He'd arrested men for less. All the same, if ever there were occasions for strong language this was another one.

'Had to leave them out there,' Rupe said, his voice shaking. 'Had to get help for this bitch. All her fault, the lot of it. Just got too much for Lew, poor bastard. Too much. Bloody hell, I don't know how I can stand this.' Shoulders hunched, he rammed his clenched fists against his temples and turned his back.

Trying to grapple with the enormity of this, of three dead and one dying, Bowler said, 'Is anyone out there now? On the farm?'

'No. Figgy drove, I knelt in the back, stop her sliding off the seat. Serve her right if she dies. All her fault, the slut.'

His first reaction, however, must have been to save the girl; if he'd been unscrupulously vindictive he could have let her bleed to death before he brought her in.

'I'll be back in a minute,' Bowler said, and beckoned to Graham Fielding as he walked over to Em. 'Graham can drive you,' he told her in a low voice. 'I'll have to stay and find out what the hell's been going on. Rupe says she — Mrs Lew — is the only survivor and there are three others dead out on the farm.' He looked into Em's shocked eyes and shook his head. 'But I'll find out,' he promised.

10

The last streaks of sunset were long gone from behind the pub by the time he came to question Rupe and Figgy over the events that had led up to the shooting. He'd helped move Agatha to his own roomier car and waved off young Graham and Em with misgivings in his heart; then he had discovered that Dick Thompson had not so far been informed of his wife's death, and so had dispatched his father Splinter out to the block to break the tragic news. He'd rung Fieldings to explain why Graham wouldn't be home; on Joan's instructions he'd trudged across the street to borrow the pub's cot from Trotter Musgrave so that she could put Cordelia to sleep; and no matter how he hurried it all took time. But at last he was free to ask a few questions of these two men, before he drove out to the farm with them to inspect the scene of the tragedy.

They'd wanted to leave before. He had to explain the importance of ringing through the news, the details, as soon as possible to his bosses in Adelaide before they'd agree to wait. He took them into his office and lit the big kero lamp that stood on the counter.

Both had refused food, but accepted cups of tea. Figgy Higgins's was getting cold on the floor by the leg of his chair; he was sitting with his head bowed into his hands. Bowler remembered, with a start of guilt, that one of the dead women was his wife. Grief was not something he had associated with that rather staid middle-aged man. Why hadn't he expected him to be upset? Any man would be. He must get his prejudices under better control.

Rupe's colour had returned; he said in a level voice, 'The slut was playing up again. That's what started it.'

'Started what? Explain.' Bowler needed details, and he'd like them fast. All the time he was asking questions he was conscious of three corpses alone, unwatched, stiffening, out there at the dark deserted farmhouse. Common humanity to the living demanded that something be done about them soon.

'I saw her, saw what she was up to, see.' Figgy lifted his head; his eyes were bloodshot, almost as though he'd been crying. He sounded apologetic. 'And I told Lew. I thought I had to, I didn't know —' He shuddered, and put his head in his hands. With his face hidden, like a child confessing sins from the shelter of the darkness behind closed eyes, he explained, 'She went off in the trap one afternoon, see, reckoned she was going to see Jack Pedler's wife. But when she came back I saw this fellow with her, a stranger, we don't know him, though later it turns out he's working for Bruce Wilson. He seemed to be — well, hiding, see, he stopped at the gate so no one would see him — and I thought perhaps she'd gone to meet him all along, and Lew should know.' He took a deep breath. 'Well, of course I'd been told about her so I suppose I took a bit more notice of what she was up to after that. But I didn't think —' He stopped, and his head sank lower.

That poor girl, Bowler thought, watched over by all those eyes. 'How long ago was this?'

'A couple of weeks or so. Don't know exactly.'

'And then?'

'Another time I saw her go off, on foot this time, down the track, and this time I happened to catch a glimpse of the same fellow riding off. So I thought I had to tell Lew, I thought it was the right thing to do. I wish — I didn't expect — how was I to know how it would end?

I'd have kept quiet.'

Bowler glanced at Rupe. 'What did Lew say?'

Figgy said, 'He was going to tackle his wife then and there, but we thought he wasn't safe, we cooled him down. Anyway, he was burning to have a go at the fellow, that seemed fair enough, so we all shut up about it and decided to watch. Perhaps we'd've done better if we'd let him get it over with but anyway, we didn't.'

Bowler let the silence hang.

After a minute Rupe said, 'Me an' Lew'd been out in the scrub block, ploughing a line for a new boundary fence. Got home a bit before sundown. Then Mum tells us Agatha's gone off again, so we followed, caught the bloke as he was riding off.'

'Just what do you mean by that?' Bowler didn't like the way neither man would meet his eyes.

'Nothing.' Rupe shifted uncomfortably on his chair. 'Well, Lew pulled him off his horse, thumped him a couple of times, then let him go. Took the bitch home with us and Lew told her to keep in her room.'

Bowler said, 'And thumped her a couple of times too. I saw her face.'

Figgy shrugged. 'Well, Lew was ropeable. After last time, wouldn't you be?'

As though doused in ice water Bowler's heart contracted. How could he tell what he would do if Joan started meeting another man? Fastidious Joan, with her ingrained codes of conduct? The very idea was monstrous; he couldn't begin to gauge what his reaction would be. He took a steadying breath.

Figgy caught his eye. He said sadly, 'Yes, and he told her if she ran off again he'd shoot her. I heard him. You did too, Rupe.'

The other man nodded, and shifted uneasily in his seat. 'Yair, yelling — Couldn't help hearing.'

The policeman in Bowler was grateful that not every man who

made wild threats of violence carried them through into action. Even one was too many. He shook his head, getting a grip, working things out.

He said, 'But if this was yesterday, what happened today? What time was the shooting?'

'Don't know,' said Rupe. 'We left after breakfast, Figgy an' me.'

'Didn't you hear the shots?'

'No. Too far off, a couple of miles away, working on the bloody fence again in the back scrub. Took dinner, didn't get home until nearly teatime.'

'Where was Lew?'

'Stayed behind.'

'Why? Just to keep an eye on his wife?'

'Yeah, that too. But he had a bit of carpentry to do.'

Something in Rupe's manner of saying this made Bowler ask, 'What was he making?'

'A door,' Rupe admitted. 'Room's only got a curtain. A door so he could lock the bitch up.'

Whatever she'd done, Bowler didn't think the unfortunate girl had deserved the treatment planned for her. Agatha had Bowler's sympathy, mainly because he didn't like either of these men much, and hadn't warmed to Lew either, and as clearly as if he'd been clairvoyant he could sense her overwhelming need to get away sometimes from her husband and the claustrophobic, over-heated house.

Had she been planning another escape, with a different man? The idea surprised him and he found it distasteful, though he wasn't certain why. Possibly because she had been so honest with him he couldn't believe she wasn't similarly honest with her husband. But if she was desperate?

He wondered if she was desperate enough to be glad to die, to escape forever from these men who had such complete power over her.

Though if Lew was dead she was a widow; she was already free of him. And he was forgetting her baby, because there was no way she would want to leave her baby unprotected. Of course she wanted to live. Perhaps there was hope for her.

But for now, he wasn't going to let these two have everything their own way. He said, 'This bloke she met, he'd be Matt Franklin. Young fellow from Edgerton, been around Kularook a week or two shoeing a few horses — mine included — and I heard he's out working for Bruce Wilson now. So I'll have a word with him, see what he says.' He saw with satisfaction the swift exchange of glances between Rupe and Figgy. 'How badly did you beat him up?'

'Didn't,' Rupe said. 'Lew just smacked him about a bit.'

'That's assault.' Mounted Constable Bowler Brown didn't care what provocation they'd had, the law was the law. 'And even if you two only gave Lew a helping hand, you're involved and it's still assault.' He knew damn well they hadn't stood idly by while Lew had a go at young Franklin; they'd probably held the poor bastard while the irate husband pounded him.

Bowler wasn't sure why he felt strongly about this. Justice was on the husband's side; most men would believe him justified in what he did, but something about the situation grated. He wasn't going to look leniently on violent men who took the law into their own hands merely because they had since suffered bereavement. Anyway, a bit of righteous indignation gave him an excuse for disliking the pair, instead of pitying them.

He'd had his fill of violence. The sort he and his mates had dealt out in the desert had been licensed, in a horrible kind of way, and at least the men they shot at had shot back; but this was different. Civilians should behave themselves. Higgins and the Benson brothers weren't even returned men, ex-soldiers hardened by the necessities of war.

He glanced out the window and decided he wasn't going to ride his horse out to their farm in the dark. Em had taken his car, so he'd borrow the pub's buckboard.

'Right,' Bowler said. 'I'll just make a phone call and then I'll follow you out. Don't touch anything until I get there.'

'You can come with us,' Rupe said, 'and drive Dick's car back. Thelma came out in that, so it's just sitting there.'

Bowler nodded as he shuffled his papers together. 'Fine.'

11

In the light of a match the clock on the kitchen mantelpiece read twenty past midnight.

Before it burnt his fingers Bowler flicked the match against the stove so that it fell safely to the cement hearth, and struck another to light the candle his wife had left for him on the kitchen table. Beside it, on a plate, lay a note: Sandwich in the Coolgardie.

There was a smell in the kitchen, familiar yet strange. He took a moment to identify it, and then smiled to himself. Baby. That's what he could smell, a baby, all the compounds of milky food and baby powder and wet naps that went together to leave a scent individual as an animal's. Who could fail to distinguish between a cow and a horse in the dark?

Yawning, he carried his candle to the back veranda, where the Coolgardie safe stood beside the back door. He hadn't waited for a meal before he left to check over the carnage at Bensons', just grabbed a handful of Sao biscuits. Joan must be making one of her spasmodic attempts at domestic competence, since she usually left him to forage for himself at times like this. More to the point, she'd put a bottle of beer in the safe too, a pleasant surprise. He took his booty back to the kitchen and bit deeply into a sandwich while he poured two glasses from the bottle, noting with satisfaction that his hand didn't shake. He set the lot on a warped tin tray and carried it up to the bedroom.

Joan had heard him come in. By the time he pushed open the door she'd lit the candle on the cupboard beside the bed and, tousled and sleepy-eyed, was hitching herself up to lean against the wooden slats of the bedhead; she threw back the sheet to let the air at her long bare legs, accepted the glass he handed her, and took a deep draught.

Deliberately vulgar, she wiped her mouth on her wrist. 'Have you heard how that girl is? Did she survive the trip?'

'Don't know. Em's not back yet.'

He saw her gauging his expression. She asked, 'Was it very bad at the farm?'

'Well, they were all dead as stated.' Bowler moved her legs aside and sat on the bed.

'Don't crack hardy with me, Bill.'

He grimaced. 'Lew Benson must have run raving mad. He shot his wife, his mother, his sister, and then turned the gun on himself.' He pushed aside his sandwich. 'The bodies were all lying tidily on beds by the time I got there. Rupe Benson said they'd brought them inside before they drove in with Agatha. Higgins seemed to think I'd be annoyed about this, but I knew why they had to.' He lifted his glass.

Joan laid her hand on his knee. 'Yes. Bill —'

'Because of the crows,' Bowler said in a hard voice. 'Because —'

'Bill, why did it happen? Tell me about them.'

He let his breath go in a long exhalation, forcing his thoughts away from the dead, filling up his memory with recent events, the incidents that had led up to the shooting as he had learned them from Rupe Benson.

He started telling her what he knew.

Then he realised that the familiar irony had been absent from Joan's voice. Did she really want to know all this? No.

Well, yes, most people liked to hear the inside information on sensational events; his wife was no different, but she might have waited until morning if she hadn't been concerned for him. She was asking questions, not because she wanted to know why Lew Benson had gone berserk with a rifle, but to help him come to terms with it. She was supportive where it mattered, he thought, and smiled at her wryly.

He said, 'It must have been a nasty shock to Lew to find she was carrying on again with another man.'

'I wonder why she came back.'

'From something she said I think it was that or starve. Her parents are dead, she's got no other relations who could give her a home, she'd have no money. I expect her choices were Lew or the streets.'

'She's qualified, she could work somewhere.'

Bowler shook his head. 'Not in this State, not with her reputation. No decent practice would take her in, even if she had the money to buy a partnership.'

In her best upper-crust English voice Joan said, 'Infidelity is always grubby —' she stumbled then hurried on, '— but I do believe that Fate has dealt hardly with that woman.'

Bowler kept his expression blank. He said, 'And you only know half of it. She's had a tough trot ever since she was little.'

'Has she?' Joan looked at him — critically, he thought — her head on one side. 'Juliet Davidson mentioned something about that at the meeting, the one where I said my party piece. What happened to her?'

'Her mother died when she was in primary school, so she grew up on an isolated farm with just her father — and half the time he was off his head. Been shell-shocked in the war. It can't have been much of a picnic for her. He got more and more peculiar as time went on, became morose, started drinking. What else did you hear at the meeting?'

'Nothing, really. It was just after she had returned, and they were being sanctimonious and throwing up their hands at her shocking behaviour, and at the same time trying to hide how delighted they were to have a new topic to be self-righteous about.'

His wife hadn't liked him sympathising with Agatha before; he stopped the words 'poor girl' before they escaped his lips. Joan went on, 'But how did she manage to get away to school, and university?'

'No idea. Probably scholarships. But her father was fifty times worse when she came back, a raging alcoholic, and finally he burned down the house with himself inside it.'

Joan said it for him. 'How ghastly. She has had a difficult time.'

He drained the bottle into his glass, threw the last of the beer down his throat, and got to his feet. 'Well, so have plenty of others. Where's her baby?'

'Asleep in Tom's room. Don't wake her.'

Bowler grunted. With the tray in his hands he paused at the door. 'Don't go to sleep, I'm coming straight back.'

But later, much later, he still woke shouting and shuddering with his wife's arms round him and her voice in his ear calling him back from the abyss.

He'd thought he was cured. He hadn't had one of those for over twelve months.

12

In the grey light before sunrise Bowler heard his car stop outside the pub, then drive down the other side of the house and into his garage. He went out in his pyjamas to meet Graham Fielding, and to hear whether Agatha had survived the forty mile drive over tracks that were ribbed with limestone on the stretches that weren't deep in sand drifts.

A rooster crowed in the yard behind the pub, and was answered by another somewhere up near the post office. The air was cool, and still. Graham, swaying with weariness, climbed out of the car, stretched himself and bent his shoulders and torso into strange shapes, trying to un-knot his stiff muscles. He seemed surprised to see Bowler, and mumbled a few responses in answer to his questions; then he shook his head.

'Em said I can crash on one of her spare beds,' he said. 'I'll see you some time next week or next year. Whenever I wake up.' He stumbled off across the rutted street towards the pub.

After that it didn't seem worthwhile to go back to his own bed. Bowler lit the lamp in his office, sat at the wide table that served as his desk, unearthed a scribble pad from the 'out' basket, and took up a pencil. He drew a careful rectangle to represent the Benson house, another at an angle some distance off to represent the long machinery shed, where Lew had presumably been working when his brother and step-father left. Then he drew in four stick figures, to show the position of the bodies as Rupe had explained them to him.

Lew was lying at the foot of the slope from the house, close to the shed, the rifle beside him where it had fallen from his hands as he died. Not far from the back door of the house Vida and Thelma lay close together, as though they had been shot as soon as they emerged. Agatha had been inside the house, lying in the doorway to her room at one end of the enclosed veranda.

Right. That was the bodies. The spent cartridge casings told a little more of the story. One was behind the two women, close to the door of the house where, Bowler believed, Lew had stood in the doorway to shoot his wife, angling a shot down the fly-wire enclosed veranda, hitting Agatha as she emerged from her bedroom. Perhaps he had called to her, to bring her out.

Then, as he had started to walk back to the sheds, his mother and sister had run out of the house behind him to see what was going on and, for whatever reason, he had turned and shot first one and then the other from barely four yards away. The two shells lying close together half way down to the shed gave the range.

He had walked on, but when he reached the shed he had apparently realised that the killings had finished him, set him apart, cut him off from any kind of a normal life; he had bent over the rifle with the barrel in his mouth and pulled the trigger. The fourth shell was in the rifle by his body.

By the time Bowler saw the bodies that evening over five hours had elapsed since Rupe and Figgy had discovered them. How long before that they had died was difficult to establish, but he was inclined to believe only a couple of hours. He was no expert on the onset of rigor, but had observed it was incomplete in all the bodies; John Shapcott or someone had told him once it took about twelve hours to complete the process. But his main reason for believing that the bodies had not lain unattended in the open air for an extended period was the limited damage done by crows.

Both women had been shot through the head; the birds had started their grisly work on their faces. Although the ravages had been sufficient to make him retch they were not as extensive as they could have been, and Lew, in the shade of the machinery shed, had not been discovered at all. A couple of hours, he repeated to himself. Probably mid afternoon when it happened.

The baby started wailing, no doubt upset to wake in a strange house, and through the wall he heard Joan getting up in their bedroom. He turned the pad face down, as though a few pencil lines could disturb a casual observer as much as the real bodies had disturbed him, and went to get dressed. Durwin, the handyman at the pub, would have finished milking by now. Bowler would feed the horses and collect the milk before breakfast.

At the breakfast table Cordelia, on the opposite corner, thumped her rusk on the tray of the pub's high chair and smiled at him, then held out her arms to be picked up.

'Not now, Tuppence,' he said, and turned to his wife. 'Agatha Benson was still hanging on when they got to Edgerton, but it's anybody's guess by now. Graham Fielding told me. I heard him bringing the car back just before sunrise.'

Joan, spooning porridge into the children's bowls, paused. 'Did he say what John Shapcott thought of her chances?'

'Not too bright. When they left he said he was going to take her to town on the Express but he wasn't sure she'd last the distance, apparently. She'd lost a lot of blood.'

Joan said, 'Last until train time, or last until Adelaide?'

'Either.'

The children were squabbling in Tom's room across the passage but Bowler hardly heard them. He was thinking that if Agatha died he would never know what had happened out there on that isolated farm; he would never learn what incident, what confrontation, what words, had finally driven Lew Benson to pick up his rifle in a murderous rage and shoot three people — four people, counting himself. Knowledge of the events wouldn't change the outcome, but Bowler wanted to find a cause, a reason. There had to be an explanation for such a monstrous deed . He didn't want to believe that the random slaughter of war might carry over into civilian life.

Joan looked at the alarm clock on the mantelpiece as Rose came in and took her place. 'You're late,' she said. A few minutes later Tom, out of breath, sneaked in when her back was turned and slid into his chair. Joan set bowls before them, saying, 'Don't grizzle to me if you're late for school, breakfast was ready on time.' She asked Bowler, 'Will you be in to lunch?'

'Hope so. May be late, though. I've got to go out to Bensons' again, and I'll have to ring around for John Shapcott and stuff for the coroner. There'll be paperwork a mile long over this lot, and you know how I enjoy that.' He frowned at his young, decorously spooning up porridge. Porridge in midsummer, for heaven's sake —why couldn't his wife feed the kids cereal, like everybody else? Not that the children seemed to mind. He shook his head.

13

After breakfast on Saturday, Bowler said, 'Joan, can you keep an eye on the kids this morning? I've got to go out to Bruce Wilson's, see if I can find the Franklin boy.' To give Joan her due she never went off on her photographic expeditions at weekends unless she knew he'd be around the place.

She was carrying Cordelia on one hip; he realised that while she was looking after the baby she wasn't going far anyway.

'Yes, that's fine. They're up at Prices', playing with their brood, but they'll be home to lunch. Bill, have you heard any news of Agatha Benson?'

'Today's report says she's hanging on, and the doctors think she's got a reasonable chance, provided there are no complications.'

'I am glad.' Joan turned her head and kissed the baby's cheek. 'That's good news for you, my girl.'

'Isn't it. Look, I'm riding Imshy, he needs the exercise. Expect me when you see me.'

A change had gone through in the night, cooling the breeze and settling the dust. The earth smelled of wet straw from the cured grasses; brilliant water-drops trembled on the mallee leaves. Bowler sat easily, enjoying the morning, yet his reflexes worked quickly enough when a bronzewing pigeon flew up and startled Imshy into a violent leap sideways. He didn't move in his saddle.

Feeling smug — he hadn't lost his old skills yet — he brought the horse under control and kicked it forward. Meaner horses than Imshy hadn't been able to get rid of him.

Before he saw them Bowler could hear Bruce Wilson shouting at his son, abusing him for some carelessness or other, and then he glimpsed them through the trees by the sheds, waving their arms at one another across the bonnet of a tourer car parked outside one of the smaller sheds. He rode past the house without dismounting.

Young Doug, a twenty-year-old copy of his strong, stocky father, was shouting emphatic denials in response to his father's accusations; he had inherited his father's temper as well as his build. They didn't hear Imshy's hoof-beats until he was almost on them, when they both fell abruptly silent.

Doug vanished into the workshop behind him. Bruce, unembarrassed, nodded to his visitor. 'G'day, Bowler. What brings you here?'

Bowler dismounted. 'Heard what happened at Bensons'?' He and Bruce, although not close friends, were both returned servicemen and met each other regularly at RSL meetings.

'Bensons! Those bastards. No, and I don't care. I don't have anything more to do with that thieving lot than I can help.'

'Why thieving?'

'Hungry bastards. Last year they were short of feed, so they pulled over a couple of chains of the old boundary fence and let most of their bloody sheep into my scrub, pushed them through the scrub, and opened a gate. The miserable brutes spent months in my back paddock. Bensons reckoned the fence fell over and the gate must have been already open. Huh!'

Bowler said, 'They've got their own problems.' He told Bruce of the slaughter. When he had allowed enough time for the other to express his shock he asked, 'Where's Matt Franklin? I heard he's working for you.'

'He's gone. He was cutting a few posts for me — one of my sister's boys, between jobs, I like to help out if I can — but he finished up a couple of nights back, wanted to get home in a hurry so Brainwave there drove him back to Edgerton.' Bruce nodded towards the workshop door, where Doug stood listening.

'Help out' indeed. Bloody Bruce wasn't one to do favours; he was as tight as a rusted wheel-nut and Bowler would bet he got his money's worth out of anyone he employed.

'What day was this?'

'He didn't have anything to do with the shooting, did he?' Bruce asked, alarmed. 'What do you want to know about him for?'

'No, of course not.' Bowler was at his most reassuring. 'It was murder-suicide all right. But they tell me he met Lew Benson's wife a couple of times, and that's apparently what set Lew off shooting every one in sight.'

'Messing about with a married woman?' Bruce's voice rose and his lip curled with distaste. 'His father'll skin the young whelp. Not that you can blame him altogether, I suppose — by all accounts she's like a bitch on heat.' He glanced uneasily at his son, as though unsure whether he should be listening to this conversation.

Bowler believed Doug Wilson's ears were not so virginal. 'Don't know about that. I don't think there was much in it,' he said. 'What day did Franklin leave?'

'What's today, Saturday? Then it was three nights ago, Wednesday. He'd finished up for me and was impatient to get home so I let them have the car.'

'According to Rupe Benson, there was a bit of a fight, reckons Lew pulled Franklin off his horse and clouted him a few times, and I'll bet the other two joined in. He probably wasn't feeling too bright.' He swung on Doug. 'He say anything about it to you?'

The youth retreated a pace, shaking his head. 'No. He was pretty maggoty, didn't say much at all.'

Bowler snorted. 'Forty miles of slow road and you didn't say much? Come on.'

Watching the policeman with a slightly speculative air Doug rubbed his neck under his ear. After a moment he said, 'We talked about bloody Spog, mostly. When we talked at all. Not that Matt gives a toss for the oval, but Spog's his uncle as much as mine.'

'Great uncle,' Bruce corrected. 'Bloody-minded old pest.'

'I thought Franklin might like to lay a complaint against Rupe Benson and Higgins,' Bowler explained. 'I'll swear they were in it too.'

'Hell's bells, he can't do that!' Bruce said, scandalised. 'Not if he's been playing up with the wife. No no, he got no more than he deserved. You let him alone, Bowler.'

'Wasn't playing up,' Doug said.

Bowler frowned. 'I thought you didn't know anything about it.'

'I know that much.' Doug set his lips.

Bruce said again, 'Let it go, Bowler. He shouldn't have been there.'

Mounted Constable Bowler Brown said coldly, 'I don't give thrippence for that. What gets my goat is these characters who think they can take the law into their own hands. What do they think I draw my wages for?'

He knew he would agree with Bruce if he hadn't admired the way young Franklin had handled Imshy when he put new shoes on him, and if he hadn't taken a dislike to monolithic Rupe in spite of an unwilling sympathy: how would a man feel to lose his whole family?

Bowler said, 'Aside from that I need to know Franklin's version of what happened, what went on to set Lew off. So he'd be home now?'

'Yeah. Reckons he's got a few things to sort out before he heads off in a couple of weeks.'

'Heads off where?'

'North? Somewhere.' Bruce shrugged. 'Brainwave there knows all about it.' He flicked his hand towards his son, like a conductor bringing in the bassoons.

The young man said, 'He's going with some scientists from Adelaide University, into the deserts out from Oodnadatta somewhere, hunting for plants and animals and stuff. He looks after their trucks and gear. He did it before, a couple of years back, and now they want him again. He's been looking forward to it for ages.'

'I see.' Franklin's departure hadn't been a sudden decision, then. 'He likes deserts?' Bowler did not. He'd had his fill of deserts in the war.

'It's because they've got him interested in what they're doing, I think, what they're finding out. Matt helps with some of the scientific things as well as the trucks and the tents.'

Bowler nodded and turned to mount Imshy, turned back. 'Rupe Benson reckons they're putting up a new boundary fence. Is that the same fence they pushed over?'

'Yep. Mind you, it was old as the hills and a couple of fires had gone over it, on its last legs I reckon. I told Bensons they'd bloody well better put up the south half or I'd sue them for loss of stock feed, but if they did that I'd put up the north. Now Matt's finished cutting the posts Doug can start digging holes for them any time. Get the damn thing fixed once and for all.'

His son bared his teeth to show his opinion of this treat in store for him.

Bowler swung into his saddle. Bugger it, now he'd have to make a trip to Edgerton to speak to Matt Franklin.

14

When she heard a car in the distance, driving up the track to the farmhouse, Margaret Franklin pushed her Mrs Potts irons to the back of the wood stove and hastily rolled up her ironing blanket from the table, rolling up the scorched brown cotton bed-sheet inside the ragged blanket like the jam inside a Swiss roll. She didn't want to be caught ironing on a Saturday afternoon since efficient housewives finished the ironing on washing day, during the working week.

This week she'd had interruptions and hadn't got the wash dried until Wednesday, so had left the ironing until Thursday; and by then she'd been too upset. She'd cried so much she'd ended up with a sick headache.

When Matt had arrived home unexpectedly late on Wednesday evening, and made his equally surprising announcement that he was leaving on the Adelaide train that same night, it had triggered a monstrous, enormous, horrendous row with his father. Margaret couldn't think about it without shuddering. Her attempts to smooth matters between the two had only enlarged her husband Bob's fury to include her too.

Matt's abrupt departure had been the last straw for Bob. He had never been able to see why, if his son had been to that god-forsaken northern country once, he would want to go again. Matt should get on with his life instead of spending months traipsing around the back of beyond digging lorries out of sand dunes.

Ever since the trip had been organised he had tried to persuade his youngest son to give it up, advancing all sorts of reasons: he'd emphasised the dangers of the deserts, so far from civilisation and help; he'd tried to convince the boy he wasn't up to the responsibilities; he'd sneered at scientific investigation as a pansy occupation for grown men; he'd dismissed the pay as peanuts. He'd nagged his son so mercilessly that Matt had slung in his job with the local garage and left home to work for his uncle in Kularook.

Margaret suspected the real reason for Bob's antagonism was not concern for his son's safety, but jealousy. He was jealous of this professor, White or whatever his name was, who had written to Matt begging him to join his second expedition; who had written a letter full of praise and affection and remembrance of past good times they'd had together. A pity Bob had ever seen the letter.

There was no doubt Matt thought the world of the professor — but then it seemed that the professor thought the same of Matt. And certainly Bob had been out of line to suggest there was something unhealthy in the professor's interest in a younger man. That's when Matt had started to laugh, started to swear, then caught his breath on a foul oath and slammed his bedroom door in his father's face, yelling that he had to finish packing.

Not that the row had been entirely Bob's fault. Matt had endured worse nagging from his father with unruffled good humour in the past, but that evening he had been edgy for some reason and Margaret thought he might have been in a fight. The bruise on his face, his split lip, might have been caused by a low branch as he was riding home after a day's post-cutting, as he explained, but they might have been caused by fists. She sighed. She hoped she was wrong. She didn't like to think of Matty, her baby, the big even-tempered sunny-natured one of her three sons, getting involved in fights.

When she heard the car pull up at the gate she bundled the ironing blanket into the clothes basket and headed for the back door. She didn't know the man who lifted his hat to her, nor did she recognise his car behind him. Youngish, casually but neatly dressed — an interesting smile, anyway, friendly but slightly raffish too.

He said, 'Mrs Franklin? I'm Bowler Brown, the constable from Kularook.'

'Oh, yes.' Margaret smoothed her hair with her hand; she had heard of him, and some of the stories. She studied him surreptitiously, curious to see him in the flesh. 'Come in. Bob won't be long.'

She ushered him in to the kitchen, a large room with a central table.

In spite of its size Bowler found it unpleasantly warm from the bright fire burning behind the slits of the stove. The air was slightly steamy, and still smelled of scorched cotton. Mrs Franklin seemed a bit uncertain, and he wondered why. Why should the appearance of the policeman from the next town make a respectable farmer's wife hesitant?

'Please, won't you sit down? Bob and the boys are at the tennis, Robbie's playing, but they should be back any minute now.'

Bowler didn't want to sit down. 'Is young Matt with them?'

'No, he —'

'It's him I came to see. I wonder, could have a few words with him?'

'He's not here.'

When he'd got over his surprise that not only was Matt Franklin not there, but had left three nights before for his trip north, Bowler said, 'But I understood he was going to be home for a week or two first.'

'We thought so too,' his mother said. She was Bruce Wilson's sister, and one of the tall ones of that tribe. The Wilsons came in two sizes: medium height and squarely built, like Bruce and Harry and Sibyl, or tall and bony, like Ralph and Mott and Spog and this woman. Her manner was quiet, even colourless; she looked tired.

Bowler said, 'So this was a spur of the moment decision.'

'I don't know when he decided. He came back from Kularook that evening with his mind made up. What did you want to speak to him about, Mr Brown?'

When he explained about the fight at Bensons', and the subsequent shooting, she looked aghast. But not, he thought, because of the murders. She exclaimed, 'Not Agatha Coleman!'

'What about her? Do you know her?' he asked, on the alert.

After a moment Margaret said in a flat tone, 'I haven't seen her since she was in her teens.'

There was a faint, though possibly unintended, emphasis on the 'I', as though perhaps Matt had seen her since. 'Was she friends with your son then?'

'No, no, nothing like that.' Her quick, indignant denial wasn't altogether convincing. She added, 'Well, they went to the same school, but they weren't even in the same class. And Matt wouldn't have seen her for years, and certainly not since she married and went to the bad.'

Bowler turned his hat in his hands, looking down, thinking. He said, 'She's only just hanging on. I was speaking to John Shapcott just now, and he says they're afraid of infection.'

'Poor woman,' Margaret said perfunctorily.

'Did Matt say anything to you about the fight?'

'He said he'd ridden into a branch. I knew there was something wrong but he was in such a state I couldn't get any sense out of him.'

'In a state? Why?'

He saw a wary expression come over her face as though she was regretting her unguarded remark and considering how much more to tell him. 'I just meant he wasn't very talkative,' she corrected herself. 'I expect his bruises were hurting him.'

His curiosity aroused, Bowler wished he was ruthless enough to follow this up, to bully her into giving him a straight answer. His interest in young Matt, however, was pretty peripheral, and he was here merely to gain more information about the incident at Bensons'. Her answer would have no bearing on the report he would write, so he decided to let the matter drop.

All the same, why had Matt Franklin been 'in a state'? From being beaten up, or for some other reason?

15

Harvest was long over. The stacks of bagged grain in the railway yards had dwindled and vanished as day by day the bags were loaded into railway waggons and carted off to the ports. Farmers at Kularook were beginning to watch the clouds and shake their heads over their rain gauges. Perhaps the next showery weather would turn into a bit of proper rain, to bring up the weeds. Then they could plough them in, and prepare their paddocks ready for seeding the grain crops.

It was the time of year when the young men of the district stopped handing their wives and mothers white shirts to wash after every weekend, and presented them instead with muddy shorts and long smelly socks. Football had taken over from cricket.

One cold and wet Friday Joan and Bowler's good friends Juliet and Archie Davidson had driven in for an evening of bridge. They put their two little girls to sleep in the Browns' own double bed, and settled down comfortably at the bridge table in front of a large mallee-root fire.

Bowler set a glass of port at Juliet's elbow, a brandy balloon at his wife's. 'Whisky for you, Arch?' He brought the glasses across from the sideboard and sat down. 'Did Joan tell you that Agatha Benson is coming back tomorrow?'

'Will she be staying with you?' Juliet cut the cards and handed them back to Arch.

'Good heavens no,' Joan said. 'We haven't the room. Em Musgrave is going to let her stay in one of her back rooms for the present. Until she decides what to do.' She smiled. 'Cordelia will be pleased to see her.'

'How is Mrs Benson? Has she recovered?'

'At last report she was rather weak, but improving. She was lucky to survive, apparently.'

'A tough one,' Juliet said, not as a compliment.

'I think she's had to be.' Bowler kept his attention on his cards, moving one across his hand. 'One heart.'

'Are we playing contract, as usual?' Juliet asked.

'Oh yes.' Bowler grinned at his wife. 'Joan's the only one likes auction, and she's outvoted.'

Archie said. 'Good. But Bowler, what was the score with young Matt Franklin? Did that woman really seduce him?'

'Hard to say. Doesn't seem likely, but Lew apparently thought so. I wasn't able to get his version of events before he shot off north, but I'll find out when he gets back.'

'What is it they see in her?' Juliet asked. 'A skinny, ordinary-looking girl like her, dressed practically in rags, and she attracts man after man without even crooking her finger.'

Archie and Bowler exchanged fleeting glances.

Joan said, 'But she's not ordinary at all, Juliet. And you're right about the rags. If you dressed her up, she'd turn heads.' After a moment she added, 'She would in Europe, anyway.'

'I must be blind.' Juliet laid down her card in suits on the table. 'You must agree I've got a nice dummy for you, partner.'

Once she would have felt put down when Joan, from her wider experience, disagreed with her; now she knew Joan was merely voicing an honest opinion and would have expected the same from her. Differences of opinion didn't ruffle Joan, and Juliet, now she understood the strength of the friendship between them could stand the strain, was learning that arguments went to make conversation interesting and didn't necessarily lead to quarrels. Or to umbrage being taken.

Once, before she knew her better, she'd been very much in awe of Joan. Whatever impressed you, Juliet thought — brains, blue blood, or money — Joan had it with knobs on. The mansion she'd grown up in, the dozens of servants, the horses and grooms, the titled cousins in Stately Homes, the Hunt Balls, the presentation at court — how alien it sounded to the average Australian woman. Yet she seemed content with her lot in this tiny Australian backwater, married to a man the rest of her family considered socially invisible.

Though you couldn't sell Bowler Brown short, either, Juliet reflected. He had his own kind of poise, a self-confidence that would be at home in any company. Almost an arrogance, though not of the puffed up kind that assumed more than it could deliver.

'Our trick I think,' Bowler said

16

When Agatha Benson was released from hospital and returned to Kularook to be reunited with her daughter she gratefully accepted Em's offer of a small room at the back of the Kularook Hotel. For the first weeks, while she recovered more of her strength, the only people she saw were Trotter and Em Musgrave and occasionally Bowler or Joan Brown when one or other of them came across the road for their milk every morning.

She had no money, and no intention of making a claim on her husband's estate or of asking her brother-in-law Rupe for any. She believed she had caused enough distress to the Benson family — with a stab of shock she realised that Rupe was the only surviving member of it — without adding a financial burden to it. So as soon as she was strong enough she did what she could to help Em in the kitchen and laundry as a small return for her bed and board.

Em wasn't worried about payment for the room. It had been a depository for crippled furniture before, so Agatha had done her a good turn since she'd been intending to clear it out for years. She was worried, however, about the young woman's health. Not so much her physical strength as her emotional well-being; in Em's opinion she was better off if she was well occupied instead of sitting around brooding.

So Em accepted the help with a good grace while at the same time, looking at Agatha's haggard face, she thought that it would take more than a few hours of housework to heal that badly-damaged spirit.

Shortly after her return Bowler came early for his milk. Em, busy cooking breakfasts at the roaring wood stove, said, 'Durwin hasn't finished the milking yet.'

'I know. I came for a word with you. Has Agatha said anything to you about what happened at the farm that afternoon?'

She turned to him, her brows raised. 'I thought that was all finished with, as far as you're concerned.'

'Couple of things I'd still like to know. The city detectives interviewed her, but they don't pass on much.' He knew which men to blame, too. They hoarded their information like bloody misers, as though it would lose its value if they shared it with him, though the buggers always expected him to tell them every last damn thing that he knew. But they were too far away to understand the local implications and he needed to satisfy himself that he had covered all the angles.

Em stirred the bacon in her frying pan. 'She hasn't breathed a word about the shooting; she just carries on as though it never happened. Probably the memory is too painful. And she's weighed down by an appalling load of guilt, anyone can see that.'

'Perhaps it would do her good to talk about it.'

Em shook her head. 'Don't try and make a virtue of your damn sticky-beaking.'

'That's rich, coming from you,. You know everyone's business in this town better than they do themselves.' He pulled out a chair and sat down at the kitchen table.

'Now come on!' She sounded slightly put out at the suggestion, which surprised him. Didn't she know how the locals regarded her? She added, 'Anyway, that's nothing to do with Agatha. She's still pretty fragile and easily upset.' Em turned the bread slices, propped in a row across the open stove door, to toast the other sides at the fire within.

'I don't know whether I should let you talk to her or not.'

'Why's it up to you?'

Smelling strongly of the cowyard Durwin Harris, a short man with the shoulders of a prize fighter, walked in with a metal milk bucket in his hand; he shied like a startled horse at the sight of Bowler, took a step back, then hurriedly put the bucket on the nearest cupboard and whisked himself out of the room. The wire door at the back banged shut.

Em looked at him with disfavour. 'What have you been doing to upset our Durwin?'

'Nothing. Just a guilty conscience. He nicked half a dozen chooks off old Spog Wilson a while back and he knows I'm on to him. Devious beggar hoped one of the footy boys'd be blamed because of their feud with Spog but I'm a couple of jumps ahead of him. He'll keep.'

'He never touches our stuff,' Em said. 'Just as well, I don't know how we'd manage without him. I'm warning you, Bowler, you can fine him if you like but don't lock him up whatever you do — I need him. Good morning, Agatha.'

With Cordelia astride her hip Agatha came in. The plain black dress that she wore habitually these days hung loosely on her thin body. She smiled vaguely on Bowler, more warmly on Em, and pulled a high chair from the corner to sit her daughter in. Cordelia beamed on Bowler, an old friend from her prolonged stay in his household, and crowed at him amiably.

Em made tea, put two cups on the table, then loaded the pot and the toast on a traymobile and wheeled it up the passage to the dining room. She glanced at Bowler as she left, but he couldn't interpret her meaning.

'Have you got a moment, Mrs Benson? I'd like to ask you a couple of questions. If you don't mind, that is,' he added. Judging by her hollow eyes it was a long time since she had last had a decent night's sleep.

'I was wondering when you'd get around to me.' She splashed milk into one of the cups and pushed the jug towards him. 'Of course I'll tell you anything I can. And Agatha's my name, we got that sorted out last time.'

'So we did. Can you bear to talk about what happened on the farm before the shooting?'

She studied him gravely while she thought about that. 'Yes, I can. In fact, there are a couple of things you ought to know.'

She'd said something like that the last time, Bowler thought. A girl who didn't live by the rules but still didn't want her actions misjudged — which of course they would be, no matter what she said. Bowler loaded his cup with sugar and took a sip; he set it back carefully in the saucer, not looking at her.

'Things you didn't tell the detectives in town?'

'Things they didn't want to know. They don't live here.'

Bowler accepted that. 'Can you tell me exactly what happened the day before? I've only heard Rupe's version so far, and he's hardly an unbiassed witness.'

'Neither am I,' Agatha said.

'I wanted to ask Matt Franklin about it but he went home that evening, packed his bags, and caught the Adelaide Express the same night, on his way north. According to his mother, he's out in some desert or other now, working with a scientific expedition.'

'Scientific? Snow?'

'He's the mechanic, she says. He looks after their lorries.'

'I see. It wasn't his fault, you know, what happened. You mustn't blame him. There was nothing between us to upset Lew, but Lew wouldn't listen at first. I know Snow from primary school, and I just happened to meet him on my way home one day and he lent me a book. That's all.' When Bowler made no immediate comment she said, 'Well, I'd hardly have come back to Lew if I meant to leave him again immediately, would I? It wouldn't have been worth the bother.'

'No, that's all right,' Bowler said, to appease the anger in her voice. 'I understood that all along.' He had, too, but on a subconscious level; that was why the introduction into the drama of another would-be seducer had bothered him. She had seemed too straight to let her husband believe she had returned for good if it wasn't true. 'Lent you books?' he asked.

'I had nothing to read, and Snow put a book under a bush for me. I was taking it back when — when —'

'When the three of them ambushed him,' he finished for her. 'Ambushed' wasn't a word he had used for a while and it unsettled him. It unsettled her too. She covered her face with her hands.

At the sight of her mother's distress Cordelia, who had been cheerfully banging a spoon against the tray of her chair, now set up a wail. Agatha jumped up, her face averted, and started mixing a bowl of cereal at a cupboard behind her. When she turned round he put out his hand for the bowl and laughed at her puzzled expression.

'Who do you think has been feeding her all these weeks?'

The child smiled at him and opened her mouth for the spoon, showing off new teeth.

His friendly relationship with her daughter reassured Agatha, as he'd hoped it might. More relaxed, she asked, 'Do you know if Snow was badly hurt? There were three of them, Figgy and Rupe were holding him and Lew was punching him and — and I couldn't help him and — Anything I said only made it worse for him.'

'A bit bruised, his mother said, but no bones broken. Not that she could get much out of him. He told her he'd ridden into the branch of a tree. He'll survive.'

'It was my fault,' she said. 'I should have told Lew, but I knew he'd never let me take the books if I did, and I was desperate for something to read. Something to do.' There were tears in her eyes but she had herself well under control. 'Such a little thing, such a small deceit, and look where it led.'

Bowler gave her a quick encouraging smile but said nothing; he continued spooning cereal into Cordelia's ever-opening mouth.

'I still can't believe it,' Agatha whispered. 'Not Lew. Why would he? Of course he was beside himself that afternoon when he saw me talking to Snow, but he'd calmed down by bedtime. He almost apologised for hitting me, said he'd forgotten I was pregnant and he didn't want to harm the baby. In the end he did believe me I'm sure, when I explained about how I knew Snow, and then told him that Snow had in fact gone off for good. I know he understood, otherwise he wouldn't have stopped shouting at me. So why then did he decide to kill me, and kill his own baby too? And why his mother and sister?'

Bowler already knew that she had miscarried after she'd been shot, while she'd been so ill; Em had told him. He shovelled the last spoonful into Cordelia and wiped her mouth with the free end of her feeder; he lifted her from her chair, settled her in his lap, and took the cup from Agatha.

'Because they saw him shoot you, I suppose.' This is weird, he thought, cuddling a baby and discussing bloody murder.

'What makes you think that?' Agatha was obviously surprised. 'He shot them first. It was them screaming and the shouting, and then the shots, that brought me out of my room.' She shuddered. 'Two shots, the ones that must have killed them.'

'Are you sure you heard that?'

'Of course I'm sure.' Her eyes were clenched tightly shut as though by blocking sight she could also block out the memory of an unbearable sound. 'I've had plenty of time to think about it. I've thought of nothing else for weeks.'

Em had come back. She was standing at the stove with her back to them but Bowler knew she was listening to every word. He said, 'I'd imagined things in a different order.'

This piece of information disturbed him, because it didn't fit the logical pattern he had constructed to make sense of the shootings. He'd need to know a bit more before he could be comfortable again.

'Agatha, you said there was some kind of row when you got back to the house after Franklin left. I know Lew hit you, we saw the marks on your face.'

Agatha nodded. 'He was beside himself, shaking me and punching, worse than he'd ever —' She hesitated. 'If he'd decided to shoot the pair of us then, when he was out of his mind with rage, I wouldn't have been surprised.'

'But what happened next morning, to set him off again?' Bowler put the cup on the table and stood Cordelia on the floor, holding on to his knees. She started worming her hand into his hip pocket.

'Nothing. Well, they were all a bit abusive over breakfast, Vida in particular. She was feeling a bit off colour, dopey and headachy, and it made her irritable, so she wouldn't let it rest. But after that things calmed down and as I said, Lew almost apologised, and then he told me I must stay in my room, and I said I would. Figgy and Rupe went up the paddock together, and Lew stayed working in the sheds. He was home at lunchtime, anyway.'

'When did Thelma Thompson arrive?'

'She came just before lunch. She didn't have the children, she'd left them with Dick's mother.'

'Then what?' Bowler knew what Cordelia was after; he assisted the child to pull his watch from his pocket.

'Then nothing for a couple of hours. Then I heard a shot.'

Bowler looked up from opening the watch. 'You said screaming, and two shots.'

'No, this was the first shot. Vida and Thelma had been talking in the kitchen, and they heard it too. I heard Vida exclaim, and the door banged shut behind them, so I thought they had gone out to see what was happening. Then I heard Vida shouting and Thelma screaming no, no, and then two shots and the screaming stopped.' Tears were running down Agatha's cheeks but she kept talking. 'I didn't know what to make of it and so I went to the door of the room and looked out because Lew had threatened me if I left the room, and there was Lew by the back door and then I was shot. I fell down. After a bit I was surprised I wasn't dead, and like a dream I heard footsteps and I thought, if he comes in I am dead, but the steps went away and there was nothing. Nobody moving, nothing. I don't remember anything after that.'

Crying too, Cordelia dropped to all fours and scuttled round the table to her mother, who pulled her onto her knee. The child tenderly patted her mother's cheek.

Troubled, Bowler said, 'So you could see Lew. Did he say anything?'

'No. I only saw his shadow, the shape of him at the back door. But it must have been Lew, mustn't it?' She sounded almost hopeful, as though she wished that after all it could have been another man shot her.

'Must have been,' he said, matter-of-fact. 'Did you hear the next shot? There must have been another after that when he shot himself.'

She shook her head, rather wildly. 'I don't know, I can't — perhaps —' She choked.

'Bowler, that's enough.' Em sat beside Agatha and put an arm across her bowed shoulders.

Bowler thrust back his chair and got to his feet. Every instinct made him restless, made him want to pace about while he sifted through this new information to see what he made of it. He stared down at the women.

'That's more than enough,' he growled. 'I'm damned if I know what to think. If the shooting happened like that, I agree, I can't see —' He shook his head. 'All right, Em, all right, I'm going. I'll come back another day.'

17

Bowler settled at his desk to make a few notes of the new facts he had learned about the order of the shots. He was interrupted by a banging on his door.

'You there, Mr Brown?' called a boy's voice. Joe, the youngest of Splinter Thompson's five sons, a lanky youth in his late teens, sidled in. Chest heaving, he puffed. 'Dad says you'd better come quickly, old Spog has just driven past in his tractor with his plough on behind, heading for the oval.'

'Damn the old pest,' Bowler said, and meant it. 'But I can't stop him.'

'It's not Spog,' Joe said, writhing his shoulders with impatience. 'It's m'brother Roy, and Bub Gregory, and a couple of others. They've gone up there to stop him. And they've taken a couple of pitchforks and Bub's twenty-two.'

Bowler shoved him aside and ran for his horse, in the yard beyond his shed. He swung up bareback and set off at a gallop through the town, leaving Joe far behind.

Old Spog had driven his tractor in through a gate at the back of the oval, where it adjoined one of his paddocks — one of his *other* paddocks, according to Spog. Apart from the remains of a secondary fence, a few rotting posts strung with sagging wires, that hinted at the oval outline of the playing area inside it, there was little to distinguish that paddock from the one beside it; both were rough with weeds and far from level.

A cold wind hunted ragged white clouds across the sky and tousled the branches of the gum trees around the perimeter. Bowler, avoiding a tangle of fallen wires, cantered Imshy around to the far corner.

Apparently he was in time. Old Spog was working unmolested at the plough, no doubt lowering the disks, while his tractor engine rumbled and popped ready to go. There was no sign of the young men who wanted to stop him.

Spog looked up as the policeman reined in his horse beside him. 'Good opening rains this last week,' he remarked, his expression bland. 'Too good to miss.'

George Wilson, septuagenarian, commonly known as Spog, was a tall, lean old man with faded blue eyes, a fierce expression, and a reputation for bad temper. A bit of a hatter, he had lived alone since his two sons, whom he had brought up single-handed after the early death of his wife, had been killed in the Great War. He also worked alone, running his farm with a tireless endurance many younger men couldn't have matched.

His feud with the footy team had started months before, towards the end of the previous season, when a couple of Splinter Thompson's sons and a Gregory or two, dropped off in front of his house after midnight, had been singing bawdy songs at the tops of their voices. On a bitter winter's night after an away match they had travelled many slow miles home seated on chaff-bags on the back of a lorry, where they had kept out the cold with flagons of cheap port. They were in fine voice as a consequence. Spog had not appreciated being woken in the middle of the night by the raucous din, and when he shouted an abusive protest they had staggered up his drive to serenade him at close quarters.

Spog had blasphemed, and fired his twelve gauge out of his

bedroom window.

There were two versions of this incident. Spog insisted he had fired in the air to warn the young men. They in turn swore that they had heard the pellets spattering in the trees close beside them, and Bub Gregory even claimed he had two new holes in the sleeve of his coat to prove how irresponsible old Spog had been. Since the coat in question was shiny with age and grime, and lacked both lining and buttons, the provenance of any additional holes was open to question.

Memory of their drunken terror and craven, speedy retreat had rankled with the young men, and so some members of the team had taken their revenge on Spog in various ways. They painted a white cross and the words 'Bring out your dead' on his dunny door; they arranged that he should be showered with several pounds of white flour when he emerged from his back door one morning; they took a bottle of red ink to his two black and white border collies so that for a while they were black and mottled pink border collies. In this last enterprise the Thompson boys had an unfair advantage: because they were neighbours, their house only a quarter of a mile away across the paddocks, they were well known to Spog's dogs, who treated them as part of the natural scenery and never barked at them.

These incidents and the theft of six of his chooks further soured Old Spog's already acid disposition. He had made wild threats against the young men but had taken no action until the end of the season when the whole team, in exuberant spirits after an unexpected win over a stronger team, had hoisted the old man's buggy to the roof of his machinery shed. A couple of the wilder spirits would have added the horse to the tableau, but that had shocked and sobered the more responsible members of the team and they had hauled their mates away before any serious damage could be done.

When he discovered the buggy Spog, beside himself with rage, had announced he would plough the town oval and plant oats. It was his paddock and had always been his paddock, and although he had previously allowed the townspeople the use of it without cost he was now withdrawing the privilege. He didn't owe the footballers any favours.

His temper was not improved by a sprained back. Always an independent spirit, he had first tried to retrieve the buggy himself and would probably have succeeded, at the cost of wrecking that venerable vehicle, if his back hadn't given out. It had finally been brought down by Spog's eldest Wilson nephew and his two sons; but one of the boys was a member of the footy team and had upset his great-uncle further by laughing immoderately during the whole operation.

After warning Spog that he took a serious view of the indiscriminate discharge of firearms Bowler had kept out of the dispute. Since nobody had broken the law it was none of his business, unless Spog chose to lay complaints of trespass or nuisance; and the chooks, as he had tried to explain to Spog, were a separate issue. He had been mildly amused by the inventiveness of the footy boys, sympathetic towards old Spog, and complacent in a detached kind of way that at least he, Bowler, knew what was going on — that he knew accurately who had done what, and when.

Even though he had taken no action over the incidents he had been watchful that no serious trouble broke out between the factions, and when the cricket season had finished peacefully, with no further move from Spog, he had relaxed, believing the crisis to be over. But now trouble loomed no matter what he did.

He couldn't legally interfere in the ploughing. He was at the oval not to stop Spog and his tractor but to prevent a confrontation that could escalate to violence if the footy boys became heated in protecting their playing field.

He scanned the road for any sign of the would-be protectors, then crossed his forearms on his horse's withers and leaned down to see what the old man was doing to his plough. Unbolting one of the disks, it seemed.

More to make conversation than for any other reason Bowler asked, 'Spog, do you have the title deeds to this paddock? Some of the boys think you gave it away years ago.'

The old man grunted. 'Course I've got the deeds. Otherwise I wouldn't be able to plough it, would I.'

'They reckon you made the land over to the District Council. If you've got the title, why don't you show it to me?'

With an enigmatic smile Spog tilted his head to look up at the policeman. The wind was whipping his overlong grey hair into his eyes.

'Well now, I don't quite know where to lay my hands on it right this minute. But it's somewhere around. It'll turn up.'

'Spog, why don't you wait until you find the thing before you begin ploughing?'

'Why would I do that? I'd miss the rains. Are you suggesting it's not my paddock?'

'I have no idea whose bloody paddock it is,' Bowler said with irritation. 'I just wish you and the footy team would declare a truce.'

'Nothing to do with those bastards,' Spog said in a lofty tone. 'I can plough my own damn paddock if I want to.'

'Certainly you can. If it is your paddock.' From his elevated position on horseback Bowler saw that the delegation coming to remonstrate with Spog had spotted the law's presence. Five young men had climbed through the fence on the town side of the paddock and now stood irresolute, heads together, conferring. He couldn't see a rifle and the one pole they carried was not a pitchfork but appeared to be a broom handle, less dangerous but still enough of a weapon if they intended threatening an old man.

Bowler straightened and waved a cheerful greeting to them. Bub Gregory waved back half-heartedly. Then all five climbed through the fence again and trudged away up the road towards the post office. Bowler wished he knew what they were saying.

Still, they could come back if he departed too soon. While the old boy fiddled around replacing the disk, Bowler slid from his horse and sat on a nearby stump with the reins through his arm.

Almost immediately the tractor engine coughed, spluttered and then stopped.

'Out of bloody fuel I suppose,' Spog grumbled, but Bowler didn't think he sounded either surprised or upset about it. Had the old pest planned this, just to tease the footballers?

'What are you going to do now?'

A gleam lit the old boy's eyes; he smiled. 'Ah. That'd be telling.'

Bowler, riding round the perimeter fence on his way to the gate, was disturbed to find a twenty-two rifle and a pitchfork hidden in the dead thistles where the young men had turned back. The bastards must have dropped them when they'd spotted him. They had been more serious than he'd imagined.

Cursing, he dismounted and picked up the weapons to take with him. He'd have to put the fear of God into those blasted troublemakers later. Even though he believed they would have done no more than threaten the old man, he didn't like the picture this conjured up. He looked along the road past the school, where in the distance he could see Spog trudging home. The solitary figure looked both vulnerable and desperately lonely.

Old Spog had seen enough trouble in his days; he was not going to be frightened by a pack of country louts if Bowler could help it.

18

Bowler found the pencilled map he had made of how the bodies had been lying at Bensons', as described to him by Rupe and Figgy. He spread it on his blotter, and looked again at the position of the stick figures. The tiny crosses nearby marked where he had found the empty shells. And Agatha was right, why had Lew suddenly decided to walk up from the sheds and start shooting? According to her there had been no further arguing to re-ignite his anger; he had apparently worked quietly in the shed all the morning, come up for lunch, gone back again. What had so enraged him so unexpectedly that he had seized up his rifle and started firing?

That was a point — where did Bensons keep the damn rifle? If Lew had carried it down to the shed with him it indicated a degree of premeditation that didn't seem to fit with the random selection of his victims. He'd fired on anyone who got in front of him when he was heading up to shoot his wife.

A further point needed explaining. If Lew had been reduced to such rage or despair that nothing would satisfy him but the death of his wife followed by his own suicide, surely he could have chosen a time or place when they were alone. He had known his mother and sister were in the house, he had eaten his midday meal with them. So had they been random victims? Did he hate his mother as well as his wife?

Because, if his mind had been made up about the suicide, he still could have let them live even though they had been unwelcome witnesses to his crime. Once he was dead he'd have had nothing to lose.

And why had he shot Agatha, if his rage had already abated enough for him to be concerned for his unborn child? None of this appeared to fit, now. And the first shot, the one that came before all the others, that one bothered Bowler considerably — what had Lew shot at then?

Where was the shell for that one? Bowler hadn't looked specifically for a fifth shell but he had gone over all the ground pretty thoroughly by the light of his powerful torch. He was sure he'd have seen one if it had been there.

If there had been five shots, either Lew was further off to begin with, or someone had picked up the fifth shell. Rupe and Figgy said they'd touched nothing. Had there been someone else at the scene?

He'd better go out to the farm and go over the ground again in daylight, even though it was a bit late to expect to find anything. And he'd better talk to Agatha again, see what else she could remember.

Bowler leaned back in his chair, linked his hands behind his head, and closed his eyes. He knew he was only putting off considering another possibility, that he could be chasing a chimera. He had no hard evidence for that fifth shot: he had only reasoned that it must have occurred if Lew fired four shots at the women first. Now he must also consider the premiss that the four shots heard by Agatha comprised the sum total, in which case the first shot fired had killed Lew.

In this hypothesis Lew Benson was innocent, as much a victim as the women had been, and some person unknown had committed the murders.

Why the devil did the business have to get complicated all at once?

If he went on with this line of reasoning he would have to start hunting for a living candidate for the murderer's role, and he had not the faintest idea where to start. Except that in cases of multiple killings, like those which had occurred here, the police had found that the victims' nearest and dearest were the most likely perpetrators by a mile. If Lew was excluded, that left either Figgy or Rupe.

But Figgy and Rupe, instead of ensuring there was no witness left to raise awkward questions, had instantly driven Agatha to town, to get help. They had done all they could to increase her chances of survival. Surely if either was guilty of the murders he would have taken care that she was safely dead before they brought her in. Why shoot her, and then save her?

So, if not Lew, who?

Did he want to go on with this? Why not let sleeping dogs lie? Bloody-mindedness, he supposed, but he was going on with it. Quite apart from Agatha's evidence that by the time of the shootings Lew had accepted her explanation, her further statement that the murderer had shot her without saying a word convinced him almost beyond doubt that the man was not Lew. No man he knew could pull the trigger on his wife without at least saying something like *Take that, you bitch*. It would have been more credible if he'd ranted and raved at her. But silence, from a man of Lew's temper? No.

The slightest possibility that a cold-blooded killer could be walking around thinking he had literally got away with murder was enough to infuriate Bowler. Although he hadn't now discarded the murder-plus-suicide theory altogether, he felt there were some strange, unexplained aspects to the crime he would like resolved before he accepted that as the true course of events.

He wanted a great deal more information before he let the matter drop.

A brisk walk might help him clear his thoughts. He'd go for the mail.

As he straightened from unlocking his postbox, Bowler saw that Aubrey Venables's sister had emerged from the post office and was pulling on her gloves at the top of the veranda steps. A light shower of rain was pattering on the roof, discouraging her from immediately stepping off. She looked at the sky.

He said, 'Good afternoon, Miss Venables. I doubt if it will last long.'

'Good afternoon,' she said, and inclined her head in a gracious nod which grated on Bowler. She couldn't have been many years older than he was, and yet her manners and carriage were those of a stiff-necked dowager of seventy. And what a waste, he thought, regarding the opulent figure which not even her firm corsets could conceal.

She caught his glance, and her lips tightened. A tight-lipped, tightly-corseted woman, Miss Venables; she kept house for her brother, shopped for household supplies, and that was all anyone knew of her. Not even her first name, Bowler realised with some surprise. She kept out of sight in the decaying old rectory her brother had bought when the Anglicans, defeated by the paucity of worshippers in the little stone church next door, had sold it off.

What did she do all day in that mouldering old house? Bowler shuffled the envelopes in his hand, checking the official ones. Her foot tapped impatiently; she was still waiting for the shower to pass.

He said, 'Good rains we've had. Has your brother started his ploughing?'

'Not yet. Thompson has walked off the place. Aubrey's waiting for him to get in touch. He has no idea when the man will be back to work.'

Where the devil had Dick got to? He'd better ask Splinter. If he'd gone off on a drunken orgy, trying to drown his sorrows in the only way he knew, he could even be in gaol like his eldest brother; though Bowler had always believed Dick to be one of the less dim-witted and criminally-inclined of Splinter's sons.

He said, 'I didn't know he'd gone missing. Can't your brother find someone else?'

'My brother is keeping the job open for Thompson. He is sorry for the man in his loss.' Miss Venables flushed, apparently realising that her tone had sounded scornful of this charitable impulse, and added, 'Tragic about his wife of course, a terrible thing, Aubrey and I feel for him. I believe his mother is taking care of the children.'

'That's right.' On the spur of the moment he asked, 'Miss Venables, do you play bridge?'

He had surprised her; she stared at him without words. Then she stammered, 'No. I mean yes, a little. We don't —'

'Would you and Aubrey like to come round for a few rubbers one evening?'

'I don't think — I really don't know what he would think, my brother, I must be guided by my brother, Mr Brown.'

'My wife will see you about it,' Bowler said. He still had no idea why he'd issued the invitation, unless it was because he had subconsciously seen her as a lonely figure. Perhaps that was it. He lifted his hat to her, and stepped out into the rain.

19

Rupe Benson and his step-father sat at the kitchen table over cups of tea when Bowler arrived in mid-morning. They hadn't heard his knocking above the rain pounding on the unlined iron roof; he'd walked in unannounced.

He heard Rupe say, 'Yes you bloody well will. Whose house is this, anyway?'

Figgy said, 'You know damn well I'd be long gone if your mother had agreed to move.' Then he heard Bowler, and with a crude oath he jumped up. 'Hell, we didn't hear your car!'

Rupe hadn't shaved for days, and the kitchen had slid a long way from Vida's housewifely standards: dirty plates and black-bottomed saucepans were piled on the other end of the table; under the leaking window the packed earth floor was beginning to break down into its original mud; the room smelt of sour food and mildew and stale sweaty clothes. Momentarily it made Bowler's nose wrinkle, but he'd smelled worse.

Much worse. Though that was something he strove to forget.

He took off his coat and shook some of the rain from it, then pulled out a chair, hung the coat on the back of it, and sat down, pushing the sleeves of his jumper up his forearms.

Rupe went to the wood stove for the teapot keeping hot on the hob.

'Fraid it's a bit of a mess,' Figgy said; he shrugged. 'I don't know how the women manage.' He glanced at his stepson and frowned slightly.

Bowler said, 'I'm not much good at batching either.'

That was a lie — he believed he was both efficient and neat whenever he had to look after himself — but he wanted to sound sympathetic if he could. These two looked tense, possibly angry, as though he had interrupted a quarrel. He didn't want them too prickly when he started asking casual questions.

He was about to state his errand, and ask whether after the shooting they had seen a fifth spent bullet casing anywhere about, and if so, where, when he realised that he didn't want to share the information that Agatha had given him.

He didn't want to explain the steps that had led him to suspect the extra shot; he wanted to investigate the possibility that it had never been fired. For the moment he'd like to keep that information to himself.

He tried to keep his face blank while his thoughts scrambled around half-formed options. He should have decided beforehand how he would approach these two.

Impromptu, he said, 'I found this letter. I was going through my paperwork the other day and I found a letter, a letter from head office I'd forgotten, weeks ago it came, wanting to know a couple more things about that shooting, a couple of things I missed in my report. Thanks.' He took the cup of tea Rupe pushed across to him. 'But I keep forgetting to ask you.' Given time to arrange his thoughts Bowler could utter barefaced lies with sufficient aplomb to be instantly believed; off the cuff he was not so sure of himself.

Both men were regarding him with some surprise. Hadn't he sounded plausible? A swirl of cold air came in under the badly-fitting door and a rain squall roared on the iron roof, filling their ears with mind-numbing sound.

They waited in awkward silence, avoiding one another's eyes. Bowler wondered what made these men so defensive in his presence.

Figgy held a paper bag of coffee biscuits towards him. He nearly shook his head, but that might look too critical, as though he was refusing hospitality for some scruple or suspicion. Unwillingly he crunched the damn thing in his teeth. Why did everyone in this bloody place buy nothing but coffee biscuits?

As the shower dwindled, as soon as he could make himself heard, he said, 'It's only those sticklers in the city.' From his tone, they could infer that his senior officers were a bunch of fussy and unreasonable fuddy-duddies wanting the t's crossed and the i's dotted, instead of a gang of hard-headed cynics not in the habit of taking any crime scene at face value.

And of course it was a crime scene, whether Lew pulled the trigger or someone else did.

Rupe said, 'Thought you'd wrapped it all up.'

'So did I, but it seems not quite. They want a couple more details. They want to know, for instance, about that rifle. Where it came from, did it belong to Lew, where was it kept, things like that.' That wasn't quite a lie. They would certainly want to know, once he told them Agatha's evidence.

'What's it matter?' Rupe asked. 'We know who fired the bloody thing.'

'For records, statistics, something like that,' Bowler said, improvising rather cleverly he thought. 'How long have you had the rifle?'

'Oh.' Rupe nodded, apparently accepting this explanation. 'Bought it when we moved here, nine — no, ten years back. Got it to keep the roos down when we cleared the first paddocks. Suppose it belongs to me, though Lew used it as much. More, probably. He liked shooting.'

'Where did you keep it?' He'd taken the rifle away with him on the evening of the shootings and hadn't so far returned it. He wasn't sure why he was keeping it. Perhaps he could get it fingerprinted. Though that wouldn't tell him much, because Lew's prints were unavailable and he could hardly round up the whole district to find matching prints if there were others on the rifle. Fingerprints would only be helpful if he was making a case after he'd caught his murderer. Was he now looking for a murderer?

Rupe said, 'Lew made a rack beside the back door one time, when foxes were after the chooks, so's he could grab it quickly.' He gestured behind him, towards the enclosed veranda. 'Out there. Been there ever since.'

Bowler wanted to ask how many people knew it was there, but of course the answer would be any blow-in who came to the house could have seen it. And it added another dimension to Agatha's objections to Lew as murderer — why would any man carry the rifle away from the house and start shooting elsewhere if his real purpose was to come back and shoot his wife?

Perhaps Lew took the weapon to the sheds with him after lunch. But if he had made up his mind to the killings before he left the house, if he had picked up the rifle to take it with him, why not start the massacre there and then, with the weapon in his hands? Why the delay?

He must ask Agatha whether she remembered seeing Lew leave the house after lunch, and whether he had been carrying anything.

If, on the other hand, Lew had left the house with no murderous intent in mind he would not have taken the rifle; instead, he would have returned for it later, when presumably he had brooded on his wrongs until he could bear them no longer. But once again, why the delay? He would have come back, picked up the rifle while the women were busy in the kitchen and couldn't see him — but why then hadn't he walked down the veranda to the bedroom, and shot his wife? In this version he had picked up the rifle and, unaccountably, walked away, until he was at that place unknown where he had fired one shot, the one that had brought his mother and sister outside; and then, by this time half-way between sheds and house, had fired on them both. And only then, after killing two people against whom he had no particular grudge, had he gone back to the house to revenge himself on the one person who was the cause of his murderous fury.

Both hypotheses appeared pretty shaky to Bowler. He could imagine no course of events to fit with Agatha's account of the order of shots fired. So what had really happened, out here on this isolated farm on a blistering summer's day?

Figgy moved abruptly in his chair. He leaned forward, glanced at Bowler, then at Rupe. He said, 'Constable, what are you getting at? Is there any doubt what happened?'

Bowler realised that he must have been silent too long. 'It's just that some policemen have nasty suspicious minds. One bloke wants to know where you and Rupe were that afternoon.' He didn't want them to think that the suspicious bloke was sitting at the table with them.

He was just getting rid of the preliminaries, he told himself; after all, did he really believe either could be implicated? Neither had any motive that he knew of. Rupe appeared too unsophisticated to have faked his agonised distress over his brother's death — interesting, that his mother's demise appeared to have touched him much less deeply — and Figgy appeared sincere in his grief for his wife.

And if either had shot Agatha why then had he co-operated to save her life by a frantic dash to Kularook?

Rupe, who had been leaning with his elbows on the table staring moodily into his empty cup, had sat up. 'They can't imagine I'd —'

'They don't imagine anything,' Bowler said. 'On the other hand, they want to know more than they do at present. It means bugger all, but once I've satisfied them about you two, that will be the end of it.'

'But we told you, Lew threatened his wife,' Figgy said. 'He said, "You try and leave me again and I'll kill you." Didn't he, Rupe?'

Rupe hitched a shoulder. 'Yeah. Something like that.'

They had told Bowler that before, but he hadn't made a note of it — he'd thought it merely the extravagant language of an angry man — and he'd forgotten. 'When was that?' Come to think of it, Lew had said something much the same when his erring wife had turned up after missing the train.

Rupe said, 'After he'd seen Franklin off the night before, when he took her back to the house.'

But not next day, thought Bowler, when he was strolling around between the sheds and the house collecting the rifle and shooting everyone in sight. There is no evidence for any anger that day. On the contrary, Agatha said she had convinced Lew that her meeting with young Franklin meant nothing, and he had acknowledged his fault in endangering her pregnancy.

He said, 'So where were you both? I know you were out of earshot, but how far away?'

'Almost two miles away, out in the back scrub. Windy day, the mallees thrashing, there wasn't a hope we could have heard shooting from there.'

'You were together all day?'

'Yeah. Making a start on the boundary fence,' Rupe said. 'The one bloody Bruce Wilson is stacking on a turn about. Figgy began digging the post-holes, I began cutting posts. I had the buckboard, so I dropped him off, then went back a bit where the trees are.'

'Could you see each other all the time?'

They considered this.

Figgy said, 'No. But I could hear his axe most of the time, and I'd certainly have heard the buckboard if he'd started it up.' He smiled faintly. 'I reckon he was there.'

'Rupe? Could you hear Higgins?' Bowler nodded towards the older man. He would have preferred to ask these questions when the men were not together, but if he asked to see them singly he would have instantly roused their suspicions against him, to say nothing of their hackles.

He wanted to keep on the right side of them.

Rupe said, 'You mean, did he walk out when I wasn't looking?' His tone was scornful. 'If he was Mandrake the Magician. He'd dug bloody near as many holes as Lew could've.'

'You're saying he didn't have time?'

'When I picked him up he'd done a long row of holes, half of 'm through limestone. The buckboard was with me so he'd've had to walk home and back, and we come in early as it was.' Rupe saw Figgy turning over his hands to look at the palms, and he snorted. 'You should've seen his blisters.'

To Bowler, it sounded as though memories of his brother lay close to the surface of Rupe's mind, as though he was not only grieving but also regretting the loss of a workmate. Perhaps he was even idealising the contribution Lew had made to running the farm.

'The dead are beyond reproach, and their deeds beyond telling' — who had said that? One of his mates in the Desert Column, he couldn't remember which. Why the hell did all his wartime memories have to come flooding back all the time? It must have been the deaths that set them off. He jerked his mind back to the present.

Figgy, in the face of this testimonial to his industry, looked uncertain whether to preen himself or to be affronted that anyone could doubt his innocence. Then, surprisingly, his face crumpled, and he covered it with his hands. He muttered, 'Look, I'm sorry, but I — Vi, my little girl, how could anyone think — Why? That's what I want to know, why did he have to shoot Vi?' He slumped forward across the table, his head in his folded arms.

Embarrassed by this show of grief, Bowler nonetheless felt sorry for the man. Poor beggar. These questions must be bringing the sharpness of his loss back to him. Not that he should need reminding if he ever looked round the kitchen. The squalor in which they now lived should be a constant reminder of how much Vida had contributed to their daily lives.

Bowler glanced at the two men, neither of whom he suspected of bloody murder, and abruptly changed his mind. They had suffered traumatic losses; both would be anxious to help him. He'd have to ask about the possible fifth shell casing or he'd never be satisfied. He said, 'After the shootings, did either of you see a fifth empty bullet casing? Somewhere round about the shed, it would have been.'

They both sat up. 'No. Why would there be five?' Figgy asked.

'Agatha heard three shots before the one that hit her. One some distance off that made the women run outside, then the two shots that killed them. So Lew must have fired at something before he shot his mother and sister and wife. The fifth would have been the one that killed him.'

'Didn't see it, and I would've if it was lying around,' Rupe said. 'Can't miss those things when they're new. Did her ladyship hear this fifth shot?'

'No.'

'There you are then. She's invented it.'

'No. You don't understand. She heard four shots, and the fourth was the one that hit her. So Lew or whoever was doing the shooting was alive then.' Spacing his words for clarity, Bowler added, 'If Lew then shot himself there was a fifth shot she didn't hear, after she was unconscious. But we have shells for only four shots, three on the ground and one in the breech. If there was no fifth shot, Lew didn't kill her. He must have died at the first shot.'

'Jesus bloody Christ!' Rupe was out of his chair, on his feet, standing staring at Bowler in horror. 'Someone *else* shot them?' More deliberately Figgy unfolded beside him, looking equally grim.

'It's a possibility, no more. But I'd like to find that fifth shell, to settle it one way or another. It wasn't in his pockets.' Lew hadn't been carrying any spare ammunition, either, which was rather odd when

Bowler thought about it. Not many men counted the bullets they'd need before they started shooting; it was human nature to grab up a few spares, just in case.

'Come on.' Rupe turned purposefully towards the door, grabbing his hat from a hook behind it. 'The rain's taken off. Let's have a dekko right now.'

Figgy said, 'How is Mrs Lew? I haven't seen her since she got back.'

'She's getting stronger,' Bowler said. 'Still pretty upset about everything mind you.'

'Half the farm might cheer her up,' Rupe said bitterly, leading the way towards the sheds. The wire door crashed shut behind them. The air was cold and smelled of wet earth and the muddy chook yard. 'Not sure if Lew left a will, mind you. Figgy's out of it. My mother didn't have a share in the place.'

Figgy said, 'I'm no farmer, anyway.'

Rupe grunted agreement. 'All the same, he's going to town soon, see a lawyer he knows. Find out where we stand.'

'Do you think Mrs Lew could be confused about these shots?' Figgy took a couple of quick steps to catch up to long-striding Bowler. 'The shock and so on? Heard four shots, but has got the order muddled?'

Bowler stopped in front of the shed at the foot of the slope. 'Don't think so. Her memory's pretty clear up to when she was shot herself. She convinced me.'

'Fair enough.'

'Is this about where Lew was lying?'

Rupe turned his head away, as though he didn't want to look at some image he still could see on that patch of muddy earth. 'Yeah.'

They separated, walking, heads bent, to search the wet bare earth in front of the shed. A tractor with a seed drill attached was pulled up at one side. 'Going to start seeding when this weather lets up,' Rupe explained. 'Get the barley in first.'

They searched the length of the shed, and in it, and up and down the slope to the house. Bowler noticed a spent shell standing upright on a beam inside the shed but Rupe shook his head.

'Put it there m'self,' he said. 'Had to shoot a dog a while back.'

Three-quarters of an hour's exhaustive searching by all three of them failed to find a fifth shell. And neither Rupe nor Figgy could think of anyone who might hate the family enough to shoot four people.

'Unless it was that young Franklin,' Figgy said. 'I doubt if he likes us much.'

'No, he'd left the district by then,' Bowler said.

20

Bowler said, 'That was Hammond, the station master, on the phone. There's a riot or something in the gangers' camp up the line. I'd better go and knock their blasted heads together.'

More resigned than angry Joan said, 'Damn it all, Bill. Will you be long? The Venables are due in an hour.'

'Hell, so they are.' He picked a slice of roast lamb from his unfinished dinner and stuffed it into his mouth. When he could speak he said, 'But I have to go, you know that,'

He was looking around for his hat; she read his quick impatience in his abrupt movements. She said under her breath, 'I know. Take care, Bill.' Aloud she said, 'Will you be back in time?'

Bowler shook his head. 'It's a fair drive, the camp's just this side of Cancanulla. But I'll do the best I can. You'll have to play three-handed until I get home.' He turned to go. 'Where's my torch?'

'On your desk.' She got up from the table and followed him to the office.

He clicked the torch on and off to test the batteries. 'Sorry to mess up your party and all that, but you know how it is.'

'It's not my party. You got me into this. I barely know the Venables.'

'So I did. I felt sorry for her, I think she's lonely. Anyway, you'll manage. You and your famous Pommy poise.'

'You're a bastard, Bill.'

He took her face between his hands and kissed her swiftly but thoroughly. 'I'll be quick as I can. Now I've got to dash — Hammond is waiting for me. As well as trying to smash up one another apparently they're trying to smash up railway property, and he's got to check on the damage.'

When Bowler walked in on the bridge party he was surprised to hear Agatha Benson laughing. He hadn't expected to find her there, nor had he imagined her capable of such full-throated amusement. Her olive skin, usually sallow, was flushed in the heat of the room; she looked handsome again, despite the unflattering black dress she wore.

They were seated round the bridge table in the sitting-room, Joan, Agatha, Aubrey Venables, and his sister. The room was warm from a mallee-root fire, brightly lit by one of the Aladdin lamps on the mantelpiece. Three of the small bridge party, bright-eyed and animated, looked up at him, but Miss Venables sat stiffly, looking down at her cards. Joan winked.

'Finish your rubber,' Bowler said, and walked over to stand with his back to the fire.

He gave Joan a quick smile of approval. She must have recruited Agatha to make a fourth after he had left.

One more hand concluded the rubber. While Aubrey was adding the scores Joan went down to the kitchen to bring the supper and Bowler followed.

He kissed her cheek and tasted face-powder. She didn't often wear it. 'What made you think of Agatha? I'm surprised she plays bridge.' He somehow hadn't associated Agatha's unconventional attitudes with card games.

'She says it was obligatory with her year of medical students. They played bridge or they went mad on night call. Anyway, she's an interesting woman and mustn't be allowed to rot away in the back room of the Kularook pub.'

'You won't get many of the respectable wives to agree with you,' he warned. 'They might turn on you too.'

She considered this briefly. 'Why should they? I'll worry about that if I have to.'

Only his Joan, Bowler thought with amusement, could be so sublimely indifferent to what the rest of Kularook thought.

Joan picked up the tray, then put it down again. 'What have you done to your mouth? And there's blood in your hair.' Her voice was carefully casual.

'Is it so obvious? I thought I'd cleaned it off. It's nothing serious, just there was a bit of a punch-up until I could make them see reason.' He took his handkerchief from his pocket and handed it to her. 'Mop it off, will you? We don't want the others to notice.'

She wet it at the tap and dabbed at his temple. 'What did they hit you with?'

'Mainly fists. Look, don't worry, it's only a bruise or two.'

'You're not getting any younger, Bill.' She picked up the tray once more.

'Don't remind me, dammit. Anyway, you've managed very well. Agatha looked as though she's enjoying herself.'

'Aubrey is too. I think he's quite smitten with her. Miss Venables I'm not so sure about, it's hard to tell what she's thinking. Will you bring the coffee pot?'

After an evening's bridge Joan should have discovered Miss Venables first name; Bowler had been wanting to know it for some time. His wife, however, would never address anyone by a first name unless given permission, so presumably Miss V. had not given permission. What a starchy old maid she was.

And yet there was something about her that didn't fit the 'old maid' tag, though Bowler couldn't have said what it was. Perhaps she'd had a riotous youth, and was now making up for it with overdone stuffiness. There's no wowser like a reformed drunk, Bowler thought, and thanked his stars he was neither.

'Well played, Partner,' Aubrey said. 'We did just beat them.'

Agatha smiled. 'A miracle then. It's so long since I played I'm very rusty. But that was fun. Thanks, Joan.'

'We must do it again some time,' Miss Venables said. 'Mustn't we, Aubrey? Our turn next. We'll arrange two tables, so Mr Brown can play too.' Her eyes met Bowler's, and swiftly glanced away, almost as though she was afraid he'd read some meanings there. What had she tried to hide? And why was he so certain that they'd wait a long time for an invitation to any bridge party of her arranging?

At the end of the evening, in spite of Agatha's protests, he walked her across the road to the back door of the pub. He asked, 'Did Matt Franklin tell you what he planned to do when he left here?'

'Only that he was going home for a week or so and then heading north.'

'Yes, well, I told you, he didn't stay at home for a week, he caught the train to Adelaide that same night. That's according to his mother. Now the station master tells me he got off here at three o'clock in the morning, said he'd be back in time to catch the day train next day, booked his bags through, and walked off into the night. But he never turned up, never caught the train. Never caught any train — Hammond hasn't seen him since. You didn't see him again I suppose?'

'Of course not. I'd have told you.'

'You can't think of any reason why he would stop in Kularook overnight?'

'No.' She sounded annoyed, and slightly defensive. 'I hardly know him, I thought I explained. When I left Edgerton for secondary school he was six. I have no idea what he's been up to in the meantime, what he does, where he would go.'

'I'll have to see if his mother can think of a reason. But Bruce Wilson told me his mother has had a letter he posted before he left

Oodnadatta, so he did go north in the end, however he managed to arrive there. Oh well, I expect he'll tell us what he was up to when he gets back.'

21

The next day was Saturday, and the Kularook football team was playing its first home game of the season. A few of them had trained once on the town common, an unsatisfactory playing field because of the scattered stones and the cowpats; now, seeing that it was yet to be ploughed, they were going to chance their luck and use the oval. Over the years they had cleared most of the stones off that. After all, they reasoned, what could Spog do? One old man could hardly evict two teams of fit players.

Before breakfast, after he had tended the horses, Bowler walked up to the oval to check on Spog's tractor. He knew there had been no more ploughing so perhaps the old pest had driven it home again.

But no, it was still standing where Spog had left it the day it had run out of fuel, still hitched to the plough and looking forlorn, like a horse left standing too long in the shafts.

Bowler leaned on the fence and considered one solitary tractor in the corner of a paddock soon to be overrun by thirty-six energetic young men with scarcely a conscience between them, eighteen of whom not only had a vested interest in preventing the tractor from ever moving again but would also rather upset Spog than not.

Bugger.

Short of mounting an armed guard for the afternoon he didn't see how he could protect the damn thing from some sort of sabotage. But while he was eating his lunch, the sandwiches Joan had cut for him and the children before she slung her camera bag on her back and rode off somewhere on Isma, he had an idea.

Across the road from the oval, behind the 'new' Kularook Hall, stood the first Kularook Hall, a small stone building that the footy teams, home team and visitors alike, used as a changing room before and after matches. There was nothing in it but a bench along one side, hooks in the wall above that, and a few chairs at one end.

Half an hour before the match was due to start Mounted Constable Brown dismounted outside, tied Imshy to the fence, and strode inside.

His arrival caused a stir. He was in full uniform: black tunic, white breeches, high black boots, with his white spiked helmet under his arm. He pretended not to hear the exclamations on every side.

His cold assessing eyes ignored the more responsible members of the team, the older married men, and studied the group who had promoted the feud with Spog. Most were in a state of partial undress; they fidgeted with the unease of doubt and cloudy consciences. Bowler smiled and Bub Gregory recoiled and tried to hide himself behind his brother. But Bowler's gaze had moved on.

He said, 'If there are any members of the teams not here at present, you can pass my message on. Spog's tractor and plough are still in one corner of the oval, and I am warning you lot not to touch it. Not today, not ever.' He saw one of the troublemakers smirking. 'However, if I find it has been damaged in some way, no matter how small, I am going to arrest — who's your best player? Graham, you'll do — I am going to arrest Graham Fielding every Saturday from now until the end of the season. As far as I'm concerned, if that tractor is damaged, Graham did it.'

'Hey!' Graham scrambled to his feet.

'Come off it, Bowler, you can't do that!' Archie Davidson was the team's captain and one of the more sober members; he sounded as concerned as the others.

'Watch me,' Bowler said. 'And if you Edgerton mob think you can do something clever just to spite me I'll have one of you too.' He gazed round the group. 'Ah. Lockwood will do nicely.'

The head of a lanky young man popped out of a red and white Edgerton jersey. 'Bloody hell! I ain't done nothing!'

'Keep it that way. Your mates too.' Bowler looked around. 'Now you know. That's all.'

He turned and went out. He could almost hear a military band playing a triumphal march to accompany his steps. Archie caught up with him as he was untying Imshy from the fence.

'Bowler, this has to be a joke. Fancy dress and all that.'

'This uniform is no more of a joke than the khaki we used to wear,' Bowler said in a hard voice. He turned, one arm across his saddle, to confront his mate Archie, who was another returned light-horseman and should therefore know better.

'No, sorry. But you don't really mean to carry out these arrests. Do you?'

'Oh yes.'

Dismayed, Archie said, 'But there must be a law against frivolous arrests.'

'I am the law and they won't be frivolous. You must be pretty bloody certain the bastards are planning something.'

Archie shrugged, and then nodded reluctantly. Bowler stepped into his stirrup and from the saddle grinned down at his friend.

'Then you'd better hope that I've changed their minds. And if they don't want to play a man short for the rest of the season you'd better convince them that I'm not joking. See you at the match.'

At the end of a hard-fought game the tractor was still in one piece and Edgerton had defeated Kularook by one goal. Best player and leading goal-kicker for Edgerton was G. Lockwood; for Kularook, G. Fielding.

'The stars are on my side,' Bowler told his wife that evening. 'That might convince them.'

22

Ossie Todd's garage stood across the side street on the opposite corner from the pub, where Agatha, on the side veranda, vigorously wielded a stiff-bristled broom to sweep away muddy residues from recent rains. When she looked up she saw the Bensons' Ford at the Super Plume pump at the garage and Ossie, head back to watch the level, pumping the handle to and fro to lift petrol into the measuring glass on top of the bowser.

Rupe leaned on the car door, fumbling in his pockets while Thelma's two children watched him eagerly; he dropped a coin into each outstretched palm and the children scampered off into Dunstan's general store next door. Their aunt, Dick's sister Dot Thompson, climbed down from the car and followed at a more leisurely pace.

Agatha felt she had never seen Rupe Benson properly before. On the farm he had barely acknowledged her presence; she couldn't remember that he had ever addressed more than a dozen words to her. She wouldn't have believed he would stir himself one inch on her behalf; and yet, according to Em, in the middle of his shock at discovering the carnage out on the farm he had, with Figgy, put all other thoughts aside and tried first to save her.

As though to reinforce her new perceptions, his craggy features were now softened into a smile as he watched the departing children.

Were his surly manners, his awkward silences, due not to dislike of her but to shyness? No, she hadn't misread him to that extent — he did dislike her — but she had misjudged him when she assumed his withdrawn attitude meant he had no capacity for affection.

Agatha propped the broom against the wall, smoothed her hair with both hands, took a deep breath, and crossed the road. 'Hello, Rupe.'

'What do you want?' Rupe pulled himself upright. He sounded suspicious.

'I wanted to thank you for saving my life.' Before she had considered her actions she had laid her hand on his arm, leaned forward, and kissed his cheek.

She was as astonished as he was. His skin was warm and smooth and smelled of shaving soap.

'I didn't — it wasn't —' He shook his head. 'Didn't do much,' he growled, flushed with embarrassment.

Agatha would have sworn nothing could embarrass stolid Rupe. 'Em tells me that I would have had no chance if you two hadn't brought me in when you did.'

Ossie unhooked the hose, inserted the nozzle into the Ford's tank, and let four gallons of petrol gurgle in. The piercing smell enveloped them like a cloud. He replaced the hose and started wagging the handle to pump up a second issue.

Rupe studied his boots. 'You didn't look too good, that's a fact.'

'Anyway, I wanted to thank you. Because I think you blame me for what happened and can't have felt you owed me any favours. Where's Figgy? I want to thank him too.'

'Figgy's in town.'

'Oh. Anyway, I am deeply grateful to you both.'

Rupe glanced up, then down again, but said nothing. She wished she knew what he was thinking. She said, 'You know I blame myself. There was nothing between Snow Franklin and me but a couple of books, but I should have told Lew. I know I should have told him, but I thought he'd be angry and I was dying for books.'

'Been angry all right,' Rupe mumbled. 'Turned out he was ropeable, didn't it? Why'd you want the frigging books so much anyway?'

'I had nothing to do. Vida wouldn't let me help her. You boys had the farm work. I had nothing.'

'You wanted to sweat like we did?' A puzzled frown wrinkled his brow. 'Still not a reason to take up with that bastard Franklin.'

'I explained that to Lew. He understood, in the end.'

'You broke his heart. Shamed him. How could he understand that?'

Agatha took a deep breath, let it go. She said, 'Rupe, I know how badly I treated him. Mind you, he wasn't —' She clipped her lips shut.

He was looking at her face now. 'Wasn't a perfect husband? No excuse. How many damn blokes are?'

'Yes, all right,' she said. 'We won't agree on much. But it doesn't matter how you feel, I won't stop being grateful. So you'll just have to live with it.'

He shrugged, and turned to the children, who came racing out of the store each brandishing a small white paper bag and calling, 'Uncle Rupe! Uncle Rupe! Look what we got!'

Rupe obligingly peered into each bag in turn. The children turned to Agatha.

Beryl said smugly, 'See, Auntie? Uncle Rupe gave us a whole sixpence each.'

'That was kind of him,' she said.

Over their heads Rupe caught her eye. 'Matter of fact Lew told me next morning you'd explained, things weren't bad as they seemed. So what happened, set him off again? Been wanting to ask you that.'

'Nothing happened. He seemed perfectly all right at lunch time, and the next thing I heard was shots.'

'Poor bastard,' Rupe said. 'Must've had a brainstorm or something.' He yawned widely, put a belated hand to his mouth. 'Pardon,' he said.

'Been up half the night, brought Figgy in to catch the Adelaide Express.' He hesitated, then explained, 'He's gone to see a lawyer, sort out Lew's affairs.'

From his tone Agatha inferred that Rupe would have preferred his brother's affairs to remain unsorted. She said, 'I won't claim half the farm, whatever the law says.'

Rupe shrugged. 'Might be yours anyway. Don't think he left a will.'

'Rupe, what do I know about farming? No, you've made it, you keep it.'

Dot came out of the store and walked over to stand close to Rupe's shoulder, an almost aggressive statement of possession. She was a sturdy young woman of about Agatha's age, with dark curls and a high colour. She stared without smiling at Agatha.

'Hello, Dot,' Agatha said. So that was where the wind lay. Seeing that she had no designs on Rupe — on Rupe! As if she hadn't made enough mistakes with his brother! — she said, 'I'll see you later, Rupe,' and returned to her broom.

23

In the late morning Agatha set up a playpen she had borrowed from Durwin Harris's wife beside the concrete underground tank behind the pub, spread Em's travelling rug beneath it to flatten the weeds, and stowed Cordelia safely in the middle of it. The child began banging a couple of carriages from an old wooden train together and laughing at the noise.

Agatha sat nearby on a kitchen chair she had moved into the cool autumn sunshine. Her long wet hair fell over her face. Slowly, almost sensuously, she combed and lifted it to speed its drying. She felt relaxed and lazy, and more serene than she had been for months.

This was due, she realised, to the bridge party. She had enjoyed herself, unheard of these days, and felt grateful to Joan Brown for inviting her, deeply grateful. For the first time in months she had been treated as a normal human being, as neither a victim nor a monster of depravity, and she had relished the unusual pleasure.

Neither Miriam Pedler, on the one occasion she had been able to visit her, nor Em Musgrave, in her daily lectures, had been able to ease Agatha's conscience. She knew they were biassed in her favour to begin with, so their words carried little weight. But the bridge party had been different. The memory of that cheerful evening, talking and laughing with uncritical and congenial people, let her hope that she would eventually recover from the fog of guilt and depression that had been with her so long.

She resented the guilt most of all. Since she first deserted her husband, and during the months she had lived with another man, she had tried to ignore her niggling conscience, acknowledging her faults yet believing she had harmed nobody except herself.

Lew, as the injured party, perhaps deserved consideration; but he had never considered her and had never shown any genuine affection for her. Like his mother, he appeared to despise her for her education, as though her different manners were a deliberate criticism of his country ways. She had been of value to him for the satisfaction of his sexual needs and for not much else, and she had felt on a par with his sheepdogs, valued for their help with the flock but shown no affection afterwards.

His mother Vida had done her best to undermine the marriage from the start, his brother Rupe had ignored her. Why should Agatha feel guilty in leaving a situation where her in-laws made her feel unwelcome and her husband used her like a chattel? Anyway, she believed that Lew, if he divorced her and remarried a country girl, would be better off in the long run.

When this didn't happen, when instead of seizing on divorce he had insisted that she return, then she had felt guilty. This magnanimity to an adulterous wife seemed out of character for Lew; she had to adjust her ideas about him. She now believed she had indeed wronged him. Her introspection and 'breast-beating' that Snow had derided was part of her attempt to come to terms with some painful new ideas about herself and her husband.

She still didn't believe it was love for her that had made him jealous: the damage had been only to his pride, his self-esteem. Though she couldn't excuse herself on those grounds. Men were so vulnerable in unexpected ways, so touchy about their damn pride (though they all seemed to think women could get on without any), they were quickly driven to insane jealousy. So because of his attempt to kill her, he had killed two uninvolved women and himself.

She had tried reminding herself that the action had been Lew's choice, that a different man would not have killed to assuage his anger, but it hadn't helped much. If she hadn't left him he would have had no reason to kill.

During the bridge party she had forgotten it. She had spent an evening as happily carefree as she had been before her marriage.

And that, of course, was the real mistake she had made. She shouldn't have married Lew in the first place. All the rest had followed.

She should have known better, but she had been extraordinarily immature, considering the years she'd spent studying and gaining experience at university and in hospitals. In her isolated years on the farm keeping house for her father after her mother had died, in her years in Adelaide boarding with an unsympathetic maiden aunt while she studied first at high school and then at university — in those years, studying long hours to support herself on scholarships, she'd had no time to develop skills in understanding other people, no time to dabble in romance. She had repressed her dormant sexuality quite as thoroughly as her puritanical aunt could have wished.

Agatha thought how different her upbringing might have been if her mother had been alive; a woman, not a man half out of his mind; and a woman not pathologically afraid of men, as her aunt had been — a woman who could have helped her understand not only herself, but the male half of the human race as well.

After all her years of study her degree hadn't been much use to her, either. She had been halfway through her houseman's year when she'd been called back to the farm when her father had become incapable of looking after himself. There she had found Lew living in the back room of the house and doing all the work on the place. The stock agent had forced her father to employ someone when it became obvious that the neglected farm was falling apart.

She'd come because reports of her father's conduct had alarmed her. She had found the truth much worse.

Frank Coleman's mental instability and occasional 'breakdowns', result of his wartime experiences on Gallipoli and in Flanders, had now become one continuous breakdown. Perhaps one continuous binge described it better, for her father had become a hopeless alcoholic.

Agatha had tried to help him, and Lew had helped her. He'd been big and dependable and, in those days, deferential and polite. Lew had put Frank to bed after his drinking bouts; Lew had rounded him up and brought him home from Edgerton when he went off raving about 'injustice' and demanding his 'rights' from the unsympathetic local council; Lew had shown Agatha where Frank had hidden his store of brandy.

The few sheep remaining on the weedy pastures Lew had shorn; he had milked the three cows, separated the milk, taught Agatha to drive the ancient Dodge so that she could take the cream cans to the cheese factory. Agatha could have managed neither the farm nor her father without Lew.

And when the final tragedy came, and Frank burned down the house with himself inside it, Lew had been like a rock, unmoved by the waves of change crashing in on her.

She knew now that in those days she hadn't begun to understand Lew. She had believed him a more sensitive man than he was, and had read her own feelings into some of his silences. And, spending so much time with him, out there in the isolated farmhouse so far from any neighbours, evening after evening reading at the kitchen table with this big, masculine presence while her father snored drunkenly in his room, she had felt the first stirrings of her passionate nature and had misunderstood herself as well. She had confused sexual excitement with love, and had been naive enough to believe that she would enjoy a slightly primitive love-making with this simple countryman.

The farm was mortgaged to the limit; she would inherit nothing. Her life now held nothing, no way forward, no goals to work for. She was starved for affection and craved stability, and saw a slightly peasant-like habit of mind as durable and somehow fulfilling. A life on the land with a man whom she believed was offering her love and protection seemed the answer to all her problems. They had married two weeks after her father's funeral and gone to live on the farm at Kularook, with his unmarried older brother and his twice-widowed mother.

She had known within a fortnight that she had made a terrible mistake. All the same, she had never intended to abandon her marriage until Monty Parmenter appeared on the scene six months later, offering escape to a more congenial kind of love.

He'd been staying with an aunt on a neighbouring farm and had borrowed his uncle's tractor so that he could contract to plough for Bensons. While he ploughed a newly burned tract of scrub he had lived with the family, camped in the shed but taking his meals with them. He'd done a bit of stump picking after that for wages, but the brothers had decided he was too slow and had sacked him. He'd stayed on with his aunt for another month or two, and when he finally left to go back to the city he'd taken Agatha with him.

He'd been about as unlike Lew as she could imagine — a sensitive, educated young man, good-looking and charming in his way. But no matter what people thought, for a long time she'd resisted him. Although now she could see that he was just a spoilt boy who expected to be given whatever he wanted, at the time he convinced her that he was deeply in love. He was captivated by her gallant acceptance of her lot, he said, by her intelligence, and by her beauty — although this, she believed, existed in his eyes only.

Their flight had been his doing. He had been so insistent, so desperately persuasive about his undying love for her, that in the end he'd worn her down, aided at the last minute by a bit of more than usual bloody-mindedness from Lew.

Months later she realised that Monty, although unlike Lew in every way other way, was just as selfish. Her needs counted for nothing if they conflicted with his.

Agatha shook her head irritably. She had been over all those memories too often; she wasn't going to start again now. She pushed her fingers up into her hair and found it was almost dry.

When her hair was neatly braided once more, the plaits pinned round her head, she asked Em to keep an eye on Cordelia through the kitchen window and crossed the road to see Joan, who had been so friendly and such good company the night before. Agatha rather hoped she could advance her friendship with Joan, and thought a visit to thank her for the bridge party a good way to begin.

'Sorry,' Bowler said, 'she's not home. She went off early this morning in search of an emu-wren.' He was standing at the counter of the police station, in the room at the front of the house, lifting up an open ledger to look under it. He waved her to a chair, but she chose to lean on the counter opposite him.

She said, puzzled, 'In search of a bird?'

'Well you might ask,' Bowler said with some asperity. 'My wife is always searching for some damn bird or other. I blame my mother-in-law, in England. For Christmas eight years ago she sent Joan an expensive camera and a subscription to a German photographic magazine, and she's never been the same since. Whenever she can she rides out into the scrub and photographs birds.'

'I see,' Agatha said, although she didn't altogether.

Bowler's critical mood vanished. He said, 'Look, she had to have something, a woman with her talents mouldering away in a place like Kularook. Don't get me wrong, she likes the place, enjoys the country life, but she didn't have enough to do. It's not as though she'd spend the time on cooking and cleaning even if she didn't have this hobby. She's not a homebody, Joan.'

Agatha thought he sounded as though he was proud of his wife's lack of domesticity, but at the same time was surprised by it.

'And can you tell me why, Agatha Benson,' he said, pointing the end of his pen at her, 'you wear deep mourning for a man who tried to murder you?'

When she had gone, he held the pen upright against the light and sighed. The kids must have been there again; the bloody nib was hopelessly spread. He'd mislaid his fountain pen and had wasted half the morning searching the office for it.

He rarely took it from his desk — for most of his writing away from home he preferred an indelible pencil — and he'd been using it only yesterday, when he'd started writing out a new report on the shootings, setting out the conflicts he saw between the various pieces of evidence in an attempt to clarify his thoughts. Had one of the children borrowed the damn pen? He'd skin them if they had.

He hated bloody steel nibs. The fountain pen, the one his mother had given him for some birthday long past, had the only nib that could cope with his strong, vertical handwriting. He valued it, however, not only for that reason but also because his mother was no longer alive. So now, as he hunted through the cupboard under the counter, he muttered lurid oaths while he shuffled the stacks of books and stationery and forms about in search of a new nib.

But there were none. He must have used the last of them and forgotten to indent for a new box last time he put in a requisition for stationery. Exasperated, he stamped off down the passage to requisition the pen with which his son wrote his homework.

24

Archie Davidson, captain of Kularook football team, thumped the counter in front of Bowler. 'You can't do this!'

'I told you I would,' Bowler said, and yawned.

In broad daylight Spog Wilson had ploughed two circuits around the perimeter of the disputed paddock; in the middle of the following night a person unknown had put an axe through the fuel tank on the offending tractor; and before breakfast the next morning Mounted Constable William Brown had driven four miles out of town and arrested Graham Fielding at his father's farm, ignoring the shocked protests of both Graham and his parents.

When Graham had yelled, 'Bloody hell, Bowler! I didn't do it, and you know it!' Bowler had smiled and said, 'Prove it.'

Which Graham could not do. His parents might believe him home in bed every night, but Bowler knew better. When he couldn't sleep for fear the night mare would ride him, he walked the rutted streets of Kularook, and several times in the dark watches he had met the young man riding into town on horseback when his parents supposed him to be asleep; or he had seen the same horse tethered, half-hidden in the mallees, near the house across the line where Bella Pitcher, an unsentimental young woman known to some as Ten-Bob Bella, resided.

Bowler had managed to hint that he wasn't going to tell the senior Fieldings of these nocturnal excursions if Graham came quietly.

Graham had gone quietly.

Bowler, satisfied that the footy boys now knew he wasn't bluffing, went unconcernedly about his business. He soon realised, as the news got around, that everybody in the district took sides, half of them outraged by Spog's callous conduct, the rest horrified by his own high-handed tactics.

When the grapevine curled a tendril into Archie's ear he'd thrust his tools into his brother's hands, jumped in his car, and driven into town as fast as the rough road would permit. Now he snarled, 'Stop playing silly buggers, blast you. I thought you were a mate of mine. I tell you what — the footy team will fix Spog's bloody tractor and you let Graham go.'

'You mob will fix the tractor, you've got that bit right, but until I'm convinced someone else vandalised it Graham stays where he is.'

The window rattled when Archie slammed the door.

The next to arrive were two senior members of the Wilson tribe, middle-aged farmer brothers, demanding that Bowler squeeze punitive compensation out of the mongrel that had damaged their Uncle George's valuable tractor when the old boy was doing nothing more provocative than ploughing his own land.

Bowler knew that it suited all the Wilson brothers to believe that the paddock still belonged to Spog. It increased the value of his farm and, since Spog was now childless, who knew which nephew might not benefit from a tidy little inheritance when the old boy finally cashed in his chips? And if a nephew displayed a zealous partisanship now, in the current dispute, he might even swing the odds in his favour.

Bowler also knew (because Em had told him) that the Wilson brothers held a longstanding grudge against Aleck Fielding who, as a young man, had resisted their plans to marry him off to their sister

Sibyl. She had remained unmarried, so the brothers, who had been forced into considerable expenditure in support of her for the last twenty-five years, had seized an opportunity too good to miss. If, on his son's behalf, Aleck had to pay out large sums to a member of the Wilson tribe it would only serve him right.

'Nothing to do with me,' Bowler declared. 'That'll be for the magistrates to decide.' All the Wilsons were a bit too hungry for his taste so he would let them stew for a while. Once the tractor had been mended they'd have no case anyway, and would be forced to simmer down and give up any grandiose ideas of compensation.

By the second day nobody had owned up to the crime. Archie was threatening to report Bowler to his superiors in Adelaide, Bowler was unmoved, and Graham remained in custody. The situation was at an impasse.

Graham meanwhile was not languishing in the lock-up as the townspeople supposed. He and Bowler had come to terms, and the young man was awaiting his fate locked in a unused room at the back of the pub, lounging in a comfortable chair and well provided with refreshments and books.

Some of the books were supplied by Agatha Benson. Bowler was surprised that she owned any, until Em Musgrave explained that they belonged to Aubrey Venables, who was currently lending her more than she had time to read. Taking his cue from Matt Franklin, he had strolled round to the pub several times with different books under his arm, making himself at home at the kitchen table and talking to Agatha as she worked.

Em was as keen a matchmaker as most gossips. 'I keep out of their way, Bowler. She's too good a girl to go to waste and I'd like to see her settled into a happy second marriage. That's the least she deserves after her dreadful first.'

'You think Aub would make her happy?' Bowler asked. He wasn't sure that he regarded Venables as a potential good husband. He frowned, trying to understand the reason for his doubts.

'If she likes him enough, and I think she does, they'll do all right.'

'In that case, fine,' Bowler agreed. He unlocked the back room and put his head in to tell his restless prisoner that he had better resign himself to a few more days in custody.

'Days!' On a rush of fury Graham surged out of his chair. 'How many bloody days? The match is the day after tomorrow.' He eyed the doorway, as though considering a dash for freedom.

Bowler grinned and stood aside. 'You can try,' he said.

Graham muttered an oath and subsided. Bowler went out to saddle Imshy. The horse needed exercise; Joan was at home and could keep an eye on the children after school; this seemed a good time to do something he had been meaning to do for over a week.

25

Bowler rode out to the Pedler farm only to find Jack Pedler wasn't home. As he dismounted, Miriam, standing at the back door with her little daughter half hidden in her skirts behind her, explained that Jack and his eldest son had driven to a clearing sale on the other side of Edgerton and the other two boys were away in the scrub with the dray, getting a load of firewood.

Bowler had never spoken to her before, since she rarely attended the various social functions that Kularook organised to keep itself entertained. Was she shy, or did bloody Jack keep her shut up? With unusual caution he said, 'Perhaps you can help me anyway.'

But she was ushering him inside almost eagerly, not waiting for his explanations. For a split second he hesitated, alarmed that this brisk welcome might indicate a hunger for sexual favours; but that was nonsense, her manner wasn't in the least flirtatious. All the same, her welcome did seem a little more than neighbourly.

He stepped into the kitchen and seated himself at the table with the width of it between them. But she was only carrying on with accepted country hospitality, making a pot of tea from the simmering fountain on the wood stove, setting out a plate of sliced cake. She was small and dark, with a square frame that would run to fat on a less hard-working woman. He thought she must have been a pretty girl once.

She put out the cups and sat down opposite him. 'Agatha was here the other day. She told me how good you've been to her.'

'Not me. My wife.'

'So what is it you want to know, Mr Brown?'

He wondered if there was some way he could wrap up his questions to disguise how his suspicions were tending; but there was not. He said, 'Anybody driving out to Bensons' has to pass this house. Can you remember back as far as the day of the shootings at Bensons'? I've been wondering whether you heard a second car go past that day. Can you remember if they had any visitors after Thelma?'

She flashed a shrewd, assessing glance at him. 'That's weeks ago,' she said, and turned to her daughter. 'You must finish practising your scales, Melissa. Run along, there's a good girl.'

The child obediently went up the passage towards the front of the house and in a moment they heard simple piano scales played slowly but accurately. Miriam said, 'Do you think now that there was an outsider involved in that tragedy?'

'I don't know. That's the trouble, I don't know. But there are a couple of odd things about that shooting, and for my own peace of mind I have to investigate a bit further.'

Why had he said that, about his peace of mind, instead of pretending this was official, as he had done to Rupe and Figgy? Possibly because she looked an intelligent woman, more probably because he was accustomed to finding women sympathetic listeners, prepared to hear him out and understand his points.

'Mrs Pedler, I'd be grateful if you didn't talk about this just yet. I'm so uncertain.'

'Oh, I'll keep my mouth shut.' She smiled down into her teacup. 'Jack told me to keep my nose out of it, but I think he's wrong. Because, Mr Brown, yes, I did hear something that afternoon, and I've been hoping for a chance to tell you. Not a car, a motorbike.'

Apparently she hoped he wouldn't tell Jack, then. He said, 'A motorbike went out towards Bensons' that afternoon?'

She nodded. 'I didn't think much about it at first, I thought Gab Thompson must be home, he used to ride out this way shooting rabbits every now and then. But his mother told me he's still away.'

'That fathead,' Bowler said with some contempt. 'His sentence still has four months to run, last I heard. So if it wasn't Gab, do you have any idea who it was?'

'No. I didn't see him but it sounded like his bike, one of those noisy two-strokes. I heard it revving and roaring through the loose sand at the turnoff, then it headed out along the track.'

'So it could have been anyone. Someone else to shoot rabbits, do you think?'

'Perhaps. We don't have so many since Jack ripped the warrens, but I don't suppose all the boys know that. Miss Venables can usually get a few, but she comes around dusk.'

'Miss Venables?' he said, considerably surprised. He'd imagined she'd occupy herself with needlework or something similarly domestic, not stride about the landscape with a gun. He remembered vaguely that Aubrey had said something once about her shooting and he'd thought it was meant as a joke.

'She drives her brother's little car out this way occasionally. She never calls in though, and she hasn't been for ages, now I think about it. Certainly not since I heard the motorbike.'

Bowler replaced his cup on the saucer. 'I'd better ask around, see if anyone knows who it was. Can't be more than half a dozen motorbikes about, after all.' He pushed back his chair and stood. 'You didn't hear any cars as well, that day? No? Well, thanks anyway. And thanks for the tea.'

The piano scales faltered, went back to the beginning. He wished he was brazen enough to take another slice of the delicious gingerbread cake. Joan, bless her undomesticated heart, fed him a steady diet of bought coffee biscuits for his morning tea and he loathed coffee biscuits. But she never listened: she believed that anyone who made a fuss about a trivial detail like the taste of food didn't deserve consideration.

So now he crunched the bloody things up without protest because he had learned the hard way that he wasn't going to be offered anything else.

26

'A picnic?' Agatha said. 'I promised Em I'd wash the front windows this afternoon.'

'Mrs Musgrave says the windows can wait.' Aubrey Venables bumped one hand against the leg of the grey flannels he wore, as though he missed the whip he habitually slapped against a riding boot. He gestured with his other hand at his Citroen coupe parked outside.

In spite of herself, Agatha was flattered by Aubrey's attentions. He had been born to wealthy parents and given an expensive education; he had travelled, he was well-read, and he had the urbane good manners of a man who customarily mixed with others of his own kind. She found his conversation entertaining, his wit amusing, his presence comfortable. He made no demands on her other than that she should listen to him, and after her years in university lecture theatres she was a good listener.

'I'd like to show you the farm, my dear,' he said. 'Then we could drive to Mount Muckle, and have a picnic lunch. It's a fine day, and the views, although not spectacular, have a certain charm.'

Mount Muckle was an outcrop of granite rocks ten miles out of town which, although not high, rose conspicuously above the scrub-covered, worn-down limestone plains all around it. It was almost the only accepted picnic spot in the district. Agatha had never seen it —

picnics had been far too frivolous for Lew Benson — so she said, 'I would like that. What can I bring?'

'Nothing but the pleasure of your company, my dear.'

'There's Cordelia,' she reminded him.

'Of course,' he said, but not quickly enough. Apparently he had forgotten he would have to entertain a baby as well for the day.

'And naturally I'll bring her lunch,' Agatha said. 'You'll only have to feed one of us.'

Bowler was called to the pub just before closing time at six o'clock. Jockey Gallagher, a small man with a hair-trigger temper, had reached the point in his drunkenness where he wanted to fight any man within a radius of three yards, regardless of their size, weight, or age. Jockey was over forty, and he tried to flatten Splinter Thompson's second son Roy, who was not only solid and tough but three times his size and ten years his junior. So Trotter Musgrave the publican sent for Bowler to stop Roy stamping Jockey into the linoleum. Although Trotter himself was big and burly enough to quell most fights this time interested bystanders shouldered him away. Too many of his customers were enjoying the spectacle of Jockey getting a thumping.

'Jockey started it,' Trotter said when the law arrived.

Bowler bundled Roy out through the corner door, gave him a shove in the back, and told him to go home before he was arrested. Then he returned to the bar and regarded Jockey with disfavour.

'What's bloody Gallagher celebrating, for pity's sake?' he asked. The six other men remaining in the bar looked at one another and shook their heads. 'Why do you go on serving him, Trotter? He's more nuisance than he's worth.'

Jockey, muttering curses, was making ineffectual swipes at the bar with a bottle, trying to smash off the end to convert it to a dangerous weapon.

'A cheap drunk,' Trotter said. 'After a pot or two you never can tell when he's going to get excitable.'

Bowler took the small man's collar in a strong grip, held him at arm's length, and twitched the bottle from his grasp. Jockey then made strenuous but unavailing attempts to kick his shins. 'Nasty temper the bastard's got.'

'Spiteful, too. Davidsons reckon he tried to fire their haystack last harvest, after they sacked the little pest and booted him off the place.' Trotter held out his hand for the bottle, and stowed it behind the bar.

Bowler tightened his grip and studied his prisoner, his head on one side. 'Is that a fact. I'd better check with them. In the meantime, you say he started this rumpus, Trotter. Right. Drunk and disorderly. A night in the lock-up will cool his temper.'

'Why stop at one?' Trotter said. 'Nobody will miss him.'

Jockey was twisting and flailing his free arm, howling oaths and obscenities, as Bowler dragged him into the street. Daylight was fading fast, the last of the sun blanketed by dark clouds billowing up in the west. They were halfway across the road when Aubrey Venables's car pulled up at the pub's back gate, and Bowler saw both heads within it turn towards him. He muttered a curse of his own and under cover of the dim light smacked his prisoner lightly across the mouth.

'Shut up,' he hissed. 'Or you'll get worse next time.' Raising his voice he called cheerfully. 'Did you have a good day?' He didn't wait for an answer but hustled Jockey into the police station before he could start shouting again.

In the car, Agatha shivered.

Aubrey reached for her hand. 'Take no notice, my dear.'

'He's a horrible man.'

'He's beneath your notice. I hope you have more pleasant matters to think about. Did you enjoy the picnic?'

'Aubrey, it was lovely. Thank you.' She couldn't remember when she had last spent such a lazy, happy afternoon. Her expectations had not been so high when they set out. Aubrey, however, was a more experienced host than she had given him credit for, and more intelligent. He had arranged everything exactly to please her.

Cordelia too had enjoyed the new sights, the new small landscapes she'd been allowed to explore. The child was asleep now, cradled in her mother's left arm.

Agatha said again, 'Thank you, Aubrey. We both enjoyed your picnic.'

Gallantly he lifted her free hand, and kissed it.

27

At the eleventh hour, on the morning of the football match, Archie arrived at the police station in company with Bub Gregory, a huge lumbering man of about thirty. The footballers had finally discovered what Bowler had known almost from the beginning, that Bub was the ringleader of the saboteurs, and so the team overcame its collective distaste for dobbing — after all, Bub was an inconsistent footballer, not nearly so useful a player as Graham — and offered him up to the law so that they could get their star goal-kicker back in time for the match.

Bowler had no evidence against Bub, and had intended his blackmail to coerce the team into providing some. Although he had remained unruffled and amused throughout the episode, he felt at the same time an underlying current of anger, annoyed that his warnings to the team had been disregarded and that they'd believed he was bluffing — he, Bowler, who never bluffed. So in a spirit of bloody-mindedness he told Archie that he was not convinced by the offer of this new victim.

'You mob have just grabbed anyone as a swap for Graham. I can't prosecute an innocent man just because the footy team says so. You'll have to give me proof, Archie, and I'm not letting Graham go until I get it. The law can't work on hearsay evidence.'

Impatient and angry, Archie swore at Bub, a rather slow-witted man, and badgered him into a reluctant confession. Bowler declared that he could take no notice of a confession obtained by threats, and waved them out of the police station; but Archie, breathing heavily through his nose, refused to go. So he ushered them down the passage to the lock-up in his back yard.

They nodded to Joan as they passed the kitchen door but didn't see the cheerful thumbs-up Bowler gave her behind their backs. At the lock-up he threw open the door and invited them to view the empty cell. (Jockey Gallagher had been hauled before a JP that morning, fined — not nearly enough in Bowler's view — and turned loose.)

Aghast, obviously fearing that Graham had been sent somewhere beyond their reach, Archie demanded, 'What the devil have you done with him, Bowler?'

Bowler merely smirked.

Archie, by this time twice as angry as Bowler, said, 'If *you* don't take any notice of Bub's confession, *I* will. I'll make him write it down and I'll send a copy to your bosses in Adelaide. *Then* we'll see what happens.'

Bowler recognised that his rope had run out. 'Keep your shirt on, Arch. All right, if Bub doesn't change his mind as soon as you've gone he can write me out a nice little confession. Once that's taken care of I'll send young Graham up to the oval. But you lot have got to get the tractor fixed before Monday or I'm taking him back.' Bowler aimed a forefinger at Archie. 'And you'd better make the team understand that if anyone touches Spog or his tractor again it'll be worse for them next time.'

'I thought the law was supposed to keep the peace in the community,' Archie said in bitter reproach as he departed. 'Not set everybody at one another's throats.'

Bowler eyed Bub, scowling sullenly by the open cell door. 'And as for you, mate, the least you can expect is a fine.'

Feeling pleased with himself, Bowler went to tell Joan about his cleverness. He couldn't find her. Then as soon as he sat down in his office she came in from her dark room and spread a dozen of her photographs across his desk. He picked up several to study more closely.

'I'm pleased with that one,' Joan said, standing behind his chair and pointing over his shoulder. 'Not all of them enlarged so well.'

He pulled the photograph free from the others he held. It showed a pair of emu wrens sitting on a twig of mallee, every detail of their tiny bodies — feet, bills, shining eyes, their fine tail-feathers — distinctly etched against an unfocused background of grey leaves.

'How on earth did you get so close?' He pointed to a print. 'Where's this one taken? I don't know that place.'

Joan craned to see. 'Oh, the galahs drinking. That's an overflow of the tank at the old Government Reserve well, in Bruce Wilson's back scrub. There's a huge tract of scrub out there, part of all the uncleared land between here and Cancanulla, so the birds are relatively undisturbed. I go there often.'

'There's nothing much cleared between here and the coast, either.' Bowler always thought the townships and settlements along the railway line were like islands, pale islands of cleared paddocks in a vast sea of dark scrub. Year by year the paddocks extended a little, and year by year the scrub retreated. One day it might all be gone. He couldn't imagine such a naked landscape in his own shaggy country. Palestine, Europe, they were different — they'd been cleared and ploughed not for ninety years but for thousands of years.

He picked up the photograph of the galahs at the well again. 'How do you get there? Is it far?' He wanted to pin-point the place to register it on his mental map of the district. Possibly from some lingering superstition, he needed to have every feature of the local terrain fixed in his mind, as though one day he might have to fight over the land to defend it against invaders as the Turks had defended their lands against him. A ridiculous idea, when the Great War had been The War to End All Wars. In a sudden mood of self criticism he thought probably this need was merely a kind of vanity, a dislike that others should know more about the place than he did.

Joan screwed up her eyes. 'About eight miles out. I used to ride out on the main track nearly to Bruce Wilson's and go in from there, but then his son Douglas showed me a shorter way, straight through Ralph Wilson's back paddocks. The southern part of the scrub belongs to Ralph so I can get to the reserve that way. Not so many gates, either.'

'You must show me one day,' Bowler said. 'The birds must be used to you, to let you get so close.'

'I've cut a couple of branches of mallee to make a kind of hide.'

Bowler put up an arm, twisted his head, and pulled her down to kiss her lips. 'I'm impressed, you know. You could sell a couple to magazines, easily.'

Joan hugged his shoulders and laid her cheek against his. 'I already have,' she said, and pointed. 'Those three.' When he said nothing, she added, 'Not for the money, stupid. For recognition.' She jerked upright, smacked him lightly on the side of his head, swept up the photographs and left.

Now he'd annoyed her.

Bowler pulled a ledger towards him but didn't open it. Joan read him too easily. She knew he resented her private income — the income that allowed her to indulge in this expensive hobby — and would have preferred her to be dependent on him for all her needs. He struggled constantly with his baser self. He wanted her to have the hobby, he was proud of her talents, even proud in a perverse kind of way of her slap-dash house-keeping. But he wished sometimes he could be generous to her in a manner that counted.

Most men, he supposed, liked to lavish gifts on their wives occasionally. Was there something mean-spirited in him that he'd like to give Joan something, sometime, and bask in her gratitude? Why did it matter, when he could provide for her and the children in every other way? He didn't want to be ungenerous, but he was unable to suppress completely his jealousy of the independence her money gave her.

Unlike most wives Joan could leave him at any time, with her children, and still live as well as she did now. Better, in fact.

Scowling at that hideous thought Bowler went back to his researches into motorbike ownership. Miriam Pedler had heard a motorbike heading out towards Bensons' on the Thursday afternoon of the shooting and, whether or not the rider had any hand in the tragedy enacted there, Bowler needed to know who he was. He opened the ledger.

The list of registered motorbikes was not long. Claud John Gregory, Conchubar Dorian Harris, Gabriel Walter Thompson, Michael Henry Wilson and Clive Cecil Wishart each owned one.

Claud John Gregory.
That was Bub. He and his older brother had been boarding with their uncle Arnie Gregory ever since their parents had moved away three years before. Arnie owned one of the small houses and shacks built apparently at random along the dirt tracks through dense mallee on the other side of the railway line. It must have been a tight fit for the large nephews seeing that Arnie and his wife had their five nearly grown-up children living with them already.

They were a ramshackle gang. Bowler wouldn't trust them with a dud penny, but he could see no reason why Bub should take to homicide. He'd never worked for the Bensons, he can't have known them more than casually, so why would he want to embark on such wholesale slaughter?

If Bowler was looking for a murderer on a motor-bike, Bub was an unlikely candidate.

Conchubar Dorian Harris.
What weird names the Harrises had. The eldest son Durwin was the

pub handyman; Con was the youngest. The second son Val, short for Valerian, had left home some years before and gone to sea (remarking, as he left, that if he didn't put the greatest possible distance between himself and his father he'd kill the bastard), and the sole daughter Calpurnia kept house for Con and her father, Old Man Harris, in a corrugated iron humpy not far from Gregorys' over there on the wrong side of the tracks. They too were a light-fingered lot — well, not Callie as far as he knew — but it didn't make them murderers. The youngest, Con, was at present working for the Davidson brothers as a wood-and-water joey, and had as few motives for murder as Bub.

Bowler reminded himself that he hadn't yet fastened the theft of old Spog's chooks on Durwin; he must get after the man. Shaking his head he moved his pencil to the next name in the book.

Gabriel Walter Thompson.

Gab was in gaol, and had been from before the shooting. His two-stroke motorbike had been stored in the back of a shed at his father's place ever since Bowler had arrested him, according to his father Splinter. The mere thought of Gab made Bowler angry — he was such an inept thief, such a slow, bumbling, dim-witted man, he should never have turned his hand to crime in the first place. Bowler still remembered his arrest with embarrassment.

Michael Henry Wilson.

Mike, Harry Wilson's eldest son, had bought a two-stroke motorbike last summer. Jean Watts, to whom he was betrothed, lived on her father's farm five miles out on the south side of Kularook, twelve miles by road from Harry's place to the north-west. Mike was not a particularly impetuous lover — they had been engaged for three years already — but his father allowed him to borrow the family car too infrequently for even his temperate wooing. Hence the motorbike.

Bowler could not see phlegmatic Mike Wilson getting steamed up enough to punch anyone, let alone shoot anyone. All the same, Miriam Pedler thought the bike she heard was a two-stroke, what Bowler's brother used to call a two-banger. Possibly Mike had been out after rabbits too.

Though most farmer's sons shot their own farm's rabbits. Why waste ammo on somebody else's pests when they (usually) had plenty at home? He could find out easily enough, however, if Mike had been further afield that afternoon, and if he had, that took care of the motorbike.

Clive Cecil Wishart.

Bowler didn't like Clive, a lazy, over-sexed man with a notorious temper who lived with his wife and ever-increasing family in a bleak little shanty on a farm east of Kularook. He was a rotten farmer, who had done almost nothing to improve his land in all the years he'd been there. Bowler could easily imagine Clive, in one of his violent rages, seizing up a rifle and opening fire on everybody in sight; unfortunately, he couldn't imagine a reason why the lazy beggar would ever visit Bensons'.

Bowler had never seen Clive's bike — it also was a two-stroke machine — and when he considered, he didn't expect to. If it was like every other piece of machinery the man owned it had been bought second-hand, then abused until it fell apart. So it probably wasn't even in working order. All the same, if Bowler ever discovered a whisper of a motive he'd get after Clive like a shot. He'd enjoy arresting Clive Wishart.

Checking on motorbikes hadn't got him very far. Probably the bike Miriam had heard was young Mike, after rabbits. Where did he go from here?

The easiest way to deal with his suspicions and uncertainties was to assume the murderer had not been Lew, and then try and find a logical suspect, someone with a motive to kill four people. Though surely only a deranged man would have a motive for four deaths — and Bowler, although he knew of a few weirdos among his parishioners, would hesitate to call any of them deranged. Obvious homicidal maniacs were thin on the ground.

Bowler swore, and slammed the ledger shut.

28

For the convenience of the farmers who chose to drive in for the football, the two general stores remained open on Saturday afternoons. As Agatha turned in to the store closest to the pub she waved to Bowler, who was strolling up the middle of the street towards the oval. The white-metalled surface glistened from the last shower of rain.

In the rather dim interior of the store two small boys were hovering over the ha'penny tray of sweets while the storekeeper, Len Dunstan, watched impatiently. Selection made, each child handed over a penny and went out clutching his booty, while Len slid the tray under the counter again and turned to Agatha. His expression hardened when he recognised her.

In tight-lipped silence he weighed out two pounds of split peas into the deep pan of his black iron scales. Carefully, he removed half a dozen little yellow pellets until the balance swung exactly level. He lifted the pan and tipped the peas into a brown paper bag.

'A pound of milk arrowroot biscuits,' Agatha said. 'And two Solyptol soaps.' She saw Mrs Dunstan's head jerk out of sight round the doorway that led to living quarters at the back. That woman had been peering at her as though she were a freak or a monster, she thought resentfully. And Mr Dunstan wasn't much better. He looked at her as though he could see her sins branded across her forehead.

Through the wire door to the street she heard thin shouts, the faint tooting of car-horns, from the oval at the other end of town; Kularook footy team must have scored a goal, and she hoped Graham had kicked it. He had been so savagely resentful of his role in Bowler's row with the footballers he deserved a change in his fortunes.

While Len swapped the two-pound weight on his scales for the one-pound weight, turned to the shelves behind the counter, and lifted down a square tin of biscuits, Agatha squatted to sort over the cakes of green soap in a box on the floor on her side of the counter; most of them were chipped at the corners; she selected the least broken and placed them beside the rest of the order.

She checked the list Em had written on the back of a used envelope. 'A bottle of coffee essence, a gross of matches, two dozen candles. Put them in Musgraves' book.' She stowed the purchases in Em's big shopping basket, called, 'You can come out now,' over her shoulder to the lurking Mrs Dunstan, and walked out into a dark and drizzly afternoon. She made a dash through the rain to the pub veranda.

On a gust of male voices Em came out of the bar into the hall. 'Damn Saturday afternoons,' she said. 'They're always bedlam. I could do with four hands in there.'

Agatha ran her hand over her wet head. 'Those Dunstans won't even say good afternoon to me. They think I'm a murderer. Everyone does, everyone blames me for driving Lew to murder. I will never fit in here. I think it's time I left.'

Em pulled the door shut behind her, nearly catching the elbow of a man standing just inside the bar. 'It's not as bad as that. You don't have to take any notice of those two, they're a pair of sanctimonious wowsers, a proper pain in the neck.'

'But I do have to take notice. Really, Em, everyone looks at me the same way. I shouldn't impose on you any longer.'

'Good grief, you're not imposing, you're an enormous help to me. And not everyone looks at you the same way — what about Aubrey?'

Agatha wasn't sure how she wanted to answer that. Aubrey Venables was certainly attentive, and had hinted more than once that his intentions were serious, but she didn't want to appear to be taking him too much for granted.

After many restless nights of soul-searching, she had decided that if he asked her, she would marry him. He could give her a life so removed from the one she had shared with Lew that her head spun at the thought of it: life in a comfortable house, a life that included books and intelligent conversation, intelligent friends, even civilised diversions like playing bridge. His consideration, his unfailing good manners, would make him easy to live with even if she wasn't passionately in love with him. Though she believed he'd be easy to love, too, in the long run, since he seemed a kind and undemanding man. And Cordelia would be safe.

If Agatha didn't marry Aubrey she would have to search for a place where her sinful past was either unknown or ignored, so that she could practise medicine and support her daughter; and, as she knew from experience, places like that were almost impossible to find while the country was trying to struggle out of the Depression. Last time she'd tried, in spite of all the letters she'd written, in spite of the advertisements she'd answered, she had found no hospital, no practice, no organisation, that had been prepared to employ her. Her reputation was too easily discovered by anybody wanting to check up on her credentials.

Which was why, when she had found herself trapped, unable to stay any longer keeping house for her fellow-medico friend and unable, despite her desperate searches, to find a position where she could support her daughter, she had approached Lew for a divorce. She believed a divorcee would be more acceptable for employment in some places than a runaway wife. But Lew had refused, and had instead sent her the price of a train ticket.

Agatha knew she couldn't stay at the pub indefinitely. True, she helped Em with the housework, but that really was insufficient return for her bed and board. When she left she would have to find a job that enabled her to support Cordelia and, in spite of the difficulties, would have to find it fast.

There would be no search, no anxiety, if she married Aubrey. She and her daughter would both be secure, their future protected.

She wasn't yet ready to share these hopes with Em Musgrave. She said, 'Aubrey is courteous enough to ignore my sticky past when he's with me. What he says when I'm not there, I have no idea.'

'I know how he speaks of you to me,' Em said with a significant smile. 'Really, Agatha, you must try to put it all behind you. It's no good brooding on the past. You can't blame yourself for what Lew did.'

'But I do, of course I do, because I knew what he was like.'

'All the same —'

'Em, I knew he'd be angry if he found out I'd met Snow even though there was nothing in it, just the loan of a few books. But never in my wildest dreams did I imagine Lew could think I was planning to leave him again.' She gave a huff of derisive laughter. 'As if I'd go through all that a second time.'

In public Em supported this version of the shootings: that Matt Franklin, out of friendship for an old schoolmate, had merely lent Agatha a couple of books, and had been misunderstood by Lew. In private, she told her husband that there must have been a bit more to it than that, because in her view Matt wasn't going to ride miles out of his way to lend books to just any old schoolmate. Agatha might not have encouraged him, but young rips like Matt Franklin didn't need encouragement.

Em didn't, however, explain her views to Agatha.

29

When Bowler arrived at the oval the Cancanulla team had just kicked a goal. From a row of cars parked on the far side of the ground came ragged cheers, shouts of encouragement for individual players from their wives and supporters, and a triumphant tooting of car horns.

'Another bloody goal,' Splinter Thompson said with an air of unrelieved gloom. 'The buggers have scored eight to our four already.'

He was standing between the goalposts, a goal umpire for the afternoon, and so no doubt knew the facts.

Bowler said, 'Archie told me they're a weak side this year.'

'So they are, usually. You know we always beat them. But now they've got hold of some new bloke — see, that ginger-headed character just went up for the mark — he's turned the bloody match around.' Splinter announced this as a grievance, as though Cancanulla were taking an unfair advantage by providing a tougher than expected opposition to the Kularook team. He added more cheerfully, 'But looks like our blokes have put Kenny on him. That might cramp his style.'

After watching for some minutes, Bowler was forced to agree — Kenny, the eldest Pedler son, might cramp any footballer's style if he didn't kill him first. What was going on out there in the middle of the oval was so close to criminal assault that if the umpire didn't stop it soon Bowler had a good mind to stop it himself.

The Cancanulla team, however, weren't going to put up with it either. After the next scrimmage in the centre, when play had momentarily outstripped the umpires, their captain emerged from the melee solicitously supporting Kenny, who was half-stunned and reeling and bleeding profusely from gashes on his calf where his leg had been raked by a sprigged boot.

Bowler turned his back, trying to decide whether he could ignore the mayhem. He didn't like Kenny Pedler, a foul-mouthed troublemaker when he was drunk (which was as often as he had money in his pocket), but that didn't mean he could let the bastard be maimed under his very nose. He saw a younger Pedler run across to help his brother, decided that just this once he was looking the other way — after all, the umpires were supposed to be out there to stop this sort of thing — and turned back to Splinter.

'How's Dick these days? I haven't seen him around.'

Splinter shrugged. 'Dunno what he's up to.'

Miss Venables had said he wasn't out on Aubrey's block. 'Where's he gone? Did he pick up his car?'

'Nope. Probably off on a blind somewhere.'

'Poor bastard,' Bowler said with feeling. 'Are the children all right?'

'Seem to be settling down,' Splinter said. 'Mind you, Shirl and the girls spoil them something rotten.'

By half time the Kularook team had rallied, and cut the difference in scores to one goal. One good forward, no matter how brilliant, couldn't in the long run drag a weaker team to victory over a side stronger on all other parts of the ground. There was an aura of self-satisfaction about the Kularook team as they squatted on the cold ground between the thistles in the centre of the oval, sucking their oranges and conferring in low tones.

'That Graham Fielding is a bloody good player, Bowler, you must admit,' Splinter urged.

Bowler hunched his shoulders inside his jacket. 'Why else did you think I arrested him?'

Surprised, Splinter said, 'I thought you had him tagged for having a go at the tractor.' He crossed his arms, and shook his cold booted feet one after the other, then propped his back against a behind-post and rubbed to and fro, like a cow against a rail.

'Not me. I knew it was Bub.'

'How'd you know that?'

Bowler flipped a dismissive hand. He'd never admit that he had an informer among those haphazard families across the railway line; he preferred to foster the myth of his omniscience. He said, 'Splinter, if poor bloody Dick has been drowning his sorrows ever since his wife died it's been a pretty long bender. That was ages ago. Don't you have any idea where he could have got to?'

'He's got mates over Dincawauta way. I reckon that's where he'd be.'

'How'd he get there, if the car's still parked at your place? Do you think he'd have caught the train?'

Splinter screwed up his eyes and scratched the back of his neck while he considered this. Hardly surprising if he itched; his skin was nearly as dark and greasy as his hair.

'Hadn't thought of that,' Splinter said.

Uneasily, Bowler wondered where the man could be. He said, 'How did Dick take the news, when you told him his wife had been shot? Did you bring him back to town with you that evening?'

'Didn't see him. I drive all that way, bloody near break every axle the old bus's got, and then the place is empty. Then Aub Venables tells me Dick came to see him that afternoon, so he was in town anyway, seems Thelma dropped him off before she left the kids with us and went on out to Bensons'. So I reckon someone else must've told him. He woulda been kicking round town waiting for Thelma, see, and word went round fast after Rupe and that Figgy brought

Lew's wife in.'

Incredulous, Bowler demanded, 'Do you mean to tell me that you haven't seen your son since before his wife died?'

He'd forgotten the match. A football soared past Splinter's head; a whistle shrilled. Splinter bent for two small white flags on the ground at his feet.

'More like it,' he said, waving them vigorously. 'Makes us even.'

'Splinter! Did you hear what I said?'

'Yair, I did. Put it like that it does sound a bit off.'

'Doesn't your wife know where he is?'

'She was saying only the other day she wished he'd get in touch. The kids are missing him. But he'll turn up, Bowler. He always does.'

'I suppose so,' Bowler said. Certainly the Thompson sons had a habit of going into smoke every now and then, sometimes on a bender, sometimes engaged in some activity they'd rather nobody knew about.

He'd better ask Trotter at the pub whether he'd sold any liquor to Dick since the shooting. And ask the stationmaster whether he'd seen him catch a train south.

'How's it going, Dad?' Splinter's daughter Dot had walked up to them with her arm in Rupe Benson's. Figgy Higgins hovered at her other side.

Bowler said 'Good afternoon,' and lifted his hat to her. He thought with wry amusement she must have a pretty powerful personality if she could drag Rupe to a football match. None of the Bensons had shown the slightest interest in football — or any other Kularook social occasion — before. Good on Dot if she was softening up the remains of that reclusive family.

Black clouds were piling up in the west. Heading home before the rain started, Bowler came across Harry Wilson's eldest son Mike, wrapped in a grey army blanket as well as his overcoat, propped on the front bumper of the family car. His eyes were reddened, his nose streamed with a severe cold, but he had apparently chosen to watch the match from this chilly perch in preference to sharing the interior of the car with his mother and two of his Wilson aunts.

Bowler placed himself upwind of the young man. 'Don't you pass that on to me,' he warned.

'I widsh I cood,' Mike said, dabbing at his nose with a bunched handkerchief. 'I dode wad the bloddy thig.'

'Mike, do you ever go shooting rabbits out past Pedlers'?'

'Whad's habbend? Somboddy shod a sheeb? Wasn'd be.'

'Nobody's shot any sheep. I just wondered if you ever went out on that track on your motorbike.'

'Pasd Pedders'? God enough flambing rabbids of our own.' He buried his nose in the handkerchief, trumpeted into it, and said more clearly, 'Don't do much shooting, actually. Leave that to m'brother. I'm a lousy shot.'

A surprising admission, Bowler reflected as he walked away. Whatever their shooting skills, most country boys believed implicitly that they were crack shots, King's Prize standard at least. He turned and walked back.

'Do you ever lend your bike to your brother?'

Mike looked horrified. 'I wouldn'd led him within twendy yards of id.' He resorted to the handkerchief again. 'He's the lunatic who topped up the radiator on Dad's last car drough the oil filler.'

'Ah yes,' Bowler said. 'I heard about that.'

'I'd break his neck if he laid a figger on it, ad he knows it.' He dabbed his nose. 'Bud Bowler, eddyone ridig from our blace to Jack's warrens would go drough the paddogs, not alog the drack pasd his house.'

That was logical. Anyone from the Wilson property riding east across the paddocks would save miles of distance — the surface of the paddocks was not much rougher than the track — and would come to the warrens before he came to the track to Bensons'.

So who had been on that motorbike Miriam Pedler had heard?

30

The rain was pelting down by the time Bowler reached the pub veranda. He raced through the heavy downpour for the last two hundred yards, then ambled in at the front door pleased to find that he was breathing barely faster than normal. As he was hanging his dripping hat on a row of hooks in the hall, Trotter Musgrave put his head through the door from the bar.

'In training for the Stawell Gift?' he enquired. 'I saw that. I wish I had your lungs.'

He shouldn't smoke so much. 'Result of a pure and blameless life,' Bowler said. 'Hey, Trotter, have you seen Dick Thompson about lately? Sold him booze, or anything?'

'Not so far as I know, though you'd have to check with Durwin and Em. Either of them could have served him when I wasn't around. He's been lying pretty low since his wife died.'

Too damn low, it seemed to Bowler. 'Em in the kitchen?'

'I reckon. Not far away, at any rate.'

She was in the laundry, feeding sheets folded lengthways through a rumbling mangle while Agatha turned the handle. Bowler leant unseen on the door frame for a moment, enjoying the view of Agatha's lithe swing and twist as she hauled the handle round and round.

Agatha straightened her back and pushed a strand of loose hair off her forehead with her wrist. 'I thought you were at the football match.'

'Too cold and too wet. Em, have you seen Dick Thompson around lately?'

Em pulled the sheet from the mangle, matched the ends carefully, and started to fold it on a wide, scrubbed wooden bench along the wall. Over her shoulder she said, 'No. Splinter seems to think he's on a drinking binge somewhere.'

'I know he does. But did you sell Dick the grog? Trotter didn't.'

'Now you mention it, no. Perhaps he had a private supply parked somewhere.'

'If he had any he'd have drunk it long ago. Damn it all, Em, you know Dick. He's got the self-restraint of a flea.'

Agatha said, 'I don't know about that.'

Bowler rounded on her. 'Why not?'

She stared vaguely out the streaming window while she considered this. 'He seemed pretty restrained in his dealings with his wife, in spite of her provocation, it seemed to me.' Her hand went to her cheek, as if in memory of Lew's less restrained responses to his wife's intransigence.

'What provocation?' Bowler demanded instantly.

'Well, she was threatening to leave him, you know. I felt quite sorry for him. There was quite a row about it. Only Lew made her go home.'

Away in the distance at the back of Bowler's mind a faint alarm bell tinkled. He said, 'What row? What happened? I haven't heard about this. When was this? How long before — ?'

She flapped a hand at him to slow down the rate of his questions. He fell silent, and watched her frowning over her memories.

Em laid the folded sheet on top of a neat pile. 'Come into the kitchen. The kettle's boiling.'

So he sat at the table in the pub kitchen drinking tea while Em took a cup to her husband and Agatha related what she could remember of the day Dick came in search of his errant wife: Thelma's determination to stay, Lew's attack on Dick, the noise and the yelling. 'But when Lew packed him off and Thelma with him, Dick didn't seem angry with her,' she finished. 'He seemed to blame the others.'

By this time the alarm bells were ringing loud enough to deafen him. Carefully Bowler asked, 'Was Dick very much upset?'

'He was furious, but they were five to one. Four to one really, you couldn't count Thelma, because whatever she said to start with, she went off quite happily with him at the end.'

Em returned; reading only part of his thoughts, she said, 'Bowler, I don't think Dick's the type to suicide, really I don't.'

'I hope not,' he grunted. Perhaps he wasn't, if he was driven only by grief for his wife. But Em didn't know about the motorbike Miriam Pedler had heard, and because of that there was another possibility. If Dick had decided to take a terrible revenge on those responsible for his humiliation he would in all probability have finished by shooting himself. Had undoubtedly shot himself as well as the rest of them. Aspects of the shooting that hadn't fitted comfortably with Lew as murderer slotted neatly into place if Dick pulled the trigger.

Dick had been in and out of the house often enough to know where the rifle was kept, so that he could count on finding it if he had ridden out with the express purpose of revenging himself on his in-laws. Then too the order of the shots was explained — Lew, the man who had humiliated him, first; then his hated mother-in-law and the wife threatening to leave him; and lastly Agatha, to remove the only witness.

Although he was keeping his expression calm, his hands quiet, inside his head Bowler was swearing. How could he have been so complacent, so negligent, that he hadn't checked on Dick's whereabouts before? He tended to dismiss the whole tribe of Thompson sons as half-witted — they took after their bloody father, didn't they? — but that didn't mean they were devoid of feeling.

With a deadly cold certainty he knew he would find Gab's motorbike missing when he went to search Splinter's shed, which he was going to do just as soon as he could leave without alerting Em or Agatha to the way his thoughts were tending. Bloody Splinter wouldn't know what he had in those tumbledown old sheds of his. Bowler castigated himself anew for taking Splinter's word for anything.

And if the bike was not there, the next thing he would have to do was drive out to Aubrey Venables's block and search for a fourth corpse. If what he feared was true, Dick had been missing too long for him to hope that the man was still alive.

When Bowler had gone Em said, 'Agatha, don't look like that. I doubt if Dick has done anything stupid, you know.'

'I can't judge any more what a man is likely to do,' Agatha said. 'I thought I knew Lew.'

'Don't start that again.' Em banged down her cup. 'It was not your fault. You never believed Lew could be blamed for anything you did, did you? There you are then.'

'Surely I should have seen it coming. That's what bothers me most. I believed I had convinced Lew. I really did.'

'Men!' Em said, getting up. 'Who knows how their minds work? I'd better see if Trotter needs another pair of hands in the bar. Last I saw half Kularook was there keeping out the rain.' At the door she turned, said, 'Visitor for you,' and went on up the passage.

Miriam Pedler walked in with her daughter Melissa. She pulled off her felt hat and shook her head to flick raindrops from her hair. Agatha flew out of her chair and hugged her hard, wet overcoat and all.

'You're looking better,' Miriam said, holding her shoulders. Melissa pressed against her mother's side.

'Feeling better, too. Starting to get over the nightmare, anyway. Take off your coat and come and sit down.'

Miriam hung her coat over the back of a chair, sat down, and began scrubbing at her daughter's sodden hair with her handkerchief. 'I was at the football but now it's raining. The boys can get on without me. How's Cordelia?'

'She's fine. Asleep just now.'

'And now you can tell me all about this new beau you've got,' Miriam said. 'And don't say "What beau?" All the town is talking.'

31

The track was more like a steeplechase than a road. Bowler's car bounced on a ledge of stone disguised as a shadow and came down with a thump that jarred his back teeth. He'd never been on this track before, had never in all his years in Kularook needed to visit this scrub block. Until Venables bought it, it had merely been part of Davidsons' back scrub, supporting mobs of emus, more roos, and a few sheep.

Aubrey Venables had paid Bub Gregory and his brother to plough in a line for the track and run up a small house, and had then installed Dick Thompson as manager. Dick had been supposed to start clearing the scrub and erecting fences to enclose the paddocks, preparing the land for pasture and crops, turning the land into the fertile, prosperous farm that Aubrey, in the first flush of his enthusiasm, had described to anyone who would listen. But through Dick's inexperience and his boss's ignorance the job was not getting done, except in a patchy, inefficient way. Bowler, a country boy, had seen it all. It seemed to him that both men underestimated the length of time that any stage of the operation would take.

He was glad he wasn't on the land. His brother was welcome to the farm.

The track rose in a steep incline, swung right round a shoulder of the hill, and divided into a loop in front of a small house. He climbed out and inspected his tyres, cursing when he found one, as he had feared, deeply scored by a stone.

The house wasn't much of a house, more like a large hut. It was a squarish box built of second-hand materials, a timber frame covered with sheets of corrugated iron of the small-ridged variety. Not all the angles were exactly square, not all the uprights were exactly vertical; it had the same air of menacing unease that a distorting mirror imparts to everyday faces. Some of the walls showed irregular rectangles of biscuit-coloured paint, old and flaking, from the iron's previous incarnation in a different building.

When he pushed open the door of this unimpressive dwelling he decided within five seconds that nobody had been there for a long time. Not for weeks, anyway. He stepped directly into the main room, which held a fireplace with a rust-streaked stove at the left-hand end, a kitchen table covered with cracked oilcloth in the middle, five unmatched straight-backed chairs pushed against the walls, and a stack of wooden kerosene cases laid on their sides beside the stove to make a set of shelves. No curtains hung at the single window facing him. To his right, in the wall opposite the stove, a door stood ajar.

Bowler sniffed, but the air, although stale, was pure enough. Without foreboding, therefore, he pushed open the internal door, and surveyed a cramped and dusty bedroom divided by a faded floral curtain. One side was filled with a wooden-ended double bed, covered by a yellowing knitted cotton bedspread; in the other stood two small black iron bedsteads made up with grey blankets. There was hardly space to walk between them.

The place felt claustrophobic. He'd rather live in a tent any day. Bowler closed the door, relieved to get into the open air, and considered where next to search for Dick's remains — if remains there were. The heavy rifle had stayed at Benson's, but Bowler knew from the register that Dick owned a twenty-two, and that rifle was not in the house.

He hadn't told anyone he was driving out here, or why. He had no proof one way or another that Dick had been to Bensons' on the afternoon of the shooting. But Miriam Pedler had heard a motorbike and, as he had feared, Gab Thompson's motorbike was missing from Splinter's shed, much to the owner's astonishment.

'I didn't notice she was gone, honest. I'da sworn she was still there,' Splinter had protested, when Bowler accused him of misleading the law.

'Not that a little perjury would worry you.' Bowler felt bitterly angry, almost more with himself than with stupid Splinter. 'Even if you had noticed.'

Splinter, ignorant that Bowler was now considering whether Dick was implicated in the shootings, had been relieved of all worry about his son's safety. With a motorbike he could have easily reached his mates in Dincawauta, so his prolonged absence could be as easily explained.

Bowler had not confided his suspicions to anyone, not even Joan. Although many signs now pointed to Dick as murderer, although he was prepared to find Dick's dead body when he searched far enough, he couldn't be certain. Caution kept him silent. If, in spite of all probability, he found no sign of Dick, he didn't want everyone in Kularook to know that he'd gone charging off on a wild goose chase. Bowler did not like to be wrong. More particularly, he did not like others to see that he had been wrong.

There had been no motor-bike outside the house when he drove up, no note on the table, no body in the bedroom. He'd expected to find all three. Perhaps, he thought sourly, still angry with himself, he was beginning to believe the myths that he fostered so assiduously — the myths of his infallibility, of his omniscience. He'd expected a tragedy all laid out for him to read like a book. Now he'd better look in the shed.

Like more substantial farmhouses, the hut had been built on a rise.

A thicket of mallee had been left beside it, but the rest of the scrub had been roughly cleared away for a distance of a hundred yards leaving the ground littered with uprooted stumps and stones. Behind the house a long-drop dunny, unroofed, enclosed in hessian walls, reigned in isolated splendour on the rough ground. The hessian curtain which substitute for a door had been looped back; there was nobody inside.

A track bony with limestone led down the slope to a corrugated iron shed, tarred black, open along one side, and about twice the size of the house. He could see the snout of a large tractor poking from it.

He stretched, and decided to walk down. Halfway to the shed his nose picked up the odour of rotting flesh, a faint, all too familiar odour, and his stomach heaved. Being braced to find death didn't make an approach to it any easier.

But what he found was somehow both less and much worse than his expectations. More disgusting, more horrible. Under a couple of banksias at the near end of the shed lay the remains of a black and white sheepdog, the collar still around the skeletal throat, still attached by a chain to the corner of the shed. The crows had been there before him.

Perhaps it was the shock; he was taken totally by surprise. Perhaps, more than he realised, his instinctive sympathy for all powerless and underprivileged beings extended to defenceless animals. Mounted Constable William Brown, hardened by the horrors of war during the long desert campaign, toughened by the demands of his more recent profession, felt his gorge rise.

Shaken, he leaned against the shed and covered his eyes with the heels of his hands, trying to drive his memories back into cover. When he removed his hands his gaze fell unwillingly on the carcase of the dog again, and he saw, where the arched bone of the skull showed through the rotting mess, a small round hole.

The dog had in fact been shot, and by the twenty-two he'd guess.

Not the lingering death that he'd imagined, then, but a quick death and so easier to cope with. But it meant Dick had come back here at some time — and almost certainly on the motor-bike, since his car hadn't been moved — shot the dog because he knew he wasn't coming back, and left again. Had he already formed his plan to shoot his wife and his in-laws? Carried his rifle to do just that, then taken advantage of a more powerful weapon when he found it easily accessible at Bensons'?

Or had he returned after the shooting at Bensons'? Disposed of the unfortunate dog, and then ridden off somewhere to shoot himself? Because a painstaking search of the shed and its environs had failed to find any trace of Dick, or of the motor-bike.

He could be lying dead anywhere and Bowler hadn't the foggiest idea where to start looking. Or he could have ridden to Dincawauta, as his father believed, either with or without that damned twenty-two.

Or he could be innocent, and merely drinking himself stupid somewhere in another of his futile attempts to dissolve his problems in alcohol.

When Bowler considered further, he saw that some of his assumptions had been made too hastily. To begin with, he wasn't sure that Dick was devious enough to plan the shootings so that they could be disguised as murders followed by suicide. Dick didn't, after all, know of the row the evening before between Lew and his wife that gave Lew a motive.

All the same, he could have gone to the shed to have some kind of a showdown with Lew and then shot him in a rage. That was the first shot. His wife and mother-in-law next, Agatha last as a possible witness. Then, in an attempt to shift the blame, shoved the rifle into Lew's dead hands before he left. It could have happened that way. The order of shots was right.

In that case, Bowler would still expect to find Dick lying beside the motorbike somewhere with a twenty-two bullet in his head.

He couldn't dismiss Dick as suspect, nor could he rule out the murder-suicide explanation. He had problems with both scenarios, but the problems were not serious. Of one thing, though, he was convinced: he didn't yet know the whole history of what had happened that afternoon at Bensons'.

32

Em said, 'Aubrey is here again. Why don't you take him into the lounge, and get Trotter to bring you a sherry? Sit down for once, and enjoy yourself.'

'I couldn't let Trotter wait on me,' Agatha said. 'Not now, anyway, when you're busy getting the dinners.'

'I can manage. How do you imagine I coped before you came? Not that it isn't a damn sight easier with your help,' Em added. 'Don't get me wrong. But now and then you should take time off. Don't you think Aubrey deserves it?'

Did Aubrey, that insouciant man to whom so much had already been given — an easy temperament, a good education, wealth enough to indulge his whims and still lead a comfortable life — deserve more? *Unto every one that hath*, quoted Agatha to herself. Did he deserve her, Agatha?

Though that wasn't really the question that bothered her; she was more concerned about whether she deserved him. Could she give him enough, in return for all that he could shower on her, to make them equal partners in a marriage? She didn't want the role of perpetual beggar-maid to his King Cophetua; she wanted to believe she had something to offer him in return.

And Em hadn't meant anything so serious by her throw-away

question. All she had meant was that Aubrey, as a persistent visitor and probable suitor, deserved to have the object of his affections sit opposite him and give him her full attention for a while, instead of flitting about the pub kitchen while he tried to converse with her.

Em said, 'Wake up, my girl. Go on, take an hour off.'

So Agatha laughed, took off her apron, and went up the passage to the public lounge to sit with Aubrey at one of the small wooden tables there. But immediately she felt shy, and wished she hadn't let Em persuade her; anyone walking in could see them there together and she didn't want to be paired with Aubrey in anyone's speculations just yet.

Aubrey, however, was delighted. He made Trotter rummage through his stocks until he came up with a very pale dry sherry unlike anything Agatha had tasted before; and, when she had sipped it and approved, he asked her permission to light a small cigar, sat back in his chair, and beamed on her. Then he set out to entertain her.

This experience still charmed her: the conversation of a man who spoke with no other object than giving her pleasure in his company. But he broke the spell when he made her laugh at a tale of his misadventures on the polo field for, although amused by the anecdote, she was reminded too forcefully of the distance between his world and hers. Beggar-maids had their pride too.

As Miriam had warned her, Agatha's fervent wish that her name should not be linked with Aubrey's in anyone's speculations came too late. Mrs Dunstan at the store had seen them speaking together in the street one day and thereafter had kept a pretty accurate count of the number of times she'd seen Aubrey's mare tied to one of the veranda posts at the front of the pub, or noticed him strolling across the road towards it. Dolly Dunstan was secretly pleased to have something to watch for in the usually boring street outside the store, and delighted to have such scandalous information to divulge to Mrs Harry Wilson and others of the Band of Hope, to whom she imparted the latest tally every time one of them visited the shop.

Local women who belonged to the Band of Hope, a so-called Temperance movement which in fact promoted abstinence from alcohol, naturally disapproved of anybody visiting the pub regularly. That Aubrey went for a reason other than tippling didn't mitigate his offence.

'He seemed such a pleasant man,' Dolly Dunstan sighed to Mrs Harry. 'I can't understand how he can be taken in by that dreadful woman.'

'Quite the polished gentleman,' Mrs Harry agreed. 'A good background, comfortable means — it's extraordinary. When there are plenty of respectable girls around, too. Not that I'd want him for my Cynthia,' she added hastily. 'Cynthia is far too young, of course. But there are others.'

Juliet Davidson (a non-member of the Band) was poking about in a barrel of axe and broom handles standing beside the counter. She lifted her head and said, 'Agatha Benson is supposed to be brainy. She probably gives him a bit of intelligent conversation for a change.'

Juliet hadn't been impressed with Agatha on the two occasions they'd met, but would happily defend her if it meant having a dig at these two wowsers. Make that three wowsers: Mrs Bruce Wilson had just alighted from the family tourer and made an impressive entrance into the store. 'We were just discussing Aubrey Venables' interest in Agatha Benson,' Juliet explained.

'Infatuation,' Mrs Bruce corrected firmly in her slow, deep voice. 'I've heard he visits her almost every day. What a man of his breeding can see in a woman like that I will never understand. It's not as though she's even pretty.'

'Not pretty,' Juliet agreed. But Joan's assessment had made her look again at Agatha; she added, 'She's good-looking for all that. When I called in on Joan the other day I saw her taking her toddler for a walk, and now she's not so painfully thin she looks almost distinguished. I suppose it's good bones, the lucky girl.'

'Whatever her bones they can't possibly excuse her behaviour,' Mrs Harry said. 'But men never seem to care as much about that as we do.'

'Perhaps Aubrey is looking for a mistress, not a wife,' Juliet suggested.

The shocking word caused a brief pause. 'Does he visit her at *night*?' Mrs Harry breathed, horrified.

'Oh, no, no. I only see him in the afternoons,' Dolly hastened to reassure them.

'You wouldn't see him if he did skulk over after dark,' Juliet pointed out, pleased with the ripples her remark had caused. 'I wonder.'

'She has the morals of an alley cat.' Mrs Harry sniffed. 'I wouldn't be surprised.'

'I cannot imagine,' Mrs Bruce said, at her most dignified, 'that even Mrs Musgrave would countenance *that* sort of thing going on under her roof. She may run a public house, but she has some principles. Really, Juliet, you should guard your tongue.'

'Just wondering,' Juliet said. Her pleasure in stirring up these smug wowsers had led her further than she'd intended. She hadn't meant to add more to the scandals already surrounding that unfortunate Benson woman. 'Anyway, of course he is looking for a wife. He wouldn't be there in daylight if he was meeting her at night. Mrs Dunstan, if you've finished serving Greta could you take my order now? Archie will be waiting for me.'

33

Darkness had fallen early on Kularook, and by six fifteen the wet and windy streets were deserted. The farmers and their wives had finished their business and gone home, the townspeople were indoors with the lamps lit and the fires alight. Unobserved, Aubrey Venables had strolled home to his house, his sister, and his dinner.

At the pub, Em was in the bar helping Trotter clean up after he had ejected the last of the day's drinkers, Agatha was in the kitchen. Watched from the playpen by Cordelia, she stood at the stove, her back to the room, making gravy to accompany the roast leg of lamb shortly to be served to the four guests currently staying in the hotel. She had put the big Aladdin lamp on the mantelpiece, so that she could see what she was doing.

Outside the window something cracked. At the same instant something smacked into the chimney breast by her head.

She glanced towards the back window, above where Cordelia sat thumping a tin baking dish with a wooden spoon. Against the outside darkness at that dim end of the kitchen the glass didn't show clearly, but it seemed to have changed somehow.

Then on a wave of shocked and breathless fear she understood, and was diving for the floor when there was another crack-smack. The window fell in a cascade of glass. Cordelia yelled.

Agatha scrambled, half crawling, for the playpen, seized her terrified daughter, and ran bent over for the door. She raced up the dark passage to the bar, to Em, to the reassuring bulk of large Trotter, and to the illusory safety of numbers.

A lightning check assured her that the windows here were frosted over; nobody could see in. 'Someone shot at me,' she said. 'Twice.'

There was a moment's frozen silence.

Trotter exploded. '*What*!'

'Through the kitchen window.'

'Bloody hell. Are you sure?' Trotter dropped the cloth he was using to mop the bar and started for the door. His wife grabbed his arm.

'Agatha says there's someone with a gun out there.'

He stopped, suddenly made aware of his vulnerability. 'Jesus! So there is. Agatha, where did the shots come from? Did you see anything?'

Agatha hid her face against her sobbing daughter and rocked her in her arms.

'Blow out the lamp, Emmie. Agatha?'

The room went dark. Trying to control her unsteady voice, Agatha told him how the shots had seemed to her. Her nerves were jumping; she was shaking violently. She stood Cordelia on the floor, sheltered by the end of the bar, and bent over her.

'You don't think anyone came inside, followed you up the passage?'

'No.'

Trotter said, 'I'll ring Bowler. He can see into our back yard from his window.' He opened the door a few inches and peered down the passage. 'There's a glow from the kitchen door, there's nobody down there.' He slipped out; they heard the front door slammed, a bolt slapped home, then his voice on the telephone behind the desk in the hall.

Em said, 'He's wrong, it's too dark outside for Bowler to see anything. Agatha, are you all right?'

'Yes,' she lied. She crouched to reassure her daughter when all she wanted was reassurance for herself. Who wanted her dead? Was this how her life would end, by unexpected shots from the darkness some evening? How could she ever feel safe again?

Cordelia stopped crying and cuddled against her mother. Agatha tried to stop shivering.

She felt a grip on her arm. Someone was striking a match to relight the lamp. The first thing she saw was a sinewy hand holding a revolver pointed loosely at the floor, but before her heart stopped completely she realised it was Bowler holding it, Bowler pulling her up with his other hand, Bowler supporting her and studying her face with great concern.

Agatha fell against him and broke into noisy tears against his jumper.

He held her in a comforting hug while she struggled for self-control. 'Sorry,' she whispered. 'Sorry. I was so frightened.'

'There's nobody there now. Whoever he is, he's gone.'

'What if he comes back?'

Trotter said, 'We'll look after you. Keep the doors locked, the blinds down.'

She pulled herself upright and smiled at Bowler. He held her, then released her arm. 'You're safe now. All right?'

'Thanks.' She picked up Cordelia, then hesitated.

'Don't go back into the kitchen,' Bowler said. 'We've checked your room. Nobody can see into that with the blind down, and if he tries he has to stand in the street where I can see him. All the same, I'm going to nail a few planks across.' That would stop the bastard breaking in, a possibility if the man was desperate enough. He wasn't going to frighten the poor girl further by mentioning that, however. 'When I've finished, you go into your room and lock the door if it makes you feel better. Em is going to get the dinner for the travellers. They've been sitting in the lounge over their cards and their beer completely oblivious to all the drama.' He laughed. 'Just as well, or we'd probably have had them running all over the place like headless chooks.'

Trotter said, 'You're not going to tell them, are you, Bowler?'

'I am not. We'll leave them in happy ignorance. In fact, we'll leave everyone in happy ignorance. Are you listening, Em?'

Em had picked up the lamp and was leading the way to the door. 'What?'

'Don't tell anyone about this.' If the bastard tried a second time he'd find Bowler waiting for him.

'All right.'

'I hope you mean it. Anyway, I'll come over later when you've got the travellers fed, and we'll sort out what's best to be done.'

34

Agatha looked as though she hadn't slept, Bowler thought. Her eyes were huge and sunken, her movements slow. She looked as rough as he felt.

He turned back to where he was digging with his pocket knife into the plaster beside the stove in the pub kitchen, trying to prise out the bullet. Em and Trotter sat with Agatha at the table.

'Somebody thinks you remember more than you do,' Bowler said over his shoulder. 'And I'm not sure how to let him know his mistake.'

'You don't think it was random, then?' Em said.

'Unlikely. No, someone's heard a whisper that I'm not happy with the murder-suicide explanation of the shootings and has decided Agatha, the only witness, must have told me something. So that makes her a danger to him, therefore she'd better be removed. So — Ah, gotcha.' He levered the misshapen bullet into his palm.

When he first began to doubt the murder-suicide theory, he'd been looking for evidence of a fifth bullet out at Bensons' farm, but with no luck. He'd come to believe he wasn't going to find it. Now he had it in his hand. He'd found a fifth bullet, though not the way he'd expected to. The fourth bullet of the original shootings had hit Agatha but hadn't killed her. It looked as though the murderer was now trying to finish her off with a fifth. Would he go on until he scored with it?

He said, 'But all the same, that means you're safe, Agatha, if you keep to the bright lights and in company. This joker doesn't want to be identified.'

Agatha shivered. 'But he could be anywhere.'

He held the little blob of metal up against the light. 'We'll watch.'

'Bowler, does this mean that it wasn't Lew shot me? Shot all of us?'

'Most probably not,' Bowler said. He pulled out a chair and sat down. 'After what you told me, I've been thinking more and more that Lew could have died with the first shot you heard. Agatha!' Agatha had gone pale and closed her eyes, almost as though she was going to faint. He reached a hand across the table. 'What's the matter?'

'Perhaps it wasn't my fault after all,' she whispered.

'It never was your fault,' Em said. 'Whoever did it, you didn't put his finger on the trigger.'

Bowler took Agatha's cold hand in a strong grip. 'In daylight you're safe. He's not going to risk being seen flourishing a rifle about in broad daylight. Is there anywhere you could go and stay for a few nights? A friend, or a relation?'

She shook her head. 'There's nobody. And even if I had money for a hotel or something somewhere else, I'd be scared on my own. I'd rather be here.'

'Fair enough. We'll keep you safe. In daylight, you keep close to home and don't go anywhere alone, and at night you stay indoors, you pull down the blinds, and you lock the doors. All right?' She nodded. 'And I'll be watching. Me and Trotter and — Anyway, there'll be a whole lot of us keeping an eye on you, never fear.' He'd get hold of a few of the old soldiers like Archie and Bruce, and . . .

Keeping Agatha safe was more important than anything else. Although he'd dearly like to catch the murderer making a second attempt, the risks were too high.

He said, 'Em, I've changed my mind. Tell anyone you like about the shootings, and say that I'm arranging a roster of a few returned men to keep watch over Agatha day and night. Not in the pub, drifting about outside. Once the word gets round, that might put this beggar off his stroke a bit.'

He wouldn't put that detail in the report he was going to write to his bosses in Adelaide, though, because he'd be in all sorts of strife if they thought he was raising vigilante squads. But as far as he was concerned, whatever a group of old soldiers chose to do in their own time was none of Adelaide's business.

What was Adelaide's business was this latest shooting. Instead of two murders and a suicide, he now had on the books what looked like three unsolved murders and two cases of attempted murder. This was serious crime.

Bowler squeezed Agatha's fingers and released them. 'You'll be right. Keep indoors today, keep away from windows. I'll get a few things organised straight away.'

He hadn't been to bed yet, but he couldn't sleep until he'd rung Adelaide to inform his bosses of these new developments. He had waited until this morning, when the man he wanted to talk to would be on duty, and now he mustn't waste any more time. They'd probably send a couple of detectives down, which would suit him: they could worry about finding the murderer, while he concentrated on protecting Agatha. He was going to get a few of the old soldiers lined up to help him. The sooner the gunman was discovered and put behind bars the better.

Now the hunt for the murderer had taken on a critical urgency. A life could depend on it.

He decided he'd better come to an arrangement with Agatha, and made her promise that after dark she would keep out of all the pub rooms except the kitchen and her bedroom. By restricting the range of her movements he could make watching easier, since there were three positions only from which a man could shoot. In the meantime he'd commission old Petersen, the town carpenter, to board up her bedroom window efficiently, and make two plywood panels that could be wedged into the kitchen windows at dusk. They wouldn't stop a bullet but they ought to deter any would-be assassin, who would have to come into the open merely to shoot at random, too chancy an exercise to appeal to a man trying desperate measures to save his skin.

When he'd seen the carpenter he went back to his office, propped his hip against the wall, lifted the telephone earpiece, wound the handle, and told Roger Price at the post office to get him the number in Adelaide so that he could report to his boss.

Then, yawning, he sat at his desk to write down everything he knew, because he'd been forced to promise his boss that a report would catch the train that day. He wished he could find the one he'd started writing when he'd first had doubts about the shootings, that sketchy report he'd begun a week or so ago, although at the time he'd not been sure that he intended it for any eyes but his own. Inexplicably, those pages had vanished off his desk. He knew he hadn't thrown them out, and he had his family far too well-trained for any one of them to lay a finger on the smallest piece of his paperwork.

He cleared his desk, put a new nib in the detested penholder, and settled down to rewrite it. His wife woke him, sprawled across the desk with his head in his arms, when the train was long gone.

The telephone rang as he was in the middle of his evening meal. Bowler called his wife to the office, away from the children.

He said, 'That was Splinter Thompson on the phone. Dick's back, and there's trouble.'

'What kind of trouble?' Joan asked.

'Splinter says he's roaring drunk and out of control. I can't wait, I've got to go now.'

Joan's eyes widened when she saw him lift his rifle from the top of the cupboard but she said steadily enough, 'Yes. But Bill —'

'Must dash,' Bowler said, dropping a handful of bullets into his coat pocket. 'Darling, there's nothing to worry about, I'll be back soon.' He pecked her cheek, swung away. The wire door clashed behind him. She heard him running across the weedy yard towards the garage.

Joan was not deceived; he was worried about this one. Her heart clenched. She wished she'd made him tell her what the problem was, and why he needed the rifle. Perhaps the 'trouble' somehow involved other guns.

And to think that once upon a time she'd imagined that when the war was over she would have no more terrors over his safety, no more nightmares of that hard, beloved body returned to her bloodied and bullet-riddled. She shuddered, her hands over her face.

Rose tugged her arm. 'Are you all right, Mummy?'

Joan arranged a smile to cover her fears and removed her hands. 'I'm fine, chicken. Come on, we must finish dinner and get the dishes cleaned up before Daddy gets back.'

How her sisters had looked down their long noses when they'd heard little Tom, when she had taken the children home on that visit to her parents, referring to his father as 'Daddy'. Joan smiled with pleasure at the memory. Her sisters' well-drilled offspring addressed the stuffed shirts who had sired them as 'Papa'. Prunes and prisms, thought rebel Joan, and then felt fear clutch her heart again. Her man, who was so different from those tame, domesticated males, had just driven off into the night towards a situation where he believed he needed a gun.

35

Attended by a couple of barking dogs Bowler drove up to Splinter Thompson's house. It looked deserted, but when he followed the track that swept round a clump of mallee to the back door he could see a weak light in the kitchen window. Splinter met him at the door, shouted at the dogs, and ushered him inside.

Even in the light of the small hand-lamp on the table he could see that Shirley Thompson had been crying recently. Fat and blowzy, her grey hair in strings, her face blotched with tears, she sat huddled on a straight-backed chair beside the table twisting her restless hands in a grubby apron. When she saw him she surged to her feet and grabbed him by both arms. She was nearly as tall as he.

'Get them back,' she whispered hoarsely, her voice cracking as though exhausted from over-use. 'Bowler, you lovely boy, you darling man, bring them back to me.'

'Of course I will,' he said, suppressing his impatience, his urgent need for swift action. 'Shirl, why don't you —'

'He was drunk, poor Dickie,' she wailed, weeping afresh. 'Oh Bowler, Bowler, he doesn't know what he's doing, he's not —'

'Hush now, Splinter will tell me all about it on the way.' He glanced up and saw two of the daughters crowding the doorway. 'Help your mother to bed, and stay with her,' he ordered. 'She's had enough.

Come on, Splinter.'

In the car, driving as fast over the pot-holed metal road as was consistent with safety, he said, 'How far ahead is he? How long after he left did you ring me?'

'No time at all,' Splinter said. 'I reckon he's no more than fifteen, twenty minutes ahead.'

'Right. Come on then, tell me the whole story. Dick was drunk. What did he say?'

'Only that he wanted the children,' Splinter said.

Reported like that, it didn't sound very terrifying. 'Go on. What else?'

'Well, he wasn't just ordinary drunk, you know, like I seen him times before. He was roaring and shouting about how Thelma had gone and he was alone, sort of crying drunk, and now there were only three of them, and he kept waving his arms round shouting some more and he scared the kids. So when he said he'd come to take them home they didn't want to go. Ran away and hid, they did.' Splinter paused to relight his hand-rolled cigarette. 'That's when Shirl put in her six penn'orth, saying they shouldn't have to go if they didn't want to, and Dick did his block, roaring they were all he had, he needed them now and stuff like that.'

When Splinter paused again Bowler said, 'Well?' Fourways Corner was coming up; he eased his foot from the accelerator.

'Well, we was uneasy, of course we was, but we thought we could talk him round. But when I took hold of his arm, just to lead him inside you understand, he turned on me and knocked me down. Took me by surprise,' Splinter explained, as though big husky Dick couldn't knock his skinny father down any time he chose.

'Go on.'

'Well then he went screaming mad, hunted out them terrified kids and chased them until he caught them, pushed his mother over and punched his sister when she got in his way, and he dragged the kids to the car, and them screaming too, and he took off. I couldn't go after them, Roy's got the buckboard, he went to a sale in Cancanulla this afternoon and he's not back yet.'

Bowler said, 'On the phone you said Dick had a gun and he was threatening the children.'

'Yair, well, we could see the bloody thing sticking up on the front seat of his car, and then he took hold of it and shook it at us. He didn't point it at anyone, not while we was watching.'

'You said his twenty-two.'

'Yair, he's had it since he was a kid.' Splinter pinched out his cigarette and tossed the butt out of the car. 'When he left he was yelling that he didn't have anything left to live for, they might as well all be dead. "The lot of us," he said. "The lot of us might as well be dead." That's what frightened us. Because he meant the kiddies too — he meant the kiddies too.'

'Bloody hell. And you think he meant to go back to the farm? Venables place?'

'I dunno where he meant to go at the finish. But to start with he said he'd come to take the kids home, so we thought that's where he meant.'

'Jesus, it'll take us all night on this bloody track.' It had been bad enough in daylight.

Bowler clamped down hard on his feverish impatience. The headlights weren't any too brilliant; probably the battery was nearly flat. He hoped he could see the hazards, the stones and the patches of loose deep sand. They wouldn't get far with a broken axle. He set his teeth.

'Where has he been all this time, did he say?'

'Nup. Too busy bawling about they'd be better off dead.'

Bowler muttered, 'I haven't seen any bloody lights ahead, have you? Maybe he's gone somewhere else. That'll be some stunt, searching the whole damn district.'

'Dunno where he would go though,' Splinter said.

'Keep hoping, then.'

So when after ten impatient miles they finally bounced up the slope to the house Bowler was immensely relieved to see Dick's Morris standing by the door, and a faint light showing in the kitchen window.

He switched off the engine. 'Thank Christ for that. Splinter, you stay here. I'm going in to see what frame of mind he's in.'

He debated whether he should point out the rifle lying across the back seat, but quickly decided not to. That was a last resort, and he wanted it in no hands but his own. The mere idea of bloody Splinter charging to the rescue waving a rifle about made Bowler's blood run cold.

He said, 'Don't on any account come in until I tell you. If he sees you he'll think you've come for the kids, and God knows what he'll do if he's got that bloody rifle within reach.'

'But I have come for the kids,' Splinter protested.

'I know that, dammit. Just let me see if he's safe.'

36

Bowler got out of the car and stood for a moment in the wide dark silence. No sound from the house. He crunched loudly up to the door. No use trying to sneak up, Dick would have heard the car so he'd know someone was outside.

'Hey, Dick!' he called. 'Have you got a minute?'

The silence rang in his ears. Had the bastard shot the lot of them when he heard the car? Hastily he wrenched open the door and went in.

On the deal table that took up most of the space in the room stood a small hurricane lantern, its weak light doing little to dispel the gloom. The two children sat at the table, huddled down on their chairs, their cheeks streaked with tears, hiccoughing every now and then from exhaustion. They stared wide-eyed at Bowler, their mouths open on their sobs.

Their father was at the stove, straightening his back from where he had been bent over the firebox trying to light a few sticks. As he came upright he staggered, supporting himself by one hand on the cold stove-top; he was swaying, trying to keep his attention on Bowler, his eyes nearly closed. In his right hand he carried his rifle. Perhaps he had picked it up when he heard the car.

And, although it was pointing towards the floor, Dick's forefinger was inside the guard, round the trigger.

Bowler said, 'Come on, mate. Let's talk about it.'

One-handed, Dick raised the barrel until the rifle was horizontal. The muzzle swung from side to side of the room as he swayed.

'Noth'n talk 'bout. You keep outa thish,' he said.

Horrified, Bowler saw the rifle pointing at the children, swinging across them, swinging back, wavering a bit when it was pointing more or less at him, moving again to endanger the children. Dick apparently imagined he was threatening Bowler.

'Th' kids shtay with me,' he announced in a truculent voice. His left hand wavered up to support the rifle barrel more securely.

'Yeah, sure, but you're frightening them, Dick. Put the gun down for now.' The poor little devils had fallen silent, huddled in misery. Their gaze shuttled between their father and the policeman. Bowler inched forward. In that dim and shadowed light he didn't think the drunken man had noticed. 'Come on, Dick. Put it down.'

'Oh, no. You take my kidsh and I shoot the lottovush.' Dick began to cry, tearing sobs that made the rifle cover great arcs of the room. 'Nothing to live for,' he roared.

Bowler watched. The muzzle swung across the children again and he flinched. He stopped breathing when the deadly black circle wobbled in line with his own chest and Dick started to lower his head, to sight along the barrel.

His muscles so tense that they hurt, Bowler prepared to drop. Urgently he said, 'Dick, come on. Let's —'

Unexpectedly Dick howled, 'Better off dead!' and Bowler started convulsively. But the rifle had moved away.

Then the muzzle was swinging back towards him, faster and faster and he was off balance and Jesus Christ he'd miss his chance he had to —

He lunged.

His left hand smacked on the barrel of the rifle, forcing it aside, forcing it down, holding it in an iron grip while with his right he chopped Dick savagely across the biceps.

Just as he thought the weapon was wholly in his own hands the damn thing discharged. The sound filled the small room, a crack that rang in his ears as though the whole kitchen had exploded. The children screamed and went on screaming.

Dick staggered, white with shock. 'Where — what —' he quavered.

'Into the floor,' Bowler said, gratified to hear his own voice steady and level. 'You *stupid* prick.'

He glanced at the children — luckily they couldn't have heard him with the noise they were making — and stepped back, his eyes on Dick, his hands automatically working the rifle bolt to eject the spent shell, to unclip the magazine. He heard Splinter outside pounding towards the door and he called, 'You can come in now.' The children would need him, a stable figure in these terrifying events. They must believe their world was disintegrating with their mother dead and their father run mad.

And indeed, when they saw their grandfather the children hurled themselves at him as though they would burrow through his clothes into his very bones. Bowler had grave reservations about Splinter, about his honesty, his hygiene, and his intelligence, but at least the man knew how to reassure a couple of little tackers. He crouched on the floor with a child in each arm and murmured meaningless, soothing phrases against their dishevelled heads.

Dick, a great blubbering mess, sprawled half in a chair and half across the table, his head in his arms, bawling threats of what he would do.

Bowler said, 'Splinter, take the children home. Take Dick's car, he's not driving anywhere. But now, soon as you like. They've had a rough night.'

He waited until they had driven off before he informed the drunken wreck that he was under arrest.

Bowler was grimly pleased that Dick had played into his hands and provided an obvious reason to lock him up. Now he could be questioned without half the district wondering why; now Bowler might get at the truth about the man's possible involvement in the shootings at Bensons'. And find out whether he could have been lurking outside the pub with a rifle the evening before.

He'd shove him in the lockup for the night, and see if he was sober enough to answer a few questions in the morning. The answers he gave would let Bowler decide how to progress from there.

Though Bowler wasn't sure whether he was hoping or fearing that Dick would prove the murderer. He almost felt sorry for the stupid bastard.

'What was all that shouting about, out the back?' Joan raised herself from the pillow on her elbow. 'Was that Dick Thompson? He sounded pretty indignant.'

Bowler nodded. By the light of the candle he carried she looked soft and vulnerable, her shadowed eyes enormous. He read the strain there, and her relief at his safe return. He knew she worried, although she would never admit to her fears, since she had been brought up to keep her emotions to herself and under rigid control. In the years of their marriage he'd taught her how to share some of her feelings with him, but nobody on earth could undo altogether the strict, ingrained training of her youth.

He set down the candle and bent over to put his arms round her, hugging her, reassuring her of his solid, undamaged presence. She said into his shoulder, 'I'm glad you're back, Bill. Are you coming to bed now?'

'In a minute, soon as I've written up a couple of things. I've arrested that idiot Dick. He can't go roaring round the country brandishing rifles and expect me to ignore it. But he's making a row because he's drunk as a lord and feeling sorry for himself over losing his wife. And now the idiot has frightened ten years' growth out of his kids he might have lost them too.'

'Brandishing rifles,' Joan said slowly. 'You knew he had a rifle when you left, that's why you took yours.' She thought over the implications of that. 'You should have told me, Bill.'

'You'd only have worried more.'

'Worried or not, I have a right to know. Don't try and protect me all the time.'

Her hair was against his mouth. He said, 'I think I'm protecting myself. In case you can't stand the strain, and decide to cut your losses and go back to England.'

She gripped more tightly and turned her face into his neck. Muffled, she said, 'Bill, you might be the most arrogant sod in Australia, but you've got me for life.'

'I've been afraid — after —'

'Don't rake over old ashes,' she said fiercely, pulling herself away to glare at him. 'I wanted to kill you — I wanted to kill myself. But I stayed then, and I'll go on staying. Why do you have to remind me of all that unhappiness?'

In the dim light he couldn't see her clearly. But there was no reservation in her words or tone. She meant it. Bowler heaved a deep breath and gathered her into his arms again.

She snuggled against him. 'Let the bloody paperwork wait,' she said.

37

Next morning, while Bowler and the children were still at breakfast round the kitchen table, Splinter Thompson walked in the back door without knocking. Joan, at the stove making a pot of tea, had her back to the room; she looked over her shoulder in surprise at this unexpected visitor.

Splinter said, 'Them kids are fine this morning, Bowler. Shirl's that delighted to get them back she'd give them the moon. And are they making the most of it!'

Bowler had slept four hours the night before, while Archie patrolled the pub grounds. On the one pm train from town he was expecting a detective — only one, they were flat out in Adelaide — whom he disliked, and with whom he had once had a very public quarrel. He suspected that someone in Adelaide was deliberately needling him.

He glanced from his wife to Splinter, who chattered on cheerfully, 'How was Dick when you left? I reckon I might go out and see how the poor beggar is feeling this morning.' He started to sit in the chair young Tom vacated for him.

Then he saw Bowler's expression and straightened awkwardly.

There was a short silence. Splinter stammered, 'I was wondering about Dick.'

Bowler buttered the last of his toast, taking his time. He laid down his knife, slid his hand into his hip pocket, and took out his watch.

He clicked it open. 'I'll see you in the office in five minutes, Thompson,' he said.

By now Splinter was as embarrassed as Bowler intended him to be. 'Look, sorry, of course, I'll just —' He reversed out of the room into the passage. The wire door to the back veranda clicked softly shut behind him.

'Finish your porridge,' Bowler said to Tom, who obediently sat down again. 'Sorry about that, Joan. He won't do it again.'

In exactly five minutes, Bowler walked up the passage to his office at the front of the house. He opened the outside door and with a grin more like a snarl waved in Splinter, who had been waiting meekly on the front veranda. 'Fancy meeting you here.'

'Look Bowler, I —'

'Never — is that clear? — never treat my house as though it were part of this office. You can walk in here any time. There, you bang on the door and wait for me.'

Splinter said, 'Sorry Bowler, sorry, I didn't think. Honest. I'm sorry, I —'

'Oh, shut up. So, what can I do for you?'

'It was about Dick. I was wondering —'

'You can stop wondering. He's in the lock-up. And if you're worried about his health, I can inform you that he thinks he's dying but it's only a hangover. He'll live.'

Splinter's jaw dropped. 'Lock-up? But he didn't hurt the kids!'

'So?'

'But Bowler, he didn't do anything!'

'Not much he didn't. Anyone who waves a rifle at me is in trouble. I shot back at the Turks, but unfortunately I'm not allowed to shoot Dick.' He cocked his head, considering. 'On the whole, I preferred the Turks. I knew why they were doing it.'

The Fifth Bullet

'But Bowler —'

'He's staying there. I'll let you know when you can have him back.' Bowler paused. Perhaps they wouldn't get Dick back; he could be a murderer. As soon as the bloody man could open his eyes without moaning he was going to answer a few straight questions. Where had he been two nights ago, when somebody had been taking pot-shots at Agatha?

Splinter was fidgeting uncomfortably. Good. It was time the law made that damn family uncomfortable.

'I'll tell you something else, Splinter, for free. Your bloody family takes the laws of this country altogether too casually. Since I'm paid to see they're kept they bloody well will be kept around here. You tell those damn sons of yours that my patience is at an end and they'd better watch out.'

What was the use. He saw Splinter smirking ingratiatingly, and he knew that the man wouldn't remember a word he'd heard once he was out the door. Blowzy slattern that she was, fat old Shirl was worth a dozen of him.

A shower of rain pattered on the roof; he heard the gutters over the veranda gurgling. 'Oh, go home, Splinter,' he said wearily.

He hauled the register from the bottom shelf, spread it open on his desk, and started checking who else in Kularook owned a twenty-two rifle.

Half-way through the morning Bowler propped himself in the doorway of the lock-up and surveyed the human wreckage stretched groaning on the bunk. 'You like a cup of tea?' he asked.

Dick Thompson started to roll his head in a negative movement, thought better of it, and said shakily, 'No thanks.'

Hoping that he might get at the truth more quickly while the man's wits were too clouded by the hangover to invent convincing lies, Bowler asked, 'Why did you take your brother's motorbike, Dick?'

'Motorbike — I didn't —' Dick's ravaged face took on an even more worried expression.

'Don't tell me you didn't take it, you clown. You rode it to your father's house yesterday when you reclaimed your car, you've had it all along. You must have taken it the day of the shootings, when your wife had the car.'

'Oh. Yeah. If you say so.' He blinked a few times in an attempt to clear his vision — or perhaps his mind, if he actually had one inside that thick skull.

'Why? Why did you need the motorbike?'

Dick groaned.

'Thelma left you in Kularook. So you must have walked out to your father's place, found nobody home, and then taken the bike. Tell me why, dammit.'

'Got sick of waiting for Thelma to come back,' he produced at last, with an air of minor triumph.

Was that because he'd succeeded in remembering, or because he'd thought of a plausible lie? Bowler said, 'Where did you go then?' When Dick closed his eyes he added, 'You're not going to sleep and I'm not going away. Once you were on the bike, where did you go?'

'Jeeze, Bowler, my head's that bad I can hardly think.'

'You don't have to think. You have to answer my questions.'

'Edgerton. That's where I went, Edgerton.'

Bowler asked, 'What made you go to Edgerton instead of home to the farm?'

Dick groaned, and clutched his head. 'I'm a sick man.'

'Don't expect sympathy from me.

'You're a bastard, Bowler,' Dick said with heartfelt sincerity.

Bowler bared his teeth. 'And if you went to Edgerton, who shot your dog? Why would anyone shoot your dog?'

Dick's face went slack with dismay. He said, 'I'm not talking to you,' and rolled ponderously over to face the wall, his mouth shut in a stubborn line.

'Yes you are. Now or later.' But after several more attempts to make him answer, Bowler gave up. 'You'll keep,' he growled, and shut the door on him.

Back in his office, Bowler doodled shooting stars on his blotter. Had that big blundering idiot really taken a rifle to sort out his problems with his wife?

38

Bowler remembered another law-breaker he'd said would keep. He must have a word with Durwin Harris, pub handyman, who was probably congratulating himself that he'd got away with nicking six black hens. The thought of a smug thief skulking among his parishioners irritated Bowler considerably. He'd been hoping for hard evidence but, since none was forthcoming, he'd have to confine himself to terrorising the man instead.

With this amiable end in view he decided to visit Durwin's small stone cottage when he went to collect his mail from the post office. Now he didn't have to meet the train — he'd received a wire informing him that the detective had elected to drive himself to Kularook, would be arriving about teatime, and would Bowler book him into the pub — he might as well get after Durwin.

The land beside the cottage was vacant, so he walked to the back of that block and surveyed the fowl-yard across a sagging five-wire fence; he didn't expect to see the hens, nor did he. He did, however, see Durwin's wife peering at him from the back window of the cottage, and so he stepped over the slack wires and went to knock on her door.

The woman who opened it was in her mid twenties, fair and plump. She would have been pretty if she had put in her teeth. Remembering, she raised her hand to cover her mouth.

'Morning, Alma. Durwin's at work, I suppose.' Since he knew very well that he was, he was unsurprised when she nodded. 'I want to have a look at your chooks. Is that all right?'

Her eyes rounded apprehensively. Slowly she made a tiny nod.

Bowler was disgusted with himself. Terrorising bloody light-fingered Durwin was one thing; he shouldn't have begun his campaign by frightening the man's wife. Now he was here, however, he'd have to go on with it.

'Thanks. I'll catch up with Durwin later.'

He went down the yard to the wire-netted enclosure beside the dunny, where over a dozen white hens and one rooster were pecking desultorily at the bare and muddy earth within it. Nothing for him there.

He wasn't really looking for evidence — his intention was merely to unsettle Durwin — but when he turned to go he saw among the weeds on the vacant block a depression partly filled with rusting tins and old newspapers. More from habit than curiosity he went over and kicked at a couple of the empty tins, and then was astonished when a newspaper parcel, wet from recent showers, burst open and spilled draggled black feathers into the weeds.

He'd actually found some evidence. Too long after the event, though, for it to be of any use to him, except to put the fear of the lord into Durwin. He glanced back at the cottage. Alma still watched from her window. He might as well give her a good story to tell her husband.

He bent and picked up a couple of feathers and studied them carefully. Then he saw something that really might be useful, and tore a corner off the sodden paper that showed its date; carefully he wrapped both feathers and paper in his handkerchief, shoved them in his pocket, and strolled on to collect his mail.

When he walked into the pub kitchen Em, at the table, was mixing batter in a basin while Agatha spooned mashed vegetables into her small daughter, who was sitting in her high chair beside it. As soon as she saw Bowler, Cordelia batted the spoon aside and held out her arms to him.

Agatha said, 'Not now, Cordelia. Come on, finish your lunch.'

'You've made a conquest there,' Em said.

Bowler smiled, and tickled the child's neck. 'Em, where's Durwin?'

'In the bar helping Trotter. What do you want him for?'

'Not sure yet.' A new idea occurred to him. 'Em, does he ever sell you any dressed poultry?'

'No, never. We kill our own birds.' She whirred the egg-beater briefly, inspected her mixture, and lifted the beater to drain it. 'Oh, yes, once. Ages ago, after the foxes got most of mine, I took two, but not since.' Her head lowered to see over her glasses she smiled at him. 'And yes, if you must know, it was about the time old Spog missed his hens. But that never even occurred to me until long after the guests had polished off their chicken dinners, or I'd have told you.'

No she wouldn't. She handled her touchy handyman with great care, afraid that he might leave her in a huff. She would do nothing to upset him.

He said, 'If you don't want Durwin to know you told me about the hens, could you invent a fictitious record book where I could have read it?'

'It's not fictitious.' She turned, and rummaged in a drawer in the kitchen dresser against the wall. 'Here, the kitchen petty cash records.' She handed him a bundle of small, cheap, paper-covered cash books, like miniature school exercise books, secured together with a wide rubber band. All, even the most recent, were dog-eared and grimy. 'Look for yourself.'

He thumbed through the pages. Em had carefully recorded all the transactions where she had paid cash for goods, mostly small sums outlaid for eggs or butter from farmers' wives. Two or three were larger — a knife she'd bought from the butcher, a bolt of huckaback for hand towels from a travelling hawker — and sure enough, there was a record of two dressed fowls from Durwin Harris. And a date.

'Well now, that's pretty good,' he said, nodding with satisfaction. Now he could really make Durwin squirm.

He took the books home with him, to copy out the relevant entry, but his mood of cheerful self-congratulation didn't last when he turned his attention to his handful of mail. The last letter he opened was from the Lands Department.

'Bugger,' said Mounted Constable William Brown.

39

The wind shuddered round the corners of the house. Bowler arranged the sticks and kindled a fire in the small cast-iron grate in a corner of his office. Joan was in the kitchen washing up the dinner dishes, the children at the dining room table working on their homework.

Dick had slept most of the day. Now Bowler, tired of kicking his heels waiting for the detective to arrive, brought him up to the office, sat him in the chair opposite his desk, gave him a heavily sweetened cup of tea, and told him that the time had come to talk turkey. Dick lowered his head to the cup and peered almost furtively from under his brows. The tall kerosene lamp on the desk illuminated his face, but not much else.

Propping his hip on a corner of the desk Bowler said, 'You must have gone to Edgerton because you were so upset when you heard your wife had been shot you didn't know where you were going.' Watching his prisoner wince, and then give a satisfied nod as though grateful for this explanation, he added abruptly, 'So who told you?'

'Eh?'

'Who told you about your wife's death, and the shootings?'

After a long pause Dick said, 'My Dad. He told me.'

'No he didn't. He drove all the way out to the block and couldn't find you.'

'Then it must've been Mr Venables. I saw him that afternoon.'

'I know you did. But that was before you went out and got the bike, before Rupe Benson came in with the news. Who was it?'

'Someone. I forget now.'

'Don't try me too high. You couldn't possibly forget a thing like that, whoever it was told you such shocking news. I want a name from you, one that I can check up on.'

'Check up on,' Dick repeated unhappily.

Bowler waited. Then he said, 'Someone heard a motorbike heading out towards Bensons' that afternoon.'

Dick slumped forward on the desk in front of him, his head in his arms and started crying noisily.

Disgusted, Bowler said, 'Tell me what happened.' He leaned and turned up the wick on the lamp, so that he could see the man better.

Slowly the story, slightly muffled from his enfolding arms, was dragged from him. Prompted by questions, Dick told his version of events.

On the afternoon of the shootings Dick had concluded his business with his boss Aubrey Venables and then waited in the street for his wife. When she didn't turn up he became impatient, and walked half a mile out to his father's house, where she'd told him she would be. But nobody was home. Not Thelma, not her parents, not the kids.

Then he became suspicious that she had gone running back to her mother, as she had done a few days before. So he'd borrowed his brother's motorbike and gone looking for her. And, yes, finally he admitted that he had ridden out to Bensons'. But he hadn't shot anybody. The victims were all dead when he got there.

He'd seen the bodies and left again immediately.

'Agatha must have been alive.'

His face still hidden, Dick shuddered dramatically. 'She looked dead.'

Bowler gazed down on his bent head and wondered whether

possibly he was speaking the truth.

'Did you touch anything? Move any part of the bodies?'

'No! No! I got out of there fast.'

'You went out there because you were angry with your wife. You thought she was leaving you,' Bowler said. 'Did you shoot her?'

'No! Nothing like that!' He sounded horrified, although he still hadn't raised his head. It seemed he preferred not to look the law in the eye while he made these protests.

'Why did you go, then?' He wasn't convinced that Dick was telling the whole truth and nothing but the truth. There was a sly streak in the man, a cautious calculation behind some of his responses. Dick was neither so stupid nor so simple as Bowler had previously believed, and now he could at a stretch see him rearranging the bodies to cover his crime.

'Look at me, damn you.' Bowler grabbed his shoulder, jerked him upright. 'Why did you go out there?' He glared into Dick's bloodshot eyes.

'Just wanted to find her,' Dick stuttered. 'Wanted to find her.'

'Why?'

Dick shook his head. Bowler waited. His anger mounted.

Something in his expression must have got through to his prisoner. Almost hysterically he said, 'Yeah, I was ropeable, course I was, course I was, wouldn't you be? I was that mad at her, I was —' He gulped, tearful again. 'But I only wanted to bring her home, Bowler. Only home. She shoulda been at home.'

When Bowler said nothing Dick, suddenly fluent, poured out the rest of the story. After he'd seen the bodies he'd gone tearing off on the bike, hardly knowing where he was going. He'd ended up at the farm, where he'd collected his twenty-two with the half-formed intention of shooting himself. He'd taken care of the dog with his first bullet, and ridden off again.

This time he took the Edgerton road. He must have spent one night in the open somewhere — he couldn't remember, he thought he'd been vacillating over whether to put an end to himself — and had then gone on to Edgerton, where he'd turned into the smaller of the town's two pubs for a few glasses of Dutch courage to assist him towards achieving his goal. Instead, he'd spent most of the day in the bar before riding on as far as Riley, where he'd fallen off his bike and into a deep sleep. When he woke up he found that sometime during the afternoon he'd hired himself out as a wood-and-water joey to a local cocky. He'd been there ever since. And, Bowler gathered, paid every Saturday and in an alcoholic stupor every Sunday.

Dick even remembered the name of the farmer he'd worked for. That part of his story at least could be checked. And it would be, Bowler swore to himself.

He wished he knew whether he believed Dick. The last part of the story, almost certainly — that fitted whether he was distraught at the death of his wife or frantic after shooting three people. He still could have done the shootings.

Bowler said, 'You were roaring drunk yesterday, far too drunk to have ridden up from Edgerton. Where'd you get the grog?'

Dick seemed relieved at a question he could answer easily. 'I bought a flagon at the pub.' When Bowler merely frowned at him he added hastily, 'Well, two flagons.'

'Flagons of what? Trotter says he didn't see you.'

'Durwin served me. Port, I bought couple of flagons of port.'

'When was this?'

Dick now had another lapse of memory. He waved his hands, and couldn't remember which day he'd arrived back. This was altogether too vague; Bowler had to know whether he'd returned before Agatha was fired at. But when he tried to bully sense into the clown he only retreated further into confusion.

Bowler swore silently. Now he had to see Durwin, and hope he remembered which day he'd sold Dick the flagons. Then he smiled.

He could do a little terrorising at the same time.

Bowler escorted his prisoner back to the lockup. Where the hell had that detective got to? Perhaps he'd gone straight to the pub. He'd find out when he went over shortly, to speak to Archie, who was helping him stand watch over the pub.

That morning he'd driven round town and the nearer farms checking on rifles and had impounded one that was unregistered. He'd checked the locks on the pub windows and the bolts on the doors. He'd given up his idea of a roster of men watching all night, because he believed he'd made the pub safe for Agatha. If she and the Musgraves took reasonable precautions the gunman couldn't get close enough to aim at her without being recognised.

Therefore Archie wasn't there to protect Agatha. He was there to help his good mate Bowler catch anyone who made any kind of an attempt to gain a sight of her. Now both Dick and his rifle were in custody, Arch might be wasting his time.

40

Matt Franklin said, 'Well, what is it?' When Bowler didn't immediately answer he added, 'Don't think His Majesty likes his surroundings much, Bowler. Looks as though he's got a bad smell under his nose.'

On the other side of the high counter of the office Bowler, turning over papers on his desk, looked up at a coloured reproduction of King George the Fifth in full naval rig, all gold braid and brass buttons, framed in isolated dignity on the end wall. 'Does he? It's probably the company I keep, all the low life I deal with.' And if Franklin chose to take that personally Bowler didn't care. He'd had a good night's sleep the night before but his temper hadn't improved. When he'd seen the young man on top of a load of mallee roots in the pub yard he'd grabbed the opportunity to get some of his questions answered.

'Why did you want me?'

'Come through, take a chair.' Seating himself, Bowler gestured at the chair opposite.

Matt, arms folded across his clammy shirt, remained standing in the gap at the end of the counter. 'Make it snappy, mate. I've left my coat in the lorry and this den of yours is like an ice-box.'

Bowler said, 'It's about that shooting at Bensons'. What were you —'

'Bensons',' Matt said. His good-humoured expression didn't

change but his voice had become hard. He'd grown up in some indefinable way while he'd been off in the desert. After a moment he walked over and sat down. Bowler waited.

Matt leaned forward. 'I know what people are saying and it's all lies. You can tell them it was entirely my fault if Lew got the wrong idea. And it was the wrong idea, bloody wrong, make no mistake about that. Mrs Benson had done nothing.'

'I'm not trying to blame anyone —'

'Good. Because she didn't encourage me, if that's what you're thinking. She was barely civil to me, if you want to know. Taking her books was my idea. She tried to stop me.'

'Yes, all right, I understand, but I just want —'

'If you understand that, then what else do you want from me?' Matt looked surprised. 'I can't help you, I've only just heard about it. And I was gone by the time it happened.'

'If you'll only shut up I'll tell you what I want,' Bowler said, leaning back in his chair and frowning in irritation. Was the beggar stalling deliberately? 'It seems you weren't. Gone, I mean. And I want to know what you were doing.'

'But I left straight after the run-in with Lew. Of course I'd gone.'

'But you came back — you got off the train here in the night and you didn't get on it again.'

'You have been busy.'

Bowler ignored this. 'Where did you go?'

'Is that when it happened? At nighttime? Well, how do you think I got out there? Flew?'

In the official, rather bored voice in which he read out charges in court, Bowler said, 'The shootings occurred at approximately two pm on the afternoon of Thursday, the twenty-fifth of February.'

'Ah,' Matt said.

Bowler had wanted to rattle the young man but apparently he'd failed. 'So now suppose you tell me why you got off the train, where you went, and what you did.'

This seemed to amuse Matt. He said, 'I can't produce witnesses, mate. After I got home I found I'd left my field-glasses behind, and I needed them for the trip. So I got off the train and went out to get them.' Arms crossed, he scrubbed at his shoulders as though trying to warm them.

'Walked out? Seven miles out to Bruce's? For field-glasses?' Bowler was not impressed by that excuse. 'Why were they so important? I thought you were the mechanic on these trips.'

'That's what I drew my pay for. But the first time I went I found there's a lot of other stuff I can help with. The glasses were a present from the Prof, as a matter of fact.'

'Bruce didn't see you. He'd have told me.'

'Nobody saw me. When I was working there I'd been sleeping on the side veranda, and kept my stuff there. I got there just on sunrise, when it was barely light and they were all asleep. So I left again.'

'What stuff?'

'There was my old coat too.'

Bowler said, 'Then where did you go? Because I know you didn't go back to catch the day train.'

Matt laughed. 'After I got there I didn't go a bloody yard further than I had to, I'm telling you. Not five more miles through the scrub to Bensons'.'

'Bruce has horses.'

'And he'd have noticed one missing.'

'Rubbish. Your uncle doesn't spend his days in his paddocks counting horses. You could easily have borrowed one unnoticed.'

'Well, I didn't borrow one of his horses. I headed back to Kularook to get the next train but I got a lift on the track. Ben Norman had been home for his holidays and was driving back to Adelaide. He picked me up.'

'All right, I can check with him. What time was this, mid-morning?'

Matt considered, then shrugged. 'It was late afternoon. But don't get excited, I told you, I was knackered, hadn't been to bed . So I went to sleep. Turned in at that old tumbledown hut just off the track, the one Bruce uses for a shed, and crashed on a pile of wheat-bags. I didn't surface until the train had gone. So I was heading back to catch the Express again when Ben came along.'

Head tilted, smiling slightly, he was watching to see the effect of his speech; and Bowler, suspicious of such a plausible story that he could neither prove nor disprove, thought it could have been concocted for precisely that purpose. And in spite of Matt Franklin's easy manner, something had happened to change him. Under the happy-go-lucky exterior he sensed a contained and rather formidable young man.

'I see. Have you ever been to Bensons'? To the house?'

Matt frowned. 'What's the problem with that? Bruce sent me over with a message once, about this fence they're putting up. But I didn't see Mrs Benson. I didn't even know she was back at that stage.'

All the same, he could have seen the rifle by the door; and he could have remembered it later. 'And when did you get back from the north?'

'Ten days ago.'

'I haven't seen you around.'

'I went home first,' Matt said, as though this should have been obvious. 'Since then I've been out in Spog's back scrub, stump picking.'

So. He was in the neighbourhood at the time of the second attempt on Agatha's life.

'Either of your uncles, Bruce or Spog, own a twenty-two?'

Matt's face went blank. After a moment he said, 'No idea. How the hell would I know that?'

Bowler realised he wasn't going to wring any inadvertent admissions from this one. Matt was very much in control of himself, and would tell the law exactly what he wanted to and no more. Further questions could wait. In time, some flaw in his story might become apparent.

He was about to tell him to get lost when Matt had the same idea. He pushed back his chair and got to his feet, a tall young man lean as a roo dog.

Bowler checked his immediate impulse to order him to sit down again — he wasn't in the army now — and said, 'Hang on a minute. I want to know why you didn't report those three, Lew and the others, for assault. I'd have done them for a quid or two with pleasure.'

'Who, me?' Lazily, the young man stretched his arms, working his stiff muscles. 'You've got rocks in your head. You really think I'd go running for the cops whenever some bastard takes a swing at me? Rats.'

'They didn't give you much chance to swing back, from what I've heard.'

'From what you've heard.' Matt put his palms on the desk and leaned across it. He said, 'Those blokes wouldn't have told you, and Mrs Benson was the only other one there. You've got a bloody nerve, interrogating her. She's been through enough. You leave her alone.'

'All the same —'

'The gossips in this bloody town give me the shits.'

'— all the same, you must have felt pretty angry. With Lew.'

'Not enough to go back and shoot him. A pity — I should have, before he could shoot Agatha. Mrs Benson, that is.'

'Don't make a joke of it,' Bowler said.

'I'm not joking,' Matt said.

Bowler stared at the young man. Bloody hell, he sounded serious. Or he was a damn good actor. On the surface he appeared protective of Agatha's name, and angry with the man who had shot her. He might be dissembling, however, to conceal a past violence, a past all-consuming rage that had included them both.

There wasn't much doubt he felt pretty deeply about Agatha Benson. But Bowler knew of cases where men had murdered women they were obsessed with rather than let another man have them. Was Franklin as obsessive as that? He had changed. Why?

Bowler waved a hand. 'Go and get your damn coat. The lock-up's full, I haven't got room for you. I'll see you around.'

'Not for a while. I'm going home tomorrow.'

When he'd gone Bowler considered. Franklin wasn't going far; he could grab him later if he needed to. He was holding Dick, however, until the detective arrived, so that the new man could decide whether to charge him with murder. He was altogether a more slippery customer.

He hoped the detective wasn't too many more days on the road; he had wired from Branden Bend to say his car had broken down and he was waiting for parts from Adelaide so he'd be a day late.

Whatever the detective decided, Bowler intended to charge Dick with being drunk and disorderly, or threatening violence, at the very least — whichever charge he could find in the books that was the most serious.

Now he had two suspects for the shootings at Bensons'. Which did he fancy?

Three suspects. Although he'd almost crossed Lew off the list he couldn't dismiss him out of hand. He'd been a violent man with a notoriously bad temper, and there still could be a reason why the fifth shell was missing. Perhaps a magpie had flown off with it: they were supposed to collect shiny trinkets. He had never himself seen them do it, and he rather thought the stories applied to European magpies. He'd better ask Joan if it was likely. She knew more about birds than he did.

In Lew's favour, his wife stated that he had calmed down, to the point where he was protective of her and his unborn child. Did some other consideration set him off again? And why had he shot his mother and sister as well as his wife? Just because they got between him and the house? But why carry the rifle away from the house in the first place? As soon as he thought of a reason why Lew could have committed the crimes, he thought of another that made it unlikely. And the more recent attempt to shoot Agatha made it more unlikely still, since that would mean there was now a second murderous gunman loose in Kularook.

Dick was a jealous man, who had been brutally humiliated by all the victims except Agatha. But was he devious enough to shoot four people in a pattern that faked murder-suicide? Was he bright enough to plan those moves in advance? Whoever had shot at Agatha the second time believed she was dangerous, believed she knew something that could incriminate him. Where could Dick have heard that Bowler no longer believed whole-heartedly in Lew's suicide?

And Matt Franklin was a tough-minded young man obsessed with another man's wife. He too had been humiliated, by Lew and Rupe and Figgy, in front of Agatha. He had been home long enough to learn of the murders, and also to learn that Agatha knew something. Franklin was certainly intelligent enough to plan murders so that they appeared to be murder-suicide, but was he obsessive enough to plot such violent and wholesale slaughter? Or cold-blooded enough to make a second attempt on Agatha's life?

41

In the pub kitchen Cordelia stood holding the rail of her playpen and grizzling because she had thrown all her toys and three saucepan lids outside the rail. Now she couldn't reach them. Agatha went over to the child and sidled up to the window — even in daylight she approached windows with caution — to see what was making the noise outside, a series of thumps and bangs and crashes not far from the back door.

A lorry was pulled up by the wood-heap at the end of the old stone stable. On top of the high load of mallee stumps a man stood astride, balanced on the uneven footing, throwing off the spiked, knotty lumps one at a time, heaving them up and swinging them out so that they fell with a crash in a pile beyond the stack of firewood logs.

Although the wind was cold and carried a fine drizzling rain he was in his shirt-sleeves, bending and heaving without pause. Agatha watched for over a minute before she was certain that he was Snow Franklin.

She had been imagining him untold miles away. At the sight of him, back in Kularook, her spirits lifted inexplicably.

He was different somehow. In contrast to Kularook skins, which had faded to a winter pallor, he was deeply tanned; he was leaner, fined down — perhaps that was it.

Em dumped a double handful of potatoes on the table. 'What is it?'

'Why didn't you tell me Snow Franklin was back?' Agatha kept her head turned away from Em.

'I thought his name might bring back bad memories.'

'I've faced them over and over, he can't make them worse. All the same, I was hoping he'd go home to Edgerton, and stay there.'

'He probably will. He's just helping old Spog out.' Em seated herself at the table and picked up her knife. 'The stumps are from Spog's back block, he's been clearing new land. Trotter offered to buy them weeks ago, so Spog's been waiting for someone to go out and pick them up for him.'

'How long has he been back then?'

'Matt? Only a day or two. He asked how you were. Seems he's only just heard about the shooting. He says he's been bush, no papers, not even a wireless.'

Cordelia squawked and tugged at her mother's arm. Agatha lifted her, set her astride her hip, and turned back to the window. Snow was standing on the tray of the lorry throwing off the last of the stumps and any minute now he would come in to say he'd finished unloading and she didn't know what she could say to him, after all that had happened. She wasn't ready; she wished he had stayed away longer. Wished he had stayed away until she was safely engaged to Aubrey, at least.

Em said, 'Trotter left a cheque for him, it's on the dresser.' She displayed her hands, wet and muddy from the potatoes. 'Give it to him, will you?'

Snow jumped to the ground and walked towards the pub's back door, holding up his wrist and smearing away blood oozing from a scratch up his forearm. There were new lines on his good-looking face, sun-bleached streaks in his damp hair. Agatha took a step back so that she wouldn't be caught at the window.

Bowler Brown's voice called, 'Hey there, Matt! Got a minute?' and when she looked again Snow had changed direction to meet Bowler at the back gate. She felt a slight disappointment, and told herself it was because she'd been braced to meet him and now she still had that hurdle to surmount.

Snow looked back, saw her at the window, and waved with a casual lift of his arm. Before she could respond he turned away and walked off with Bowler, across the road towards the police station.

The pub kitchen was a warm refuge on a cold afternoon. At one end of the table Aubrey Venables sat with an empty cup before him; at the other stood Agatha, her back to the wood stove, her hands in a large china bowl of flour, rubbing in dripping for pastry. Em had disappeared, taking Cordelia with her.

'You would enjoy London, my dear,' Aubrey said. 'All the theatres, and art galleries, and the history lying about everywhere waiting for you to trip over it.' He smiled, inviting her to share his enthusiasms. 'The theatres in particular are superb — we have no actors to match them out here.'

His smile was full of boyish charm. Intended charm, Agatha believed, but genuine charm all the same. In spite of his years there was something very young and innocent about Aubrey. It was surprising how simple and unaffected the man was, considering that he divided the human race quite naturally into two tribes, peasants and gentry. He was a strange mixture.

She said, 'I've hardly ever been to the theatre, Aubrey. I've never had the time or the money.'

'Then it will be my pleasure to introduce you to it.' He reached into his inside pocket for his cigarette case. 'My very great pleasure.'

And just what did he mean by that? Agatha kept her head bent and concentrated on her hands, squeezing and rubbing the flour between her fingers. She raised her brows. 'In London?' she asked.

'Would you fly to London with me, sweet Agatha?' he asked, cigarette case on his heart, the other arm thrown out dramatically.

'What are we waiting for? Let us leave immediately — now, this instant!'

Agatha laughed. 'Just flap our wings.' She looked up, and saw Snow Franklin standing in the doorway. She was disconcerted — she'd forgotten Snow — but he smiled at her, and came into the room.

'G'day, Aub.' He pulled out a chair and sat down.

Aubrey had stopped laughing. 'Good afternoon, Franklin.' He started to put his cigarettes away, then offered the case to Snow, who shook his head.

'Trotter left your cheque on the dresser, Snow.' Agatha found herself flushing — or was it the heat from the stove? 'Can you get it? My hands are covered in flour.'

Snow got up, picked up the cheque, read it, then folded it into his inside coat pocket. He sat down at the table again. She had been hoping he would go once he had been paid; she felt uncomfortable, though she didn't know why. He seemed perfectly self-possessed.

Aubrey, though, was fidgeting. He said, 'Really, you know, I don't think you should be here.'

Obviously Snow was one of the peasants, Agatha thought. Not that he appeared in any way put down; he leaned comfortably back in his chair.

'Why not?'

'After all that's happened — Mrs Benson's good name — I mean, if you keep visiting — People will talk, you know, people will talk.'

Snow studied him speculatively. 'I hope not, when you're here as chaperone, mate. Though you can clear out if you like. Agatha doesn't need any protection from me. I've always been straight with her.' He tilted his head, looking up into her downcast face. 'Haven't I, Agatha?'

She couldn't meet his eyes. 'Oh yes.'

Aubrey said, 'She needs protection from anything that leaves her open to slurs and innuendo.'

'Can't quarrel with that.' When Aubrey started to speak again Snow cut him off with a raised hand. 'All right, you've made your point, I'll keep this short. Agatha,' Snow said, and waited until she looked at him. 'You're probably trying to forget about the shooting. I've only just heard, or I'd have written or something. All I can say is, I hope you can forgive me for not listening when you tried to send me away. I was plain selfish, I know that now. Can you forgive me?'

He was very much in earnest. Immobilised by her floury hands, embarrassed by Aubrey's presence, Agatha tried to think of the right response to this.

When she didn't answer he pushed back his chair and got to his feet. 'Yes, well, you can't blame me any more than I do myself. When I think how close —'

'I don't blame you,' she said. 'There's nothing to forgive.'

'But there is, dammit. You know how much there is. You could have died because of me — you very nearly did. You know damn well it was all my fault.'

'No,' she said.

'You can't honestly say that.' He stood watching her; then he shrugged. 'But it's kind of you, just the same, and I will try to bear my guilt lightly.' He laid his knuckles gently against her cheek; when she looked up he smiled at her. 'See you around, eh?' he said. 'So long, Aub.' And he was gone.

'He must think you're easily swayed,' Aubrey said. 'Trying to get round you like that. Insinuating beggar.'

Agatha said, 'But he meant every word.' She heard the lorry start up in the yard.

'A bit late in the day for that, isn't it, my dear? As he said, if he'd considered you in the first place the tragedy would never have occurred.' Aubrey glanced at her closed expression. He said more generously, 'But then, I suppose youngsters are always thoughtless.'

'Youngsters?' Agatha said. If anything, Snow had made her feel the junior in that exchange. 'Oh, I was thoughtless too.'

Neither Snow nor Aubrey had said anything about the shots fired two nights before. Perhaps Em wasn't spreading the word of her guardians as fast as Agatha hoped. She glanced at the window. Soon it would be time to put in the plywood shields.

42

Durwin Harris had had a full day to worry over what Bowler might do next, which was too long. Now that Bowler wanted to ask him about selling alcohol to Dick he couldn't find him.

Intending to continue with his planned harassment at the same time, Bowler had retrieved the feathers from under some papers on his desk and walked across the road in search of his victim.

Durwin must have seen him coming. He was nowhere to be found, though Bowler searched the pub, its sheds, and its paddocks. When, thwarted and irritable, he returned to the police station, he was wishing he'd let the matter of the blasted chooks alone. Now he wanted Durwin on a more important matter the bloody man was dodging him.

He wouldn't get away with it for long. Bowler would call at the cottage on his way home from the post office after lunch.

Roger Price the postmaster was a dark, pessimistic man of about Bowler's own age, who, because his lungs had been damaged by mustard gas in the war, had been forced to accept a lowly, ill-paid job with the Post-Master General's Department, a job more usually undertaken by indigent widows. Since he never spoke of his health few people knew of his disability. Bowler was one of the few who did.

His lungs didn't prevent Roger from collecting and retailing gossip as avidly as Em Musgrave, leaning on his counter at the post office and chatting with his customers to glean his facts as she gleaned hers over the front bar of the pub.

Bowler stood in the post office doorway to watch Miss Venables pull a couple of envelopes from the boxes outside. He lifted his hat. She nodded coolly and walked away down the street, choosing to negotiate the muddy puddles pitting the unsealed surface rather than wade through the thick wet weeds growing on the verges. She held her well-shaped figure erect and stepped with a dancer's precision.

'I can't make that woman out,' Bowler said.

Roger looked up from weighing a packet on the letter scales. 'Who do you mean?'

'Aubrey Venables's sister. She's an odd character. Half the time she seems angry whenever she runs into me and I can't imagine what I've done to upset her. I tried to be sociable, in fact. We had them round for cards, and a fat lot of good that did.'

'You know, I'm not so sure she is his sister.'

'What do you mean, not his sister?'

Roger looked round swiftly. 'Don't say I told you, but letters come to their box addressed to Miss Chapman, L Chapman, and she tucks them in her bag and takes them home with the rest. And I never find them again readdressed in the outgoing mail.'

'Bloody hell! You think she's a ring-in?' Taken aback, Bowler gave a snort of incredulous laughter. All the same, that might explain a few things; he'd known there was something off-key about her; he'd been right all along. He started turning possibilities over in his mind. Then he said, 'Perhaps she sends the letters out in different envelopes. You'd never know.'

'She might, I suppose. But why buy a stamp when she could re-address it for nothing? She's been getting them ever since they moved here, Bowler. Surely in that time she could have let whoever it is know about the mistake.'

'Does she get other letters addressed to Miss Venables?'

'No. Only the Chapman ones regularly. And I'll tell you something else — one day a Chapman letter came without a stamp, so she had to come to the counter and pay a fee to get it. Always helpful, I pointed out that if she readdressed it there and then whoever it was really meant for would have to pay the fee, not her. And she was terribly embarrassed, all hot and bothered because she couldn't think of anything to fob me off with, but she insisted on paying and taking it away with her. Said she'd "deal with it" at home.'

'If she's not his sister Aubrey Venables has got a bloody cosy little setup there,' Bowler said. 'The things money can buy! And yes by God, it would explain why Miss Whoever-she-is doesn't like Agatha Benson much. She thinks she might lose her meal ticket.'

'From what I hear, she's lost it,' Roger said. 'Some of the footy boys are laying bets, not whether but when he pops the question.'

'Are they indeed.'

'Be your age, Bowler. It's only the odd bob here or there, nothing for you to get official about. But it's no wonder la Venables hates Mrs Benson.'

'Hate is a pretty strong word. Why do you say that?'

'Miss Venables was buying stamps the other day and Mrs Benson came in to collect a parcel for the Musgraves. If looks could kill . . . And don't say I told you any of this,' Roger added, low and emphatic. 'I haven't told you a thing.'

'I'm not going to spread the word. Not yet, anyway.'

A startling theory was burgeoning in his mind, one he wasn't going to tell Roger. Whoever she was, according to Miriam Pedler this woman shot rabbits for sport. What if she was the one who'd shot at Agatha? She had no reason to commit the murders out on the farm, but she might think that whoever was responsible for those would also be blamed for these more recent shots. And if she was the sniper, had she been shooting to kill, or merely to frighten? He'd better have a word with her, and let her know he had his eye on her. And he must also, as soon as possible, get hold of her firearms, whatever she used on the rabbits. If he had to, he'd invent a reason. Perhaps tell her he had to check everybody's, or something.

He turned to Roger. 'And you damn well keep your suspicions to yourself too, for the time being. How much do I owe you for that?'

Roger lifted the packet off the scales and read the address. 'What's Joan sending home to her mother?' He flexed it between his hands. 'Photographs, I reckon. See? I know most of what goes in or out of this town.'

'For your information they're the latest snaps of the children. And you are not supposed to talk about any of it.'

'You know me better than that.' Roger tried to sound hurt and indignant.

'I know you very well indeed,' Bowler said. 'That's why I mentioned it.'

He scooped up his change and walked out. A cool breeze was ruffling the puddles in the road, the bare fruit trees in Roger's back garden clicked softly. Around the corner in the next street stood Durwin Harris's cottage.

43

Bowler caught Durwin unawares. The man had gone down the yard to throw a bucket of kitchen scraps to his chooks when the policeman strolled down the vacant block next door.

'Ah, Durwin. I want a word with you.'

The handyman, a blocky figure in navy bib-and-brace overalls, dropped the bucket and glanced round as though assessing his chances of making a dash for it.

Bowler smiled nastily and stepped over the fence. 'Where do you think you'd get to? Come on, you've got to front up to me sooner or later.'

'What d'you want?' Durwin demanded in a surly tone.

'When did you sell Dick Thompson a couple of flagons of port?'

'Eh?' He sounded confused. Obviously he'd been braced for a different question.

'You sold Dick some grog. What day was that?'

'Oh. Yair. Oh, one day last week. I didn' know he was back, surprised me, came roarin' up on Gab's motorbike when I was knockin' off one night. I mean — I was knockin' off early that night.' He glanced apprehensively at Bowler. 'Real early.'

'Selling stuff after hours, eh? You are going the pace, Durwin. But I might overlook that if you tell me about Dick. What day last week?'

The Fifth Bullet

Durwin frowned. He lifted his hands, as though to count on his fingers, then thought better of it and thrust both deep into his side pockets. 'Fridy,' he said. 'Musta been about Fridy.'

'I don't want "about" Friday — was it on Friday?'

Durwin breathed heavily for a few moments. 'Yair, because I didn' work Satty last week. Fridy it was.'

'Right.' Bowler saw Durwin relaxing. 'About that other business.' When the other said nothing he explained, 'Old Spog's chooks.'

'Dunno nothin' about 'm.' Durwin stared earnestly into Bowler's eyes.

'All right, you don't know nothing about them.' Bowler took the two black feathers from his pocket and smoothed them between his fingers, noting that, despite the cold breeze, Durwin's forehead was wet with perspiration. 'I could point out that your double negative makes an admission of sorts but — '

'Me *what?*'

'— but I might be prepared to ignore the theft, to say nothing of selling alcohol after hours, if old Spog found six new, young black hens in his fowl yard one morning.'

Durwin appeared mesmerised by the feathers and incapable of answering.

'Durwin!' His head jerked up. Bowler said, 'I have the date Spog reported the theft, the date of the newspaper these feathers were wrapped in, and the date you sold chooks to the pub. What's it going to be?'

The man's shoulders slumped. 'Where'd I get black uns? Mine're all white.'

'Buy them off your sister. And do not nick them off her, because I'll be checking with Callie myself. And checking with old Spog, too. Young birds, mind, not tough old boilers. See you around, Durwin.'

Pleased with a job well done — Spog would now have replacement chooks without Em getting upset because he'd fed her handyman into the legal system — Bowler was walking home towards his front gate when he met Agatha, holding Cordelia by the hand, who had just come out.

'We've been visiting Joan,' Agatha said. 'Now we're going for a walk.' Cordelia dropped to a squatting position and began lifting small stones in the weeds under the five-wire fence that enclosed the yard behind Ossie Todd's garage. 'She is good to me.'

'Joan doesn't deal in good works,' Bowler said. 'She asks you over because she enjoys your company, and for no other reason.'

'All the same, I am grateful. She makes me feel very welcome.'

'There you are then.' Ossie really should cut those damn weeds and clear up the rubbish he'd dumped against the fence. 'Come on, Tuppence, you're getting all dirty.'

He lifted Cordelia, but she squawked 'No, no!' and struggled to be put down again. Slightly hurt — he'd thought he was a friend of hers — he set her on her feet.

She immediately squatted again, tugging at something caught under a large stone. Bowler crouched beside her, smelling the baby soap on her skin and in her silky fair curls. For the sole purpose of taking it from her he helped her extract her find from under the stone.

She immediately pushed it into her mouth, watching him defiantly as though daring him to stop her.

'Here, no you don't. What have you got there?'

Bowler prised open the small fist and removed from her grasp his fountain pen.

His fountain pen. He stared at it, astonished. How had it got out here?

'What's that?' Agatha asked.

'My pen. I lost it several weeks ago. I can't imagine how it got here.' He sat back on one heel and slid the smooth dark cylinder between his fingers, almost caressing it, while he considered the puzzle. 'But I am very very pleased to see it again, Tuppence, so thank you.' He leaned sideways, one hand to the ground, and kissed the child's cheek. She smiled and kissed him back, loudly.

'Clever girl,' Agatha said fondly. She took Cordelia's hand and tugged her upright. 'We'll see you later, Bowler.'

'Yes, sure,' he said, his attention fixed on poking at the rubbish. How the hell had his pen got wedged under a stone out here? He lifted the stone further, as though searching for clues to whatever witchcraft had translated his pen, and saw a couple of sheets of torn and muddy paper.

He stood up and smoothed them out. They were the pages of the report he'd begun when he'd first had doubts about the murder-suicide theory of the Benson shootings. The report he'd begun, and then lost.

He glanced at the office on the front of his house. They couldn't have blown here, nor could he have dropped them. They'd been deliberately hidden under the stone. Some bugger had been ratting his desk.

He never locked any doors, on the house or the front office. Who had walked in and helped himself to the report and the pen? And when? And why that report? Did someone want to know his views on the shooting?

Taking the pen was odd, if the thief had then discarded it almost immediately. Perhaps the pen had been caught up in the report. He sometimes used the clip on the side of the pen as a kind of paper-clip, to hold pages together, so perhaps the pen had been clipped to the report.

Bowler didn't like this at all. Gunmen roaming the streets at night, break-ins in his office — what on earth was Kularook coming to?

44

Aubrey Venables was having difficulties in his wooing, chiefly in finding a place in which to pursue it. His own house was impossible, because of the presence of Miss Venables, tight-lipped and narrow-eyed; and at the pub his snatched tête-à-têtes with Agatha were constantly interrupted by every blow-in in the district.

Now Matt Franklin's reappearance gave his plans added urgency. He didn't like the man's easy familiarity with his intended bride. Immediately he planned another elaborate picnic. By moonlight.

Bowler, consulted by Aubrey, vetoed this instantly, saying it would be sheer lunacy for Agatha to be abroad in the night when the gunman still hadn't been found. So Aubrey had suggested to Agatha that she should sneak out one evening and join him. They would slink away so quietly that neither Bowler nor anyone else would know they were at large.

Although she felt both too caged and too visible at the pub, where she couldn't avoid meeting people unexpectedly in the kitchen and passage, Agatha had rejected this proposal emphatically. Indoors was bad enough. After night fell she was always on edge, watching strangers and locals alike with tense suspicion, afraid that any one of them might suddenly whip out a concealed gun. She didn't know who had shot at her. It could have been anyone.

In daylight, with other people, perhaps she would venture forth. But not in the evening.

Aubrey had been forced to revise his plans, and arrange a lunchtime picnic. At noon on Friday he drove Agatha out to Red Rab's, a ruined cottage half a mile south of the township. He'd spent an hour during the morning clearing fallen stones and rubble from beneath a large pepper tree, so that he had a smooth place to spread his travelling rug. He'd wheedled Em not only into supporting his plan, but also into cooking and packing the food — roast chicken, sliced ham, thin bread and butter, tinned asparagus — for what he intended as a romantic feast for two. He had a thermos of coffee, fruit cake and chocolates. He had a bottle of wine. He had spared no effort or expense.

The sky remained overcast, but Aubrey was not deterred. The rug was spread and he was unpacking his hamper when a wet wind swirled through, whipping up the long drooping fronds of the pepper tree and whisking a linen table napkin high into the top branches. Seconds later the first heavy shower poured down.

They grabbed up everything and raced for the car.

Agatha laughed, and shook the rain from her hair. 'Wrong time of year for picnics, Aubrey. We might as well go home.'

But instead of taking her to the pub he drove her back to his house and avoided the problem of an unwelcome third at their feast by setting out the picnic in an old, spider-ridden summerhouse at the bottom of the overgrown garden. The roof was mostly intact, the sides were protected by a wooden lattice loaded with asparagus fern creeper. He flapped around with the remaining table napkin and cleared away the most obtrusive spider webs, then brought a card table from the house so that they could eat in comfort. After that he carried on with the picnic as though they were outdoors on a balmy evening with the moon beaming down.

Agatha, reclining on the rug thrown over an old cane lounge, admired his resourcefulness and was amused by his make-believe.

As they finished stacking away the remains of the picnic the sun shone through briefly, winking in the raindrops spangling the shrubs, painting dark shadows into the corners of the summerhouse. She smiled at Aubrey as he raised his glass to her and drank the last of the Riesling. Then he sank to one knee on the dusty floor and formally proposed marriage to her.

She was unprepared for the formality and taken aback by his outdated belief that a gentleman should kneel to his lady. Although more than a little embarrassed, and stammering slightly, she accepted him. She hoped he didn't feel let down, since she could only summon words much less formal than his.

To her relief he expressed himself more than satisfied. He carried her hand to his lips. Then, as though greatly daring, he kissed her cheek.

Agatha choked down hysterical laughter. Here she was, the district's scarlet woman, and he was treating her like a teenage virgin he didn't want to frighten by a display of physical ardour. Perhaps she should initiate a more fervent kiss. But no. This temperate demonstration of his affection suited her well for the present. There was plenty of time.

They might have stayed longer in the summerhouse but Miss Venables heard them, and came looking for them. She appeared as Aubrey was tenderly kissing the finger upon which he had just placed, in spite of Agatha's protests, a large diamond ring.

Agatha received the full force of the woman's smouldering, malevolent gaze. Uneasy, her rather dreamlike state shattered, she scrambled off the lounge and asked Aubrey to drive her back to the pub. She checked in hastily with Em and went straight to her room, to compose herself before the busy time in the kitchen preparing dinner.

Cordelia was asleep in her cot, taking her afternoon nap. Agatha sat down on her bed. She crossed her arms and gripped her own shoulders, her head bent, her thoughts racing.

Em called her name, but she ignored it. She wanted a little time alone.

45

When the children came home from school that afternoon Bowler, sitting in his car with the engine running, told Tom to hop in.

'We won't be too long,' he said. 'Your mother knows we might be a bit late for dinner.' With the boy nursing his school satchel beside him Bowler drove out of town, across the railway line, heading east. He wouldn't explain their errand to his son but conversed airily about the boy's progress at school.

Tom put up with this for the first mile. Then he said, 'Dad, why don't you dry up? If you won't tell me where we're going or what we're doing, fine, you're hatching something and want to surprise me. But don't expect me to listen to all that drivel.'

Bowler laughed. 'We're going to Fieldings'. I have to see Graham.'

'You're not going to arrest him again?'

'No, Graham is safe from me this time. How do you know about him being arrested?'

'All the kids know. If you hadn't let him go in time to play in the match our lives wouldn't have been worth living at school. It was bad enough as it was.'

'Damn it, Tom, I didn't think of that.' Bowler felt contrite. He'd been so bloody pleased with himself and his solution for his row with the footy team he hadn't considered how his actions would reflect on his children.

'Rose got into quite a fight about it,' Tom said.

'Rose fighting? I don't like the sound —'

'Rose can look after herself,' her brother said with evident pride. 'Even the big kids don't tangle with Rose.'

'Don't they?' Bowler didn't know whether to be gratified or horrified by this piece of information about his slight, angelic-looking daughter. 'What about you?'

'Not me. I'm a peaceful guy.'

'You won't get much peace if your mother hears you using that American slang,' Bowler warned.

'She won't hear me. Do you think I'm stupid?'

'No. I don't think that,' his father said.

At the Fieldings' farm he drove down the track beside the house to the sheds behind. Graham, wiping hands streaked with grease on a piece of grimy rag, came out of the machinery shed to meet them.

'Round the back,' he said. 'She's ready waiting for you.'

'Go and see,' Bowler told Tom, and pushed him out of the car. At a more leisurely pace he followed with Graham. 'I'll write you the cheque before I go.'

Tom ran round the corner of the shed and skidded to a halt. 'Dad!'

Tied to the fence by the reins of her bridle stood a black mare, aristocrat in every line of her. She lowered her head and turned, ears pricked, towards the boy.

'Do you like her? Her name is Iolanthe.'

'Like her!' breathed Tom.

'She's not up to my weight now,' Graham said. 'And my sister has her own horse, her show-jumper. This one's been turned out for a while, but I worked her a bit this morning and she should be all right. All the same, you'd better watch her. Not that she's vicious or anything, it's just high spirits.'

Bowler said, 'Think you can get her home in one piece?'

Tom was holding out his hand so that the mare could breathe on his fingers. 'Her or me in one piece?'

'Both of you,' his father said. 'I promised your mother I wouldn't get you damaged. She seems to think that's important, for some reason.'

Tom grinned. He rubbed the mare's forehead, stroked her nose, scratched under her jaw, all the time murmuring softly words meant for her alone. Slowly, so that she could watch what he was doing, he untied the reins and led her towards the two men.

He walked up to his father, slid his arms round his ribs inside his coat, and rested his forehead briefly against his shirt. Then he stood back. 'Is that my saddle too?'

'Yes, it's the right size for both of you. Be careful with it — I think it's lined with gold, the amount ruddy Graham wants for it. Come on, up you go.' Bowler gave his son a leg up and adjusted the stirrup leathers. 'Take her quietly for a while until she's used to you. I'll be along soon.' He watched horse and rider walk off round the house towards the road and turned to Graham.

The young man said, 'Brace yourself. I haven't told you yet what I want for the bridle.'

Bowler smiled. 'I should have got him a horse last year, when the old pony died. He's been missing his pony.'

He fished his cheque book from his inside coat pocket, his fountain pen (his miraculously restored fountain pen, his cherished pen that he carried from his office only when he had cheques to write) from his outside pocket, and leant on the Chrysler's bonnet. As he made out the cheque he said, 'Graham, I've had a letter from the Lands Department. They searched the records and the town oval belongs to Spog.'

'Oh, hooray. That's all we need. Does the Council know?'

'They do by now. So I think it's high bloody time the footy team simmered down and made its peace with the old boy. Can't you talk sense to your mates?'

'I've tried, dammit. Do you think I want to be shut up again?'

'Garn, you had it easy.'

'Not so damn easy. It took me weeks to explain to Mum, and I think she's still suspicious I've been up to something. You really put my weights up with Mum, blast you.' He took the cheque, blew on it to dry the ink, and stowed it in his shirt pocket. 'But I hear Matt Franklin is back, I'll get onto him. If anyone can make that old pest see reason Matt can. He's Spog's blue-haired boy.' Graham apparently heard the sarcastic tone of his own voice and added, 'Give him his due, he's good to Spog. Gives up weeks of his time doing the work the old boy can't manage on his own.'

'Does he? Well then, you'd better convince him the town needs that oval more than Spog needs a crop of wheat. And make your mates see reason too.'

'Yeah, I'll have another go at them. But I give you fair warning, Bowler, next time I see you coming I'm heading for the hills.'

46

Detective-sergeant Ron Macrea walked into Kularook at twenty minutes past midnight on Saturday morning. His car had broken down for the fourth and final time three miles north of the town and he had been walking in the pitch dark on a rough track for over an hour, intermittently rained on by heavy showers. He was no longer young and his shoes were thin.

A few glimmerings of moonlight broke through as he reached the metalled road of Kularook's main street, in time to allow every dog in town an excellent view of him. He was accompanied by frantic barking as he passed from house to house through the sleeping town.

His feet were hurting, he was wet, tired, thirsty, and probably developing a cold. Bailed up by Archie Davidson carrying a Lee-Enfield rifle tucked under his arm, Macrea gave a huff of pure terror and jumped back three feet. He had strayed into nightmare. Macrea was not a returned serviceman. Although he would never admit it to his fellow officers, firearms in any hands but his own frightened him rigid.

Archie shone a powerful torch in his eyes. 'Who the hell are you?'

Macrea identified himself and tried to see past the torch. 'Is that you, Brown?'

'No, Bowler's asleep. This is my watch.'

The Fifth Bullet

'Get that thing out of my face. You are?'

'Arch Davidson. I'm a mate of Bowler's. Half a sec, I'll go in and wake him up.'

'What are you doing with that gun?'

'Making sure nobody shoots Agatha Benson. Look, let me get Bowler, he'll explain.'

'I'll talk to Brown in the morning. Where's the night bell on this hotel?'

Archie escorted him to the front door, rang the bell for him, and introduced him when Trotter, blinking sleepily behind a flaring candle, finally staggered into view. He waited long enough to hear the detective's tale of misfortune, then he crossed the road to inform Bowler of these developments.

Surprised to find the place locked up, he knocked on the bedroom window until Bowler got out of bed and came over.

Archie explained what had happened. 'But I reckoned I'd better warn you, Bowler, he seems pretty fed up. Yeah, well anyone would be after all that trouble with his car but he seems a bit extra. Watch out for squalls in the morning, I'd say.'

Bowler scraped his bristly chin with his thumb. 'You know, Arch, you'd better make yourself scarce. This joker might kick up if he thinks I've been arming civilians. Are all the lights out at the pub?'

'Last one went out half an hour ago. I was on my way to tell you I was knocking off when this joker appeared. Incidentally, what's the strength of locking this place up like the Adelaide Gaol? Afraid the gunman is coming after you too?'

'I think someone ratted my desk the other day. Arch, is it still raining?'

'Off and on. Right now it's pissing down'

'Don't sound so bloody cheerful about it. All right, you go on home. I'll check around a bit before I turn in again.'

At breakfast time next morning Bowler went over to the pub. He was well rested — he'd quickly fallen asleep again after he'd made a thorough check around the pub when Archie had gone — freshly showered and shaved, and wearing a clean shirt. He'd recognised in time that he was dressing to create a good impression, as though he cared what this detective thought; and so he'd drawn the line at a tie. The man would have to put up with him tie-less.

Macrea was in the dining room, just finishing his bacon and eggs.

'Good morning.' Bowler pulled out the chair opposite and sat down.

'Ah, Constable Brown.' Macrea did not look rested. His eyes were heavy and red-rimmed, his nose inflamed.

'Sorry I wasn't awake when you got in last night. Archie did wake me, but he said you were going straight to bed.' Bowler had a fine line to tread here: this man was a sergeant, with probably twenty years more experience than he but, since they operated under different chains of command, wasn't automatically able to order him about.

Macrea buttered a second slice of toast. 'Who's that Davidson anyway? Another of you left-over war heroes? I might have known it.'

Bowler had forgotten the man's open dislike of ex-servicemen, another reason for the ill feeling between them. With deliberate malice he put it down to a guilty conscience, and ignored it when he could.

'Of course,' he said heartily. 'Don't think I'd trust a civilian.' The bastard could take that any way he liked.

'So what was he doing? Does Inspector Smith know you've recruited a private army down here?'

'No. But I can't watch all the time. Smith would expect me to protect the girl.' He hoped the detective wouldn't put two and two together and realise that Archie had been there to catch the gunman, not to stop him, seeing that Bowler believed the precautions he'd taken at the pub, the windows blocked and the good solid doors bolted at night, would prevent further attacks on Agatha.

The detective growled, 'A rifle seems slightly excessive.'

'This other joker was armed,' Bowler said. 'The bullets looked like twenty-twos.' He reminded himself that even detective-sergeants, like blowflies and death adders, had a place in the scheme of things. Unfortunately, he couldn't deal with the one in the same way he'd deal with the other two. 'Incidentally, I've sent Ossie from the garage out to tow your car back. He's a pretty good mechanic. You tell him what's been going wrong and he'll fix it for you.'

'Thanks,' grunted Macrae. The word obviously cost him an effort.

Em came over and refilled Macrae's cup from the large white enamel teapot she carried. 'One for you, Bowler?'

He shook his head and pushed back his chair. To the detective he said, 'Come over to the office when you've finished, and I'll fill you in. There's a few things to add to that report I sent to Adelaide.'

In the office half an hour later the detective laid the pages of notes face down on the desk in front of him. Bowler, sitting opposite with his hands linked behind his head and his chair rocked back to two legs, waited for the response.

'That's comprehensive,' Macrae said, unable to keep the surprise from his voice. 'You've been pretty thorough, once you had suspicions the matter wasn't straightforward. Though I see you haven't discounted the murder-suicide theory altogether.'

'Agatha — Mrs Benson — has other enemies who could be responsible for the second shots. I'm not sure about Rupe Benson; at a pinch he might be unwilling to share the farm with his brother's widow. He blames her for the whole mess, anyway. But there's a woman too.'

'A woman!' Macrae's voice rose incredulously.

Pleased to have shocked him, Bowler said, 'She believes Mrs Benson has stolen her brother, upsetting the cosy little nest she's made for herself keeping house for him. And she's competent with guns, goes rabbit shooting for sport. It could have been her. But I've had a word with her, and lifted her rifle off her. She should be harmless now.'

He wondered whether Miss Venables's fears were well-founded. When he interviewed her he hadn't been able to make up his mind whether she had felt strongly enough to take up a rifle to get rid of her competition. She'd been evasive and resentful, but so were plenty of innocent people in the face of police probing.

'Good God. Sounds pretty far-fetched to me. What's her name?' Macrea hurriedly dragged out his handkerchief and sneezed into it.

Bowler said, 'I don't know her first name. She's known as Miss Venables.' He certainly wasn't going to tell this bastard what Roger had told him in confidence, seeing that his previous quarrel with Macrea had arisen when the detective had told too many of the wrong people some information Bowler had given him. 'And yes, she probably is a long odds candidate, but I haven't written her off for all that.'

'It's a cold trail,' Macrea said. He picked up the notes and flipped over a few pages.

'Where do you want to start? Dick Thompson's out on bail over the incident with his kids, but I know where he is any time you want him.' Bowler had made Shirl Thompson, the only one with any sense in that family, understand that her son would be in worse trouble if he tried to hide now. She would keep Dick in order and available.

'What about Matthew Franklin?'

'He's out at Spog Wilson's I think. And I can soon round up anyone else if you tell me who you want.'

'Better begin at the scene of the crime, I suppose, and then interview this Rupert Benson and his — stepfather, is it?'

Bowler nodded. 'You can take my car. I'll tell you how to get there.' He didn't offer to drive, because he had better things to do. Macrea wouldn't want his company anyway.

So when he'd gone, Bowler saddled up Imshy.

47

When he arrived at Spog Wilson's the old man met him at his back door and ushered him into the kitchen.

'Yeah, six of them,' Spog said. He waved Bowler to a chair at the kitchen table and went to the stove for the kettle. 'Woke up this morning and there they were. They're not the same hens, but I'm pleased to see them just the same. Any idea who left them?'

Bowler shook his head.

Old Spog gave a slow smile. 'You mean the beggars just had a change of heart? Pull the other one.'

'I doubt if there was more than one bloke involved.'

'And I'm sure you'd know.' Spog, his back to the room, poured boiling water into a teapot. 'Well, if he's one of those damn footballers, I suppose I'll have to let them have the oval again. Young Matt's been at me about it already.'

Bowler started to correct this misapprehension, then let it pass. 'Where is Matt? Is he about?'

'He's gone home. Got a few things to do after his time away.' Spog set out two cups, complete with saucers and teaspoons, and a plate of rock-buns. 'I reckon his mother wants him home for a bit, anyway.'

Bowler fiddled with a teaspoon, surprised by the man's careful arrangements. Did he bake the rock-buns himself? And not many men who lived alone bothered with saucers. 'Does he talk to you about the work he does on these trips? He says he's the mechanic, looks after the lorries.'

'That's right. But he does a bit more than that.'

That's what Matt had told him. Perhaps the old boy knew a more specific answer.

'What more? Why would he need his field-glasses so much that he'd walk out to Bruce's in the middle of the night to get them?'

'Walk?' Spog said, sounding surprised. 'What —?' He stopped, frowning.

'Didn't he walk?' Bowler's mind was sifting possibilities at lightning speed. 'He borrowed one of your horses.'

Spog nodded, a small, abrupt movement. 'Didn't he tell you?'

No indeed he hadn't. Bowler, very much on the alert, realised that Spog would shut up immediately if he realised his great-nephew had told a different story. 'I must have misunderstood,' he said casually.

Not casually enough. 'What did Matt tell you, then?' Spog asked suspiciously.

'Don't remember exactly. I just assumed he'd walked, I think.'

'It's a hell of a distance to walk, even in daylight.'

'Yeah, seven miles there and seven miles back.'

Spog said, 'But —' He shook his head, stirred the pot, clapped on the lid, and poured tea into the two cups.

'But what?'

'Nothing. Wasn't anything. Forgotten what I was going to say.'

Like hell he had. Pretty obviously, there was something about the distance involved that Matt hadn't told him. Bowler said, 'Did he wake you, when he took the horse?'

Munching slowly on a rock-bun, Spog took his time over his answer. 'No. I didn't even notice the colt was gone until it came home next day with the stirrups over the saddle and a note tied to the bridle. But he knew it would be all right with me, Matt did. He's welcome to borrow a horse any time. He knows that.'

'Why didn't he bring it back himself?'

'I reckon he told you that.' Spog said, with a private smile. 'He met that Norman boy on the track, could give him a lift to town, so he turned the colt loose.'

Bowler had so many questions tangling in his mind he didn't know where to begin. But they'd have to wait until he could get hold of Matt himself. And he'd lent his car to bloody Macrea so he couldn't immediately set out for Edgerton to confront the slippery bastard.

'Is Matt coming back, do you know?'

Spog appeared amused, as though reading his mind and understanding his difficulties. 'Yeah, in two to three weeks. I don't know, whenever he's ready. He reckons he's going to dig a well I need, out on the scrub block.'

Two or three weeks was too damn long. Bowler hoped Ossie at the garage was busy fixing Macrea's car because he wanted his own back urgently.

So, since there was nothing he could do for the moment, Bowler stayed, discussing the weather and the state of the crops, the price of wool and the cost of shearers, until he had finished his tea.

He couldn't blame Spog in spite of the frustrating attitude he'd adopted. However misguided, he was a decent old boy who was genuinely fond of his devious great-nephew Matt.

48

The news of Agatha Benson's engagement to Aubrey Venables spread through Kularook like a bushfire before a northerly. The grapevine was always at its most vigorous on Saturdays, when so many of the farmers drove in to collect their stores and watch the footy. They collected their mail from Roger Price in the morning, and often had a drink in the pub during the afternoon.

Em, sincerely pleased for her protégée, couldn't keep such a splendid piece of news to herself, so Roger had learnt it early. By teatime not only the townspeople but almost everybody else in the surrounding district knew of the astonishing good fortune which had befallen that undeserving Benson woman.

Agatha kept out of everybody's way all day. She needed time to become accustomed to wearing Aubrey's ring. When she'd first studied it in detail she had been startled to find it was set with no fewer than five diamonds, two large and three enormous. She was self-conscious, knowing that such a bauble was far too dramatic to remain unnoticed for more than ten seconds by the seasoned observers inhabiting Kularook.

'It was my mother's,' Aubrey said, when he called in at the pub on Sunday morning. He couldn't keep away, and had visited his betrothed every few hours the day before to rejoice in his good fortune. 'I know it's old-fashioned, but I could have it reset if you like.'

'No thank you, Aubrey. I think it's beautiful as it is.'

Agatha felt embarrassed to be carrying the equivalent of a large sum of money pinned to her finger but Aubrey had been hurt when he'd found her in the kitchen and seen that she wasn't wearing the ring. Was she trying to hide her engagement? Had he done anything to offend her?

'Dear Aubrey, of course not,' she said with an affectionate smile. 'It's just too beautiful. I'm afraid to wear it.' She couldn't explain that it also made her ashamed for some reason. Perhaps her subconscious believed that she with her flawed history shouldn't be matched with its dazzling perfection.

He said, 'I hope you haven't had second thoughts since Friday.'

'No. Have you?'

The idea seemed to surprise him. Then he laughed. 'Gentlemen are not allowed second thoughts, my dear. We have to be sure before we ask our ladies. When can we be married?'

Agatha tried to hide her shock. She felt the question was too much and too soon for her to answer. Yet she had promised to marry him, so surely the time was a minor detail. She twisted the ring on her finger and light from the window sparked into her eyes. The ring was like the question: too big for comfort.

'Give me time to get used to the idea,' she said. 'Time for your sister to get used to it, too.'

Miss Venables's cold fury when she had broken up the picnic was still vivid in Agatha's mind. The woman hadn't said much, merely makeweights like 'So there you are' and 'I might have known', but the venom behind the words was unmistakable.

'We needn't regard her,' Aubrey said. Which seemed a pretty cavalier statement whichever way she looked at it.

Em bustled into the kitchen, saw them standing by the table, and halted abruptly. She said, 'Shall I go away again?' Aubrey beamed and shook his head. 'You're a lucky man, Aubrey.'

'I know it, dear lady, I know it well. A pearl beyond price.' He took Agatha's hand and stood back from her as though admiring a work of art that might escape him unless he kept it tethered.

Hot and uncomfortable under their scrutiny she flushed, then slid her hand from his and turned away.

'I've just finished squeezing this orange juice for Mr Macrea. I'd better take it to him,' she said, and went away to the small room where Ron Macrea lay in bed.

In spite of his best efforts to carry on the detective had succumbed to a raging headache and a worsening cold. His eyes burned, his throat was raw, his muscles ached and twitched. He thanked her for the juice, but after she had gone he flounced angrily about in his bed, unable to get comfortable.

He was tense with frustration. He couldn't stop worrying about his investigation; he couldn't get on with the job; his throbbing head hurt like hell and confused his thoughts. Later, when at last he did fall into a light doze, he was almost immediately jolted back to consciousness when Bowler breezed in.

He dragged his gritty eyelids open. The view did nothing to improve his mood. The sight of Bowler, disgustingly healthy and stalking to and fro in the small room, set his teeth on edge. And he could tell the beggar was pleased with himself, no doubt delighted to have the city detective confined to bed and out of his hair for a couple of days.

If Macrea didn't look out Brown would be running the investigation for him. He'd been forced to put him in his place once before, when the cocky bastard had tried to tell him his job.

He said, 'It's Sunday for God's sake. You don't have to work on a Sunday.'

Bowler came away from the window. 'You're never really off duty in my job.' He picked up an ashtray from the bedside cupboard, turned it over, put it down. 'If somebody needs me, I go.'

Self-righteous bugger. Did he think detectives worked office hours? 'If it's anything about this murder case, leave it alone. You'll only muck it up.'

'No, nothing to do with that. Alec Fielding's got a mob in and reckons he's missing some sheep. He wants me to check his tally, check the paperwork, make it official. I'll have to have a dekko.'

'Just forget about the shootings. I've taken over now.'

'Of course you have,' Bowler said, far too heartily to reassure Macrea. He straightened a picture, a steel engraving of a London street scene, on the wall. 'Of course. Though if there was anything I could follow up for you —'

'No! I'll be up and around tomorrow, I can carry on then.'

'Goodoh. I'll see you tomorrow.'

When he had gone Macrea went over this conversation in his aching head, and realised unhappily that Brown, the bastard, had only agreed on who had taken over the case; he had made no promises to leave the case alone.

49

'Agatha's got a finger-full of diamonds fit to blind you,' Bowler told his wife. 'Aubrey has popped the question. You'd better go over and wish her joy or whatever the stunt is.'

'I saw her yesterday. I was surprised he'd finally plucked up courage.' Joan was sorting some of her prints on the kitchen table. Rose leaned on the back of her chair and studied the photographs almost as closely as her mother did. 'Somehow, I never believed he'd do it.'

'Why not? Wasn't he supposed to be in hot pursuit?'

'If a man gets to his age without marriage he's not always in a hurry to change his circumstances.' Joan put two nearly identical photographs, of a frogmouth on a dead branch, side by side and cocked her head at them. 'To a man in that position too many changes can look daunting. Already he has a comfortable home, his sister to cook and clean and darn his socks — what else does he need?' She looked up into her husband's eyes, and smiled. 'Well, I mean if he's managed so long without it.'

'Without what, Mummy?' Rose asked.

'Without a wife,' Bowler said. 'But Joan, Roger thinks he might not be so deprived anyway. Perhaps *la soeur n'est pas une soeur.*'

'Your accent is vile. All the same, that's interesting.' Joan sat back, smiling faintly, and considered this. 'Why does he think that? No, tell me later. But if it's true it makes Aubrey's proposal even more surprising.' She handed one of the photographs to Rose. 'I think that's the best one. What do you think?'

Bowler said, 'So you've already seen Agatha.'

'Certainly I have. I thought she probably needed a little moral support.'

'Why moral support? Isn't he the catch of the season?'

Joan twisted her mouth. 'That depends on what you want to catch.' She stood up and began gathering up her photographs. 'Bill, do you know where Tom has gone?'

'He's ridden out to see Mott Wilson's boys. I gave him permission. Didn't he tell you?'

'He did, Mummy, I heard him.' Rose snatched up the second photograph of the frogmouth, to compare them more closely.

'I expect I was busy.' To Joan such a memory lapse was a trivial detail. 'Come on, we'd better get Daddy some lunch. I can see he's getting impatient.'

'I'll get my own if you feel like that about it,' Bowler said.

Joan's manner changed instantly. She smiled lazily and made bedroom eyes at him. 'How do you know what I feel?'

The diamonds were also in Agatha's mind, uneasily weighting her thoughts much as they weighted her finger. A smaller ring, she assured herself, wouldn't have chafed her spirits so. Her richly decorated hand was constantly catching her eye unexpectedly, constantly surprising her, constantly setting her thoughts on the step she had taken. It was done now. Why was she still going over and over her engagement in her mind, as though she was still to be asked, still to decide?

The scene in Aubrey's summer-house replayed over in her mind. She couldn't leave it alone, as though it was unfinished business.

She had done it. She had told Aubrey she would marry him, had committed herself and her future to him. Probably she was only testing the idea, trying to see how her life would run now, seeing a calm domesticity without any violent ups and downs, seeing security, seeing Cordelia safely provided for. Yet she still had an uneasy feeling that there was more to come.

Perhaps on one level, she thought restlessly, she didn't believe her luck. Or perhaps didn't believe she deserved it. For whatever reason something, subconsciously, was bothering her.

His sister's hostility made her uncomfortable, but she could understand that. No devoted sister would want her brother to marry a woman with a chequered history like hers. All the same, if her past sins didn't worry Aubrey Miss Venables' views were irrelevant, and she wasn't going to let the woman upset her.

Round and round, over and over. What was preventing her from letting go of the past and concentrating on her future? Though probably this turmoil in her thoughts was only natural. Of course any momentous decision so recently taken would still occupy her mind.

She couldn't discuss her engagement with Em, because Em was preening herself on her success as matchmaker. Confident she had seen the possibility long before either of the principals, Em believed it was her machinations alone that had then brought Aubrey's courtship to such a satisfactory conclusion. She saw only a flawless whole, the marriage of her erstwhile poor and unfortunate protégée into comfort and luxury.

Agatha wanted to examine her position more critically. She wanted to see Miriam Pedler.

She found Trotter in the closed front bar, leaning on the counter with the week's newspapers spread in front of him, in the usual aroma of beer and stale cigarette smoke.

'Trotter, could I borrow your buckboard for a couple of hours this afternoon? I'd like to go out to Pedlers'.'

He took the cigarette from his mouth and smiled on her benignly. 'Course you can, girl. I never use the thing on a Sunday.'

Agatha had forgotten the implications of Sunday. Miriam's husband and sons would be at home too, not working outdoors as they normally did. Still, it had to be today or not at all. 'I'll put some petrol in tomorrow.'

'Nah, don't bother. We've never got around to paying you wages, all the things you do for Em.'

'I get my board and keep,' she said. 'That's more than wages.'

'Don't you believe it.' Trotter went back to the racing results.

The pub's buckboard was an early T-model Ford with the back seats cut off and a small tray fitted; Trotter used it only to collect his kegs and cases from the railway station. The canvas hood had disappeared at the time of the major surgery, so the driver was exposed to whatever the weather happened to be providing at any time. Sunday was cold and windy with showers threatening. Agatha left Cordelia in Em's care and drove out to see Miriam.

The rain held off. Agatha turned the car off the track to the sheds and pulled up at the back of the house. She realised she had never been to the front door, didn't even know what the front of the house looked like since the pines hid it from the road. Just as she had never been in any of the front rooms, only the kitchen. The hearts of our farms are the kitchens, she thought.

At the foot of the slope she could see Jack Pedler and his three sons down by the horse yards working with the Clydesdales. They appeared to be breaking in a couple of young horses to work with the team, which was a stroke of luck for her, as it meant she could try to explain her unease to Miriam over cups of tea at the kitchen table without the embarrassment of the men overhearing her.

And Miriam, once she had hugged her friend and exclaimed at the diamonds, was wholly reassuring.

'It's only left-over guilt,' she said. 'Truly, Agatha, you must stop feeling guilty. Let go of the past.'

'I don't think I'll ever forget how Lew died.'

'I don't expect you will. But you don't have to remember it every waking minute.'

'It's hard not to. Something as big as that.'

'Look, this is a wonderful chance for you. A new start — you should look on it as a new start, for you and for Cordelia.'

'She will be protected now, at least,' Agatha said.

'And you.'

'You're right, most of the time I feel that I don't deserve this. And yet I'm not just using Aubrey to insure our future, you know. I do believe I can make him happy.'

'Of course you can,' Miriam said. 'Of course you can.'

Later, as Agatha was leaving, Miriam said, 'I don't know Aubrey at all. You must bring him out one afternoon.'

Agatha was startled by the idea she could 'bring' Aubrey anywhere. And yet why not? She had already decided that she must be an equal partner in this marriage.

50

On Monday Ron Macrea was still too ill to get out of bed. With total hypocrisy Bowler made sympathetic noises while in his heart he rejoiced. He still had a free hand.

After lunch he got out his car and set off for Edgerton.

It was mid-afternoon before he reached Franklins' place. The track, always a slow one, had been washed out in places by the recent rains, exposing more of the dangerous reefs of limestone lying on the surface. He'd been forced to drive long stretches in second gear.

When Bowler came within sight of Franklins' homestead, he stopped a couple of hundred yards down the track, at the foot of the hill. In spite of the many old gum trees surrounding it he could see another car parked in front. Someone else was visiting. He'd have to find some way of getting Matt on his own.

He was impatient to confront that young man. Young Matt had been lying in his pretty white teeth and Bowler was going to enjoy ramming his lies straight down his throat.

People who lied to Bowler both offended him and angered him. They must think he was stupid, or they wouldn't try, and he was deeply insulted if anyone thought he was stupid. On the other hand they wasted his time, which made him angry.

'G'day, Bowler,' said a voice from the sky. 'What can we do for you?'

He twisted his head. Matt Franklin was leaning down from the saddle of a tall chestnut horse which was backing and shifting beside the car. Over the sound of his still-running engine Bowler hadn't heard the unshod hoofs on the damp earth.

Matt gazed at him in an assessing manner. 'I expect you're looking for me.' He scratched his cheek with the small stem of green mallee he carried as a switch. Then he smiled. 'There's a mob up at the house I've been trying to avoid, so I'll meet you at the sheds. Just carry on along the track there.' The horse leapt forward into a canter, keeping to the verge, leaving the track free for the car.

The track led round the base of the hill to the heart of the working farm, the sheds and workshops, the machines and haystacks. Bowler parked in a kind of court between them. Beyond the machinery shed he could see a long brush stable and a group of Clydesdales dozing, rumps to the cold westerly wind, by a windmill and tank. Several more huge gums grew close to the sheds and flavoured the breeze with the scent of eucalyptus.

Bowler pulled his jacket collar higher and huddled down in his seat, wishing he hadn't left the side-curtains at home. The same cold westerly was blowing through his car.

Matt cantered up and dismounted. When he had turned the horse loose through a gate near the stable he walked back to where Bowler waited.

'Come into the grain shed, out of the wind.' He pushed open a wooden door. 'What brings you here?'

Bowler smelled oats, and mice. 'You. Or more accurately, the tales you've been telling me.'

Matt didn't answer. He propped himself on the stack of filled grain sacks against the back wall and watched Bowler settle himself on a smaller pile at the side. Light came through a gap between the corrugated iron walls and the roof; the floor was powdery earth flecked yellow with spilled grain. Something rustled and scurried in the corner.

Bowler said, 'Well? Are you going to revise that bloody rigmarole you told me?'

'What rigmarole?'

'You told me you walked out to your uncle's after you got off the train.'

'No I didn't, I said I went out. You were the one said I walked.'

'Don't you split hairs with me, you bastard.'

Matt smiled. 'I just didn't bother to contradict you. Actually, I borrowed a horse off Spog.'

'I know that now, no thanks to you. But I don't think you went directly to Bruce's either.'

'The problem is,' Matt said, 'You're liable to get quite the wrong idea.'

Very angry indeed, Bowler said, 'This is not a bloody party game. Murders have been committed — people have been killed, you stupid bastard — and I am trying to find out who killed them. Do you think I drove all the way down here just to fill an empty afternoon? Do you think I enjoy being lied to? At best you are hindering me in uncovering a murderer. At worst you are making me believe *you* are the murderer. I don't know what the flaming hell you think you're doing but I've had enough. Unless you give me some straight answers I'm arresting you here and now and sending you under escort to Adelaide on the next train. I'll let the blokes in town sort you out.' He snapped his mouth shut, breathing deeply and trying to get his temper under control.

Matt's amiable mood evaporated. In a hard voice he said, 'You go right ahead. D'you think you can bully me like you bullied Graham?'

As furious with himself as he was with Matt, Bowler gritted his teeth. He, who never bluffed, had just had his bluff called. Why had he made such wild statements? Still, he wasn't going to get anywhere by antagonising the bastard further.

'Look, just answer a couple of questions, will you? And truthfully, if you can manage it.'

His milder tone lowered a few of Matt's hackles. 'Depends.'

Bowler said, 'Where did you go once you'd got the horse?'

'I went out to collect my field glasses, I told you.' Matt paused, then shrugged. 'But I hadn't left them at Bruce's, I'd left them in the scrub, where I'd been cutting posts.'

No wonder he hadn't wanted to admit this. That would be the scrub that was only a couple of miles from the Benson house.

'What time was this?'

'As fast as I could get there on horseback after I'd got off the train. Before sunrise, anyway. I'd left a whole pile of stuff there, the axe and whetstone, my coat, Aunt Cora's billy, the glasses hanging on a tree, completely forgotten them. Well, I was pretty steamed up after bloody Lew and the others had had a go at me. I needed the coat and the glasses, and I wanted to return the other things before I went north.'

'And when you'd got them, which way did you go?'

'Back to Bruce's through the scrub, the same way I'd been riding while I was post cutting. There's an easy way along that new fence-line they've ploughed provided you watch for the empty post-holes — they're a bit dangerous for horses. Then a track leads to the homestead. I left the stuff on the side veranda without anyone seeing me and rode on to the hut. And went to sleep. I told you all that.'

'You had time to ride back to Bensons' during the afternoon.'

'So did a lot of other people and like them, I didn't. Why are you so bloody sure it wasn't Lew? Everyone else thinks it was.'

'Several reasons. But it seems unlikely now, since somebody took another potshot at Agatha —'

Matt jerked upright, his fists clenched. 'Shot at Agatha? What —?'

'— last week. Don't worry, she wasn't hit. But Lew didn't fire those shots.'

'What happened, is she —?'

'Didn't you hear about that? Somebody fired twice through the pub kitchen window, no idea who. Missed her, though.' If Matt was acting surprise he was pretty good at it. But the rest of his story . . .

Bowler didn't know what to think. He believed it as far as it went, but there was that long gap in the afternoon when the young man claimed he was asleep and Bowler wasn't sure what he believed about that. The young pest had time and enough to ride back to Bensons' and still meet his mate on the track when he said he did.

Urgently Matt said, 'What are you doing to protect her? Is she somewhere safe?'

'A couple of us are watching. Nobody gets close to the pub at night any more, not without me knowing it.'

'Why, for God's sake? Why?'

'I think someone believes she knows more than she does. It was only after I talked to her that I began looking for a different murderer. I think someone is afraid Agatha saw more than she did, that afternoon on the farm.'

'Count on me, I'll help keep an eye on her.'

'Not sure if I should,' Bowler said, and was rewarded by the rising fury in Matt Franklin's face. A new thought occurred to him. Deliberately he added, 'Though I might get Venables to help, now she's engaged to him.'

Matt went still. He almost stopped breathing.

After a moment he said, 'She's not.'

'She got a massive great diamond ring from her fairy godmother, then.'

'No. Not to that gutless wonder.'

'Sorry, mate.' Bowler now was slightly ashamed of himself. He'd been angry, but tossing that news at Matt so abruptly was a dirty trick. He didn't like to think he was quite so spiteful.

'All right,' Matt said, purposeful, now snapping out of his shock. 'You can give me a lift back to Kularook. Give me five minutes to get my gear.' He turned a stony face to the policeman. 'That's the bloody least you can do.'

'I don't know. What sort of strife are you planning? Do you want to upset Agatha? Thump Aubrey?'

'I'd be afraid to thump Aubrey. My fist might go straight through him. No —'

'Why do you want to come then?'

'Don't be stupid. I want to talk to Agatha, that's all.'

'Good intentions aren't always enough,' Bowler said.

Matt looked him in the eye. 'I am not a murderer, you pig-headed bloody copper. Why the hell can't you get it into you thick skull I'm on your side? Some bugger shot Agatha, and if I knew who he was I'd take him apart with my bare hands.'

His words hit Bowler with unexpected force, and carried complete conviction. Abruptly, like a conversion to a new faith, he knew Matt had not committed the murders, was not trying to hide anything, was merely trying — as any man might — to keep his affairs to himself. Much as Bowler would have done in his shoes.

'Go and get your traps. I'll wait.' He'd misjudged him. He owed him a lift.

Matt ran up the slope towards the house, leaving Bowler to reflect that, after the hours he'd spent constructing a case against him, now he'd have to dismantle it and convince Macrea that the evidence against this young man was irrelevant.

Which left him with Dick as prime suspect. And how did he feel about that?

51

The pub kitchen was warm and mostly dark, lit only by a small lamp on the table in front of Agatha where she stood washing up the dinner dishes. Not many dishes, as the bedridden Macrea was the only house guest. For once Em was off duty, playing cribbage with Trotter in the empty lounge.

Agatha slopped the dishrag against a plate. She had recovered from her alarm at the idea of an early wedding, had faced that, had accepted that. She was wearing his ring — well, when she didn't have her hands in washing-up water she was wearing his ring — and she was permitting Em to tell the world of her engagement.

She'd had three days to get used to the idea. She shouldn't be feeling unsettled still. She propped a plate on a teacup on the draining tray and reached into the bowl for the next.

The wire door at the end of the passage closed and light footfalls approached the kitchen. Agatha thought it was probably Durwin, until she remembered he had gone home as soon as he'd finished the milking.

The back door! Like an electric shock knowledge exploded in her brain. Not bolted!

Terror seized her, heart and mind. Who was coming? Would a rifle come poking round the door jamb?

Even as these thoughts raced through her mind she saw the gate to the cellar steps was ajar and in two fast strides she was halfway there.

'There you are, you bitch,' Miss Venables said.

Her hands were empty.

Agatha stopped in her tracks and sucked in a huge breath of air. Her heartbeats slowed. She walked back to the table, into the light.

Arms akimbo, Miss Venables stood and stared at her, studied her face and her figure, her clothes and her hair, with slow and insulting thoroughness.

'Get your claws out of Aubrey.' The woman's voice was gritty with loathing and the intensity of her emotion. Her hair, normally neatly waved, frizzed out in an untidy tangle round her head.

Agatha wasn't going to argue with her. That was probably what she wanted, a nice vulgar slanging match. Well, it took two to play that game. What a nerve the woman had, bursting in like this, abusive, issuing demands. What right had she to interfere? Her brother was surely entitled to make his own choices without reference to her.

Her furious descent on the picnic had been bad enough, but this was worse. She was carrying on as though she was the one who'd been insulted.

Miss Venables eyes narrowed. 'I can't imagine what he sees in you. Skinny and sallow, that's what you are, Bitch.'

Unable to deny these charges, Agatha took up her tea towel to have something to do with her hands. She couldn't stand passively under an attack like this but she couldn't think how to counter it. Or how to shut the unpleasant woman up, or how to get rid of her.

Planting her fists on the opposite side of the table Miss Venables leant her face to within a foot of Agatha's. 'If you don't leave him alone, you'll be sorry. I'll make you sorry, Bitch. Understand?'

Agatha's hands moved routinely, drying the plates, while she looked steadily into those angry eyes.

Her silence only enraged her visitor further. 'You stuck up whore,'

The Fifth Bullet

Miss Venables hissed. 'Answer me!'

Agatha set down a dry plate on the stack, picked up a wet one. Miss Venables seized the top plate and hurled it against the cast-iron front of the wood stove. It smashed loudly and comprehensively. Chips of china flew in all directions.

'Hey!' Agatha flung down the towel and rushed round the table to protect the rest of the crockery from this lunatic just as the mad woman reached past her, snatched something from the table, and ran from the room. The back door slammed.

Em hurried in. 'Is everything all right?'

Agatha was shaking, her guts knotted. 'I think we forgot to lock the back door. Miss Venables came.'

'What on earth did she want?' Em stared in surprise at the mess of china chips in front of the stove. 'Did she smash that plate?'

'To tell me hands off Aubrey. She was very strange.' Agatha looked at the table-top. What had the woman taken?

Em went out to lock the door. She was away several minutes, and when she returned she said, 'Your other beau is here. He wants — What's the matter?'

Agatha said incredulously, 'That mad woman has stolen my ring.'

'Stolen? She can't have.' Em sounded as disbelieving as Agatha felt.

'I'd taken it off while I was washing up. It was on the table there, just beside the bowl. She grabbed it and ran. So now what do I do?'

'You'll have to go and tell Aubrey.'

'I can't go anywhere after dark without Bowler's permission. Anyway, she might be lurking.' Although Miss Venables had used only words to attack her, Agatha felt she was so unbalanced she might resort to physical violence next.

'You'd better phone him then. Immediately. Before his sister has time to lose the ring.'

'Do they have the phone on? Yes. Yes, I'll do that.' An unwelcome thought occurred to her. 'Em, that was her mother's ring. Perhaps it belonged to her, and not to Aubrey. Perhaps he had no right to give it to me.'

'You'll still have to tell Aubrey, so he knows where it is. And when you've finished with him, someone else wants a word with you. Though I tried to put him off I had to say I'd ask you. Matt Franklin is outside.'

'Damn Matt. I don't want to talk to him.' Agatha pressed her palms to her temples. 'That damn ring must be worth a fortune and the mood she's in that woman could do anything with it. Throw it in the nearest rubbish pit, drop it down a well, anything to spite me. I wish I'd stuck to my guns when Aubrey gave it to me, but I couldn't convince him I'd rather not wear such a fearfully valuable thing. And you can tell Snow to get lost.'

52

Soon after breakfast next morning Agatha walked round to visit Aubrey in person. She came back in a sombre mood, and in answer to Em's questions said shortly that Miss Venables still, presumably, had the ring. She had charged in the night before and gone straight to her room, locking the door behind her, and had emerged this morning without the ring, refusing to say where it was. Yes, Aubrey was most upset.

Em, unable to elicit any more information from her, went out to the laundry. Agatha seized the broom and began sweeping the kitchen floor, pushing the broom with hard short strokes, bending the bristles, thumping it down.

A voice from the doorway said, 'You're at it again.'

Snow was propped against the doorframe, hands in his pockets, watching her.

She straightened, scowling, pulling the broom handle to vertical in front of her as though to shelter behind it. 'What? What do you want?' She felt defensive. After the stormy emotional weather she'd experienced at Aubrey's that morning she felt too drained to for a passage at arms with Snow. He took altogether too much for granted.

He shook his head. 'You're not safe running around loose. Tell me, just for the record, what weird kind of standards do you use when you judge a bloke?'

This was about Aubrey, she thought resentfully. She might have known how it would be once Snow heard of the engagement. 'That's nothing to do with you.'

'I'm curious, that's all. The workings of your mind are beyond me.'

'Fine by me.' She turned her back and resumed sweeping, hoping he'd get the message she didn't want to talk to him. Hoping he would go away.

'Hey!' he said. 'I'm a friend, remember?'

She paused, but didn't turn. He certainly had done his best to befriend her, in the weeks leading up to the shooting. He'd lent her the books and, although she'd been on edge during their brief meetings, his obvious pleasure in her company had restored a tiny amount of her self-esteem. It wasn't his fault she was so tightly wound she could scream. 'This is none of your damn business. I don't want to talk about it.'

'But I do. And you can't get out of it, because you're not the only one involved in this. You knew damn well that I was only giving you time to get your breath before I asked you myself. To marry me, I mean.'

'Now wait a minute.' This time she did face him, this big, serious young man regarding her steadily from the doorway. 'I didn't know that. And don't you go all indignant on me, I hadn't the foggiest idea of your intentions. You might have wanted a mistress, you might have wanted a casual roll in the hay. That's the usual reaction from men who know my history.'

'Has some bastard been putting the hard word on you? Tell me who and I'll knock his block off.'

She shook her head impatiently. 'It's over now. Forget it.'

'You can't have believed that's all I wanted.'

'Even if I didn't, you're a bit sure of yourself if you imagined I'd automatically say yes.'

He twitched his shoulders. 'Of course I didn't expect that. But I did expect a bit of time to try and persuade you. And I don't care what you say, you must have known that.'

'Well I didn't. And what's more —'

'All right, forget about me for the moment. Why don't you take a long hard look at bloody Aubrey?'

'I have, and he's —'

'You can't have, or you wouldn't be letting yourself in for such a disaster. Aubrey's a self-indulgent fool who imagines his money can buy his dreams. For God's sake, the man's a perpetual adolescent. He fantasises about a farm and imagines he can conjure one up in a couple of years out of a scrub block that's more limestone than soil, and all without dirtying his hands or raising a sweat. He's an idiot.'

Agatha said, 'He is not. It's just you don't like him.'

He tilted a hand. 'I can take him or leave him.' His tone changed. 'Where's your ring? Bowler said you were loaded with diamonds.'

'They're with Aubrey. And this isn't about him, is it. It's about you. You're jealous, so damn jealous you can't see straight.' She wished he would go away, just go away and leave her in peace.

'Jealous or not, I can see a bloody sight straighter than you do.'

The broom handle clattered to the floor; she covered her face with her hands. 'Can you? I doubt it. Now go away.' Her voice was strained, and partly muffled. She couldn't take any more. 'Just go away.'

'Look, I didn't mean —'

Her endurance cracked. 'Go away!' she shrieked. His presence, his criticisms, were too much; she didn't want to argue, she didn't want to discuss anything. 'Go away! Go away! Go away!'

'All right! All right! But —'

Em rushed into the room, shoving him aside so strongly that he staggered a few steps into the room. Fiercely she demanded, 'What have you been saying to her? What have you been doing to upset her?' She wrapped her arms round Agatha, who hid her face on her shoulder.

'Trying to get her to change her mind. What did you expect?'

Em said, 'You ought to have more sense. You should have stayed away.'

'No I shouldn't. All right, I'm going now, but I'll be back.'

'We'll see about that,' Em said.

53

Furious with Agatha, furious with Aubrey Venables, furious with himself, Matt charged towards the back door of the pub. He skidded to a halt when he found himself face to face with Macrea in the doorway.

'Franklin? I want a word with you.'

The detective, although his head was still thick, had dragged himself out of bed to continue his investigations. He had to keep ahead of that bastard Brown, who hadn't wanted to tell him where to find this particular suspect. Trying to sabotage the inquiries, without a doubt, trying to make him look a fool. He'd been forced to lay down the law in no uncertain manner before Brown would tell him that Franklin was not only back in Kularook but actually in the pub at that moment. He said brusquely, 'Come on up to the lounge.'

'Who the devil do you think you are?'

'Detective-Sergeant Macrea. I want —'

'Some other time,' Matt said, and pushed roughly past him. The wire door crashed shut behind him.

As soon as Macrea had got over his surprise, he went after him. He got to the street just in time to see Spog's bay colt disappear round the corner at a fast canter. And when the detective crossed the street to the police station, to try and galvanise Bowler into joining him in the chase, he got no help.

Bowler said, 'He's not absconding. He's staying with his uncle, and we can find him any time we like. But not now. Later.'

'I don't like his attitude.' Macrea mopped his nose. He didn't like Brown's attitude either: the man was altogether too sure of himself, too patronising. 'He seems to think he can choose his own time to talk to us.'

'I'll take you out there this afternoon,' Bowler promised. He lifted his heavy rifle from the top of a cupboard. 'Now I've got to go out to Davidsons'. A stray dog, harassing sheep, it's already killed one. Sorry, but I'll need the car. Do you want to come too?'

'No. I've got to get some kind of a statement from Thompson so I can either charge him with murder or let him go. You can't keep him on bail forever.'

'I'll keep him as long as I need. If you decide you can't charge him with the murders, then I'll arrange for a hearing on what I've charged him with already. Whether or not he shot the Bensons, don't forget he very nearly shot me. And in case you're wondering, I consider that a crime even if you don't.'

Macrea smiled thinly. 'I'll use this office, if that's all right.'

Surprised that the detective thought he even had to ask, Bowler said, 'Of course it is. Any time. Here's his phone number. I've got him lined up to come in whenever you ring.' He turned to go, then halted, irresolute.

He had the sudden feeling that he should be telling Macrea some piece of information. Something he had heard in the last couple of days niggled in his mind, something he should sort out, and pass on. But he couldn't think what it was, who had told him, why he felt it had relevance.

He shrugged, and went out to his car.

When Bowler returned in the late afternoon they drove out to Spog's place, but neither Matt nor his uncle was at home. They walked through the unlocked house and checked the four sheds. Six black hens rushed to the wire of their yard and stood, necks bobbing, eyes peering about hopefully for food, as they walked back to the car.

Bowler tried to reassure Macrea. 'They haven't gone far. This is a farm. Not many farmers are home at this time of day. They'll be working out in the paddocks somewhere.'

'Stop telling me the obvious,' Macrea said angrily. 'I know it's a farm. What I don't know is how you can be so sure that Franklin hasn't decamped.'

'Why would he? He knows I don't suspect him of any part in the shootings now.

'*You* don't — what about me? He hasn't satisfied me by a long chalk.'

'Well, he doesn't know that,' Bowler said reasonably. 'He's still around. Look, that's Splinter's place over there, the house with the mallees around it. How did you get on with Dick? I'll take you over so you can have a word with his family as well, if you like.' He trod on the self-starter; the engine fired. 'I'll be interested to know what you make of that lot.'

Macrea grunted. Brown might be interested, but Macrea doubted if he would tell him.

54

Trotter put both fists on the bar and leaned towards the little man. 'I'm not serving you, Gallagher. I don't like the colour of your money. Get lost.'

'He's with me,' Harry Wilson said. 'I'll keep him in order.' Harry only visited the pub when he came into town without his wife. Mrs Harry was one of the town's leading wowsers and regarded strong drink with frequently proclaimed abhorrence.

'How?' Trotter demanded. 'The man's a menace, fighting drunk after two beers.'

'He's working for me. I'll watch him. Pull him a beer, Trotter, and one for me.'

'Put in a slug of arsenic while you're about it,' growled a voice from the other end of the bar. 'Do the town a favour.'

Rupe Benson, for only the third time Trotter could remember, was lined up with the rest of his customers. He had a Gladstone bag at his feet and was making his beer last, filling in half an hour until train-time. He turned, holding his schooner glass, and gave Harry an unfriendly stare.

Beside him Figgy said, 'Who's the little bloke? What's he done to you?'

'Don't wind him up,' Trotter said. Jockey Gallagher had grabbed his beer and was casting murderous glances at Rupe over the rim as he gulped it down.

'Worked for us once,' Rupe explained to his father-in-law. 'Lazy thieving beggar. Lew threw him off the place.'

Bowler was watching from the doorway leading to the entrance hall. He'd come into the bar looking for Macrea to tell him that his car had been fixed, and stayed to see what Jockey was up to. He noticed the irritating little sod, for all his truculent manner, was keeping on the far side of Harry.

Harry said, 'He does all right by me.'

Rupe put his glass on the bar. 'Lucky you. Come on Figgy, drive me to the station. I've got a train to catch.'

As they were leaving Bowler saw Jockey lean on the bar and thrust a foot backwards to trip Rupe. He said, 'Go ahead, Gallagher. Always room for one more in the lockup.'

The small man adjusted his weight and withdrew his foot. Bowler said, 'Harry, if you buy him beer Gallagher's your problem. I'm not going far — if he starts any strife Trotter only has to yell.'

'There's no need for threats,' Harry said. 'I'm taking him home in a minute.'

Macrea wasn't in the lounge, the dining-room, or the kitchen. There he found Em. She'd covered the table with a grey blanket spread with an old sheet and was working on the pub's constant backlog of ironing. A basket of damp, tightly-rolled washing lay at her feet.

'Macrea went across to the store with Agatha, to carry her basket,' Em said. 'I think he wants to buy a paper, too.'

'Well, tell him his car's fixed, Ossie says he can pick it up any time. Good as new, he says, if not better. Em, what's that brown horse doing in your yards? I saw it when I fed mine this morning.'

Em carried her boat-shaped iron to the stove, put it beside two others on the hot surface, unclipped the handle, clipped it to another; she rubbed the sole over a clump of rags to ensure it hadn't collected grime from the stove; then she thumped it down on a heavily starched damask table-napkin.

'That's old Spog Wilson's buggy horse,' she said. 'He always leaves it with us when he goes away.' The fire in the stove was burning fiercely, the job was hard work; in spite of the cold, she was sweating.

Frowning, Bowler said, 'Leaves it with you?'

'Leaves his buggy here when he drives in for the train. He went to town yesterday.'

'I'd forgotten he doesn't have a car. I wonder why he went.'

'No idea.' Em shook her head. 'Matt Franklin went with him.'

'Matt did? For heaven's sake don't tell Macrea. He'll think the beggar's absconding again.'

'Too late. What's more, he blames you. Macrea says if you'd helped him chase after Matt yesterday morning you'd have got him before he caught the train.'

Alarmed, Bowler said, 'He hasn't put out an alert in town, has he? To arrest him?'

'You'd better ask him.'

'Oh well, he'll simmer down when Matt comes back.'

'I don't think he is coming back,' Em said. When Bowler exclaimed she added, 'You'll have to ask Agatha that one.' Quickly she said, 'No, don't. Not yet. She's furious with him. I was at the clothesline, and I couldn't help overhearing them when Matt was unharnessing the horse, before he caught the train. But by the time she'd finished with him he was as furious as she was. It's a wonder he didn't murder her then and there.'

'That sounds as though you're sorry for him.'

She shrugged. 'I suppose so. A bit. He's carried a torch for her for years, and now he's lost out for the second time. It's a bit much when she yells abuse at him as well.' She smiled. 'He's an engaging young devil when he isn't blazing mad.'

The overnight gale was blowing itself out when Bowler went to feed his three horses next morning. The clouds scudding across the heavens were mostly white, not grey.

Tom's little mare seemed to be settling down well. When he looked across the road he saw that Spog's brown buggy horse had disappeared. The old boy must have come home on the Melbourne Express, which reached Kularook about midnight.

Durwin, in his old army greatcoat, was carrying a shining metal bucket towards the cowshed. Bowler called a cheery good morning but the handyman plodded on without turning his head. Sulky bastard, Bowler thought, conveniently forgetting what Joan said about his own capacity for carrying grudges.

Next he approached Macrea, who was breakfasting in the pub dining-room. The detective said no, he hadn't asked anyone in Adelaide to arrest Matt Franklin. He was trusting to Bowler's assurances and expected to see the young man shortly, on his return to Kularook. With a confidence he was far from feeling, Bowler agreed.

'How did you get on with Dick yesterday?'

'I haven't finished with him yet. I'll tell you when I'm convinced enough to charge him. And now I have my car there's others I want to see, too. There's plenty to do before I can see my way clear.'

Bowler said, 'Anything I can do, let me know.'

55

Bowler was heading for the back door of the pub when Em, standing at the stove, beckoned him into the kitchen. The room was full of breakfast smells, wood smoke overlaid by frying bacon and toasting bread.

'I'm worried about Agatha,' she said.

He lowered his voice. 'Where is she?'

'She's gone. Here, read that.' She held out a crumpled piece of paper which she removed from her apron pocket without taking her attention from the frying pan.

On a page from a ruled writing-block he read: *Dear Mrs Musgrave, Everyone blames me for driving Lew to murder. I will never fit in here. It is time I left. Aggie.*

He stood, trying to make sense of the note. 'She's really gone?'

'Her room's empty, her things have gone. But it's a funny message. She never calls me anything but Em, and you know her views if anyone calls her Aggie. All the same, I know it's her writing.'

'Yes it is.' He'd become familiar with Agatha's handwriting when she was convalescing in Adelaide after the shooting, and Joan was sending her regular bulletins on Cordelia's health and well being. Agatha had always answered these letters promptly and gratefully. 'But the rest of it . . .' He frowned.

'Oh, I've heard her say that, or something very like it. I thought she'd got over it, that's all.'

'But Em, why would she go now? She's just got engaged to Aubrey, you'd think she'd be happy to stay. She is making a new start.'

Shaking her head Em said, 'Yes, I must explain about that. Hang on while I take these breakfasts to the dining room.' Quickly and neatly she slid bacon and eggs to three plates, filled two racks with toast, loaded a large tray, and headed out the door. 'Back in a tick.'

When she returned she seated herself at the table and waved him into a chair opposite. 'Agatha made me swear I wouldn't tell anyone, but in view of what's happened I think you'd better know, Bowler. Last night she was so miserable and upset she finally admitted to me that she had broken off the engagement the day before, on Tuesday morning. She wouldn't say why, just that she had.'

'Hell, that was quick. Just about a world record, I'd say.'

'Don't joke. She was deeply depressed about the whole thing. I don't know whether that batty sister had anything to do with it.'

Bowler read the note again. 'Yes, she sounds depressed. What do you mean about the batty sister?'

Em recounted what she knew of Miss Venables's visit to Agatha on Monday evening, and the theft of the ring. 'I suppose that sort of spitefulness might upset her enough so she'd want to get out of the engagement and go away. All the same, something's not right.'

Perhaps Agatha had discovered the truth of what he and the postmaster suspected, that 'Miss Venables' was not Aubrey's sister. If she had found that the man she had agreed to marry possessed a mistress already installed in his household, that could very well have induced Agatha to break off the engagement. And made her feel miserable afterwards, at the betrayal of her trust, at the loss of her hopes.

Bowler realised Em was still talking. '. . . if she'd written, "Dear Em, thanks for your help but I have to go, etcetera etcetera" I'd feel happier about it. "Mrs Musgrave" indeed. Or if she'd signed it properly. What could possibly have made her sign a nickname she detests?'

He shook his head.

'Bowler, can you find out where's she's gone? She's got no family, very few friends. I can't imagine how she will manage.'

He said, 'I'll do my best. But she's of age. My mob won't search for her.'

'At least ask at the station and see which way she went. She left in the night so most likely she caught the Adelaide Express, but she could have taken the Melbourne train if she'd wanted to.'

Trotter came in and went to the stove to pour himself a cup of tea from the large enamel teapot on the hob beside it. 'How does the letter strike you, Bowler?' he asked. 'Emmie's all worked up about it, but it seems pretty straightforward to me. This tea tastes like tar,' he added. 'How long's it been there?'

'Can I show it to Joan? Tell her?'

Em waved her hand. 'Yes of course.' She got to her feet and began making a fresh pot of tea.

He nearly missed Joan. Riding Isma, with her camera bag slung on her back, she had just turned out of their yard into the side street; she reined in when she saw him. They met in the road.

Joan listened, and read the note attentively. Slowly her expression darkened with concern. She said, 'Something was seriously wrong when Agatha wrote that message.'

'Em's worried, too.'

'Perhaps a breakdown.' Joan held the reins in one hand, the letter in the other while she studied it. Isma stamped sideways, and tossed his head against the bit; she controlled him with unconscious ease. 'It might be that. She could be so disgusted with herself for some reason that she believes she shouldn't be familiar with Em, and the hated nickname is all she deserves — some cockeyed reasoning like that. If so, she's ill. Otherwise someone else dictated it. Either way she needs help.' She handed the letter back to him. 'You'd better make a few enquiries, Bill.'

'Someone else dictated it' — at those words Bowler had to repress a shiver. He hadn't even considered that the unknown gunman might have had a hand in Agatha's disappearance, and he should have. But he didn't want to alarm Joan.

'You put everything so clearly,' he said lightly. 'What would I do without you?'

She grinned, and leaned from the saddle to dab a swift kiss on his lips. Then she urged Isma forward. The sound of trotting hoofs receded up the street.

Bowler went back into the pub, to look for himself at Agatha's room. He needed to sort out his thoughts, too. He was glad Em was too busy in the kitchen to come and supervise him.

In the bedroom, the window was still solidly boarded up. The bedclothes were thrown back on the bed as they would be on any morning, without any signs of outside interference; so were the blankets in the cot. The dressing-table was bare, its drawers empty. The door of the narrow wardrobe hung ajar on half-a-dozen empty coat-hangers. Everything looked as normal as it would do if Agatha had packed up in the night and left, taking her baby with her.

He'd better walk over to the station, and check which train she'd taken.

56

Spog's bay colt was tied by the reins to the pub gatepost and Matt Franklin was in the kitchen conferring with Em when Bowler returned.

So Em had been mistaken. He hadn't stayed away. Bowler, relieved that at least he wouldn't have to make excuses to Macrea, nodded to him. To Em he said, 'A long shot, but I checked with Aubrey too, in case she'd gone to him for refuge. Neither he nor,' he hesitated, 'nor his sister has seen her since Tuesday morning.'

He wasn't going to tell them what 'Miss Venables' had said when he asked politely if they'd seen Agatha. In a perfect passion of rage she had said, 'That woman in this house? I'd claw her eyes out. I have lived with that man for sixteen years — lived a lie. I have given up my family, all hope of a normal life, of making friends or having children, for him. And then he proposes to provide for me by finding me a job as housekeeper-nurse to an invalid cousin of his so that he can marry some whore who's caught his eye. Can you imagine what that job would be like? And I'm supposed to be grateful. I would kill myself first.'

At his most formal — he didn't like to hear Agatha called opprobrious names — Bowler said, 'Did you tell Mrs Benson of your relationship with Aubrey Venables?'

'Of course I did. That took her down a peg or two, I must say, and a good job too. And him. No wedding bells for him now, the two-faced bastard, she very smartly told him it was all off. And now he's furious and says I have to go. I'm not going to take that lying down, I can tell you. Because it's all her fault, that harpy. She bewitched him.'

So he knew the truth now. He'd tell Joan of course, but nobody else. He'd rather admired 'Miss Venables' in her justifiable wrath, and there were too many gossips in this town to —

'Hey!' Matt held out his hand, waggling it impatiently. 'Can I see that note?' Bowler woke up and handed it to him. He read it twice, swore violently, apologised to Em, then handed it back. He looked blank with shock, as though he'd been sandbagged. 'She's in trouble,' he said.

'What are you going to do?' Em asked.

'Do?' Matt still looked dazed. 'Find her. We must find her, she's in trouble. I think she was forced to write that. She must have been, and she used the wrong names so we'd know.' He walked to the door, turned, came back, walked to a window. Bowler knew how he felt, wanting action yet not knowing where to begin.

'Joan thought she'd been made to write it, too.' Bowler added, 'And whatever trouble she's in, we mustn't forget Cordelia is in it with her.'

Swinging round, Matt said, 'She didn't catch a train, did she?'

'Not to Melbourne. But the later train — the station master isn't certain. She didn't buy a ticket, and he didn't see her, but she could have slipped aboard at the last minute when he was talking to the guard, and then bought her ticket on the train.'

'I don't think she did. The beds have been slept in. Why would she go to bed if she was waiting for a train?'

Bowler hadn't stopped to listen. He'd headed for the front of the pub and was going through the building systematically, bedroom by bedroom, window by window, looking for a place where someone could have broken in. The doors hadn't been tampered with; he could find nothing.

He ran out the back door to check from the outside. On the side veranda the wooden trapdoor to the cellars under the bar looked secure. But then he saw a pale yellow splinter at the edge of one of the planks across it.

He knelt to inspect it more closely. The hinged wooden cover was pretty roughly made and had warped. Someone had prised a plank up, to get a hand inside and slide the bolt open, and then pushed the plank into place again, hoping no doubt to hide all sign of a forced entry.

That opening had been designed for barrels, not people, but where a beer-barrel could go, so could a person.

Bowler got to his feet and dusted his knees. An explosion of blasphemy filled his head. His guilt was twisting his heart like a tourniquet. He'd believed he'd made Agatha and her baby safe, and he had not. They had trusted him. He closed his eyes.

Matt was standing over him. In a voice that creaked with strain he said, 'That was forced? Well, that proves it.'

'Yes it does.' Bowler stared at the wooden square. There was something he should remember.

'Where do we start?'

We? thought Bowler. This was his job. However he felt, he had to try and find her. He knew it was too late, but he must find her. But perhaps he could do with help.

He'd trust Matt ahead of Macrea any day. Not because he believed the latter was anything but a good detective and a good policeman — he was demonstrably good at his job — he just didn't believe that he and Macrea could cooperate efficiently in a search like this. Cross-purposes he could do without.

To Matt he said, 'Ask Em and Trotter if they have any idea when this happened, what time of night. Can they remember any unusual noises, anything, after they went to bed. Whoever it was would have come up from the cellar into the bar, and their bedroom is the only one he had to pass to get to Agatha's. Though it's unlikely they heard a thing, with all that wind we had last night. When you've done that come over to my office and we'll think where to go from there.'

He wanted to re-read some of his notes. There was something niggling at the back of his mind, some small detail he was overlooking. Whoever had abducted Agatha it wasn't likely to be Dick, watched over with an eagle eye by his mother, or Miss Venables. He'd checked on her, and anyway, she had no reason for jealousy now the engagement was broken.

He was pretty sure he was looking for someone else.

57

By the time Matt arrived, Bowler had his desk covered in papers, from the copy of his report to Adelaide — several sheets of hand-written notes held neatly together with a paper clip — to odd-shaped scribbled-on fragments torn from his jotter. He scowled at them. They hadn't told him a thing.

'Musgraves didn't hear anything,' Matt said.

'Didn't really expect them to, but we had to ask. All the same, I'd guess it happened before three in the morning. It was arranged to look as though she'd caught the train, left of her own free will, and that's about when the Adelaide Express leaves. We weren't supposed to start asking questions so soon.'

'Not soon enough!' Matt exploded. 'She could alert us, but not soon enough!'

'She did her best, her intelligent best.' What had happened to all that intellect now? 'Have you put your horse away? Come on.' Bowler swept the papers into a heap and jumped from his chair. Action was what he needed, anything to keep his mind off his guilt, his heavy load of dread. He was halfway down the passage to the back door before Matt caught up with him.

'Get a move on, he's had her for hours. I wish I knew who the bastard is.'

Matt said in a flat voice, 'She could be dead a dozen times by now. Where the devil do we start?' He scrambled into the car seconds before Bowler took off, grabbing at the top of the door to keep his balance as the car swerved into the road.

'We start by checking if Dick Thompson was accounted for all night.'

But after a wild careering drive out to Splinter's place Shirl was able to convince them that Dick hadn't strayed. His bed was in a sleep-out; he'd have to pass through her room to go out. Anyway, she said, he'd had a few beers before he turned in and had kept her awake by snoring all night.

Bowler drove back into Kularook. 'Now we start knocking on every door in town and finding out if anyone heard a car in the night.'

'Why a car? He could have just walked her off —' Matt put his head in his hands.

'No, he's trying to maintain the fiction that she has left of her own accord. So he'll take her somewhere away from town. I expect he'd already picked the spot.'

Without lifting his head Matt said, 'You mean somewhere he can bury her and she'll never be found.'

'Yes.' Bowler glanced at him. Though the young man hadn't been toughened by war — that grim training school where men learned to suppress grief, and rage, and guilt, so that they could get on with the job in hand — he was tough enough, it seemed, to face appalling facts squarely. 'So I believe he'd need a car. He didn't drive up to the pub or I'd have heard; we get so few cars after dark they always wake me. But he can't have left it far away. Someone might have heard which direction it was heading when it left. We'll start with good old busybody Roger.'

But Roger couldn't help them. They left Bowler's car there and walked to all the nearer houses. They went back for the car. They knocked on more doors, asked more people. Nobody had heard a car in the night. Both men became monosyllabic, their tempers wound tighter and tighter as their frustrations grew. The morning was advancing and they still had no lead.

Matt turned on Bowler. 'Haven't you any idea who it could be? Isn't that your job, tracking down criminals?'

'Keep your hair on. Yes it is, and no it isn't. I'm not a detective. It's really more Macrea's job than mine. But it was a cold trail before anyone thought of murder.'

'Surely to God you've got *some* suspicions.'

'I did have. I thought it was you, didn't I? Then I thought it was Dick. It's almost certainly the same man who shot Lew and the rest. Do you know anyone else with a grudge against the Bensons?'

'Uncle Bruce doesn't love them much. No, forget I said that, I'm not serious. What about this bloke Agatha ran off with? Could he —'

'Unlikely. He abandoned her. There's no reason why he would now hunt her up and start shooting.'

'A neighbour, then. Jack Pedler's got a short fuse, they could have got under his skin somehow.'

'There's another neighbour with a short fuse. Another of your uncles, Harry Wilson.'

'Oh hell. I give up.'

They were heading out for the schoolmaster's house, next to the school on the edge of town, when they saw a horse and rider approaching fast, galloping hard towards them on the soft dirt beside the metalled road, throwing up clods in their wake.

Bowler exclaimed, 'That's Joan!'

What the hell was going on? He drove on to the verge, stopped the car, and scrambled out.

'Bill!' She hauled Isma to his haunches and almost fell from her saddle into her husband's arms. He held her tightly; she was trembling, from fatigue or emotion. 'Bill, I was coming for you. I found Agatha's clothes, buried, someone's been trying to hide them and —'

'Take it easy,' Bowler said with reassuring calm. He led her to the car and seated her on the running board while he knelt in front of her, holding her hands. Isma, blowing hard, stood with lowered head behind him.

'A dog or a fox had started digging them up,' Joan said. She bit her lips to stop them shaking. 'I recognised her things. What's happened, Bill?'

'She's been abducted. We think our murderer has taken her. Darling, where was this?'

'The Government Reserve well, out there in the scrub.' She waved her arm vaguely towards the north. 'I go there for birds.'

'I know the place.' Matt was crouched beside Bowler, listening to every word. 'Where did you see —?'

'In the corner of an old sheep yard, over near the mallees.' Joan glanced at Matt, then looked steadily into her husband's eyes. 'I heard a shot,' she said. 'A fair distance off to the north of where I was, but unmistakable.' He heard Matt suck in his breath.

'How long ago?'

'However long it has taken me to ride in. Not much more than an hour — I've been hurrying.'

'We'll go and look,' he said.

'He's armed, Bill.'

'So I will be too. Darling, we'll be careful.'

'There's two of us,' Matt said.

'See? Now you go home and don't worry. Try and reassure Em if you can. I don't know how long we'll be.' He stood, and pulled her up after him. When he had tossed her into her saddle he said, 'You'd better tell Macrea what's going on, if you can find him. Apologise from me, if you like. I should have told him before we left but I couldn't see his car and we didn't have time to hunt him up.'

'You don't think there's much hope for Agatha,' she said, a statement, not a question.

'Not now.' Bowler would never insult Joan by offering her less than the truth at times like this. 'But I can't let him get away with it. Can I?'

'No.' Joan leaned down, one hand on his shoulder, and kissed him hard.

Matt watched her ride on. 'You're a lucky bastard, Bowler.'

'Tell me something I don't know. Bugger, now I've got to go back after all, to get my rifle.'

58

Matt borrowed Spog's rifle.

They got more petrol from one of Spog's forty-four gallon drums. Spog cut them thick wedges of bread and mousetrap cheese. Matt lifted a three-o-three rifle from a rack on the wall, lobbed it on the back seat beside Bowler's, then showed him a way in to the Government Reserve by backtracks and farm tracks, faint and rarely used, behind Ralph Wilson's home paddocks. Here and there Isma's galloping hoof-prints showed clearly in the damp earth.

As they threaded through paddocks, along fences, through wire gates and along overgrown tracks, Bowler said, 'It's lucky you know the way. I'd be lost by now.'

'This is all Uncle country.' Matt waved a hand. 'Bruce's that way, we're on Ralph's here, Harry's joins over there. Spog and Mott have scrub blocks that join Harry's western boundary. I've ridden over most of it at some time or another, with Doug or some other cousin.'

'Our man wouldn't have come this way, would he?'

'No, there's a track in from the main road north of Kularook, but it's a lot longer. That way he'd miss all the houses, nobody would hear him. And there's another track from the reserve out the other way, towards Pedlers', he could drive out that way if he wanted to. It's part of the old Gold Escort route.'

'He might be gone already.'

They fell silent. They both knew the murderer had taken Agatha and her child for one purpose only: to get rid of them permanently, and hide them where they'd never be found. He'd abducted them because he intended their disappearance to look natural, otherwise he might as well have shot them in their beds. But once he'd got them there was no reason for delay.

If he'd taken them before train time he'd had over nine hours to silence them. Bowler's guts twisted. He was conscious of how badly he had failed the girl he'd come to like and admire, and the friendly little child who had trusted him.

What was Matt thinking? Probably the same, to judge by his set expression.

Bowler said, 'I wish I could offer you a glimmer of hope, mate, but it's been too long. He's had more than enough time.' He couldn't be more specific, though he wasn't usually mealy mouthed. But in the face of Matt's heroic self-control he couldn't bluntly state the obvious. Whoever had abducted her had a rifle which, although only a twenty-two, a bloody pop-gun, was enough.

'If you're trying to warn me to face facts, I am facing them. Trying to,' Matt emended. 'Trying to believe she's probably dead.' He shuddered.

A mile into the scrub after they left the cleared paddocks they came to the Government Reserve, an open area fifty yards across ringed in thickets of old mallees, a few small gums, and dense melaleuca brush. A neatly built circular parapet of local stone, green with moss and ferns, topped the shaft of the old well; a single strip of rusted iron jutted from it, all that remained of the windlass frame; the ground around it looked soggy under a thick mat of coarse grasses.

A modern windmill had been erected over a bore nearby and beside it a long galvanised iron sheep trough ran out from a tank streaked orange with rust. To judge from the overgrown nature of the sheep-paths no stock had used the trough for many months.

It was a silent, gloomy place under the overcast sky. It smelled damp, of mud and stale water and rusting iron.

They found the disturbed patch of earth in the derelict stockyards in the place Joan had described. It was half hidden under a fallen branch, which had been dragged across in an attempt to hide it. There were signs where an animal had dug, and more disturbance where Joan had pulled a couple of garments from the dirt.

Whoever he was, the murderer had been unlucky with that nosy fox after the care he'd taken to conceal his digging. He'd cut the matted grass into squares of turf, and carefully fitted them back again; he'd arranged the fallen branch naturally.

Matt's jaw hardened at the sight of a tan blouse and a small blue knitted cardigan. Giving vent to a prolonged outburst of violent profanity he walked away towards a tree, where he stood, his back turned, resting his forehead and his raised fist against the trunk.

Bowler finished uncovering the clothing in the hole and found at the bottom a cheap cardboard suitcase, smashed flat. He sat back on his heels and thought about what he could see. The murderer had come prepared — the digging had been done efficiently, with a spade — so they were right, he had intended burying more than a bit of luggage. Carefully, scrutinising even the smallest rabbit scratching, Bowler scouted the whole clearing in a search for any other patches of recently disturbed earth. He found none. By the time he'd finished, Matt had joined him again.

Bowler said, 'Come on, mate. His car tracks go this way.' Like an automaton the young man followed him.

Once they were through the thick melaleucas the car tracks became confused; they turned on themselves, and went back; they seemed to run in circles. Although they searched all likely hiding places they couldn't find the car, which didn't surprise Bowler — the murderer would be long gone — but he did need to find more tracks. Otherwise they wouldn't know where to look for further digging.

'Which way did he go? Can you see?' Matt asked.

'No, the tracks are all mixed up.' Bowler stood frowning, then pointed with his shoe. 'That one looks more like a motor-bike than anything. But he couldn't carry them on a motorbike.'

'Perhaps he scouted the place on a motorbike.'

'I checked all the motorbike owners. They're out.'

'Someone who could borrow a motorbike, then.'

Bowler sighed. 'This goes on and on. I'm buggered if I know what I think.' He gazed around at the dark scrub which ran unbroken to meet the bowl of the leaden sky in every direction. 'I don't know why he moved on. But the shot Joan heard was further from the well than this. She would have known if it was so close. That snooty mob she belonged to in the Old Dart were always shooting something — it's one of the reasons she fell out with them — but it means she does know what gunfire sounds like.'

Matt, his eyes on the ground, his face expressing no emotions whatsoever, shrugged.

Bowler glanced at his set face and kept his next thought to himself. He kicked with his heel at the hard grey earth, woven through and through with roots from the dense low bushes — this was hard ground for digging. So why had the bastard moved on, out of the clearing?

He laid his hand on Matt's shoulder. 'I'm sorry, mate, but now I start looking for a grave. Do you want to wait in the car? I could be hours.' He waved widely. 'It could be any bloody where.'

'No, I'll help.'

'Just on the remote chance he's still somewhere about, bring your gun.' Bowler reached into the back seat of his car for his rifle. Even twelve years on, the Lee-Enfield felt as familiar in his hand as an extension of his own arm after his years of living and sleeping with one, cleaning it and oiling it and firing it and then relying on it for his life. He slung the familiar weight on his back and dumped a couple of clips of bullets into his coat pocket.

He'd seen enough of the way Matt handled his rifle to be reassured that the young man was competent with firearms. But nobody knew the rules as well as an old soldier. He added, 'But we keep in sight of each other at all times.'

Matt bared his teeth in a sardonic grin. 'If any one shoots you, it won't be me.'

'Better not be,' Bowler growled. He moved slowly and systematically through the scrub, scanning the closer areas carefully before moving further out. Matt followed a parallel path. Together they searched the mallee clumps, scouted from the low, scrub-covered dunes, poked about round a couple of big rabbit warrens.

The sun was sinking towards a ruff of darker clouds above the western horizon. They climbed a small hill, and from that slight elevation began a detailed scrutiny of the bush, of the dark, everlasting scrub, for signs of recent interference.

Then several hundred yards away they saw crows circling, and a wedge-tailed eagle sinking down from its high airborne vigil.

Bowler's heart sank with the eagle, to a terrible, gut-wrenching despair. But he managed to grab Matt. 'Careful. We don't know for sure that he's gone.'

They trod quietly through a stand of wattles, and looked between the leaves. The birds were busy on a fresh carcase. A brownish carcase, a carcase covered in fur. The crows were attacking a dead kangaroo.

Bowler straightened, and swore. Matt, pale as death, was hanging his head and breathing hard, as though he'd been running.

In his normal voice Bowler said, 'That's a recent kill.' The animal had been shot in the chest and had bled to death.

'He's run mad, then. He's shooting anything that moves.'

'But what if that was the shot Joan heard?' Bowler walked over, scattering the crows into the air. 'A bit odd, wouldn't it be?' The crows settled into the tops of mallees nearby, prepared to wait.

'You tell me,' Matt said.

Bowler was assessing the place the roo had fallen, the angle of the shot, the direction from which the rifleman had fired. 'It was a bloody sight later than I would have expected him to be still hanging around, and why the hell would he open fire on a roo?' He walked round to view the carcase from the other side. 'What if —'

There was a crack, and a bullet sang between them.

'Christ!' They dropped flat and wriggled apart, unslinging their rifles.

'Don't think much of his shooting,' Matt said. 'Where did it come from?'

'That hill, I think. Bloody hell, he is still around. You keep in cover. I'm going after him.'

'I'm coming too.'

'Mind you, I think that shot was only meant to frighten us, to make us keep our distance.' Bowler saw a flurry of movement in bushes on the skyline; he snapped off a shot at what he thought was the shoulder of a fast-moving figure. 'That should frighten *him*.' The report of the heavy rifle sent the crows streaking away into the distance, cawing madly. He said, 'I couldn't see him clearly, mainly the bushes moving, so I don't think I hit him, but that should keep him quiet. Now he knows we can shoot him a long time before he can get close enough to shoot us with his piddling little twenty-two.'

Unless, of course, the man was hardy enough to stick around and lay an ambush. Rifles at the ready, they dodged from mallee to mallee, from banksia clump to banksia clump, towards the small dune.

Bowler pushed between two fat barrel-shaped banksias, cursing as their serrated leaves scratched his hands. In the middle of the clump he saw a patch of bare sand before the burrows of a rabbit warren and to one side, almost hidden under low branches, he saw —

'Matt!' he roared. 'Matt! Here!'

He dropped to his knees and lifted Agatha from a deep sandy scrape where she had been huddling, curled around Cordelia.

She tried to smile at him, but her mouth trembled. Her eyes were huge, her pale face bruised with exhaustion.

'Agatha! Hell, we — Oh, Agatha!'

59

Bowler knelt on the sandy earth and hugged Agatha fiercely. She was damp, excruciatingly stiff, and shivering with cold. She put her arms round his neck, weeping silently against his coat.

Matt burst through the bushes and snatched her into his own arms, lifting her against him and holding her so tightly she could hardly breathe. Bowler patted her shoulder, rather as though she was a dog that had done something clever.

Agatha had been watching the sun moving imperceptibly down the sky and wondering when it would be dark enough to move. It seemed as though she had lain for a lifetime in the hollow she had dug under the banksias, cuddled round her baby to keep her sheltered from the cold wind. Her clothes were still wet from the overnight storm; she was exhausted from tension and lack of sleep. She had been braced for unwilling action, for danger and critical decisions, as soon as the sun went down. And now, abruptly, the nightmare was over. These two tall, competent men looked capable of banishing any number of nightmares.

'My two favourite fellers,' Agatha said unsteadily. She had never felt anything so reassuring as the solid strength of Snow's arms around her. She realised he was muttering something, but it wasn't endearments. So softly she wasn't meant to hear he was swearing, breathing terrible, heartfelt oaths into her tangled mess of hair.

Bowler bent for Cordelia. 'There you are, Tuppence. Am I glad to see you.' Whimpering softly, the child snuggled into his neck.

'Who is he?' he demanded, pulling his coat around to shelter the child and turning on Agatha. 'Who is this bastard who's been shooting at you?'

Agatha raised her face from Matt's shoulder. 'I don't know, I couldn't tell.' Her voice was gruff from weariness. 'Like a stranger, muffled up, I couldn't see his face. And he whispered, a sort of hissing. He could have been anyone.'

'A big man?' Bowler asked, thinking Dick was pretty hefty.

'No, smallish I think. Hard to tell in the dark. He had a knife, you see, and he had Cordelia.'

'How did you get away?'

'He made me drive so he could hold her and keep the knife threatening her. So when we got here I turned off the lights and swung the wheel so the car swerved and he lost his balance, fell against the door, and I could grab her as I jumped out. Before he could recover his balance or put the lights on again.'

Bowler nodded. 'Good girl. How did —? No, it doesn't matter, you can tell us all the rest of it later. Can you walk, do you think? It's going to rain in a minute, and we must get you back to the car.' He smiled down on Cordelia and tickled her cheek with one finger until she smiled back. He made a strangled sound in his throat and gave her into her mother's hands.

Matt could take Agatha back; he'd have to keep on after the gunman. The sun was low, and the light would begin to fade once the sun had set. He'd have to start at once, or he would have no hope of seeing the bastard before dark.

'Matt, take my car and get these two back to food and shelter. Tell Joan what I'm doing, but tell her my fire-power is twice the other bloke's, and I'll get him before he can get me. Now I'd better check that hill.'

Matt said, 'How will you get home?'

Briefly, Bowler thought about that. 'I don't know. And I'm wasting time, I've got to get after him now. It's not worth your while coming back for me, I could be any bloody where in an hour or so. If I do chase him north, which is the nearest house? Who is closest?'

'Bruce is about four miles that way.' Matt waved vaguely to the northeast. 'Once you get to his cleared paddocks any track will take you to the house. Benson's boundary is a couple of miles or so north west of here, the house more than a mile beyond that.'

Looked like he was in for a bit of a walk whichever way he went. 'All right, I'll walk out.'

Thank heaven he'd dumped his handcuffs in his pocket along with his ammunition. If he did have to walk out with a prisoner at least he wouldn't be at risk of losing him. He glanced at Agatha, pale, exhausted, standing only with the support of Matt's arm around her; at Cordelia, drooping half asleep against his other shoulder.

'Look, don't muck about, get those two home. Tell Joan she'll see me in the morning.'

'All right,' Matt said. 'See you then.'

Bowler banged him on the back, took up his rifle, and set off at a fast pace.

He remembered something. He hadn't wanted to tell Matt this while the young man was trying to come to terms with the probability of Agatha's death, but now everything was changed. Bowler stopped; turned.

'Hey, Matt!' he called. 'Something you might like to know. She's broken off with Aubrey.' Bowler strode on.

Agatha said, 'I was going to tell you.' She'd had long frightened hours to wish she had been more open with Snow.

'Later,' he said. 'Now we have to get you home.' He set Cordelia on her feet, stripped off Agatha's wet coat to substitute his dry one, and saw the right sleeve of her woollen jumper was dark with dried blood. 'Jesus Christ! What happened?'

Carefully he started to turn back the sleeve, but stopped when she yelped.

'It's stuck, Snow, leave it, it's not bleeding now. He slashed me as a warning of what he'd do to Cordelia if I made a sound or didn't do what he asked.' The terror came flooding back and she shuddered so violently she nearly fell. His arms came round her again. She wasn't alone any more.

'Do you want me to carry you? Here, lean on me.' Then he lifted Cordelia again and wound his free arm round Agatha's waist. She leaned against him, smelling his sweat-stained shirt, his grubby skin. He smelled delicious, male and normal and unthreatening. She remembered dimly she'd been angry with him, but couldn't remember why. How could she have possibly been angry with Snow, who had come looking for her when she needed help most?

60

When Joan had been unable to find Macrea she had left a message for him with Em and gone home to shut herself up in her dark room, the small cubby Bowler had sealed off for her in a corner of the garage, for most of the day. She developed her last film, printed it, and made enlargements of the photographs she liked. While she was working it was easier to forget that Bill had driven off again to confront an armed man.

She had trained herself to hide her fears from her children. They came home from school quarrelling noisily as usual and she told them only that their father had gone out looking for Agatha, who was lost somewhere. She would elaborate on that story only when she had to.

They weren't interested in details anyway, being far too wrapped up in their own concerns to bother themselves with grown-ups' business. Joan gave them each a slice of bread and jam to keep them going until dinnertime and turned them out of doors. Their quarrels were mainly for adult consumption anyway. They went off amicably side by side in search of their friends.

Joan stirred up the fire in the kitchen stove, loaded in more wood, and set the kettle on to boil. She stood in the middle of the kitchen, teapot in hand, and had an image of herself as though at the stake, her fears licking up like flames to torment her.

These terrors were the price she paid to the jealous gods for the gifts she had been given. During the war she had accepted them in that spirit: if the gods had contrived an improbable meeting between a farm boy from the back-blocks of South Australia and a gently-nurtured girl from an aristocratic English family half a world away, she owed them a debt. Joan, half pagan, paid without complaint, in case one day they would demand more payment from her and take Bill. Once the war ended she'd imagined the debt was squared. Now she knew better.

She put the teapot on the hob and shook her head. Matt Franklin was with him. Matt would have returned by now if anything had happened to Bill. Her reason accepted this reassurance yet the tight band round her heart didn't loosen.

A knock at the front door startled her. But it wasn't news, not news of any kind, only a big middle-aged man. 'Mrs Brown? I'm Ron Macrea. You wanted to see me?' He sounded impatient, as though he didn't have time to run after females.

She invited him in. Seeing that she was making tea he consented to sit down in the kitchen and share it, but his manner was awkward and abrupt, as though she was forcing hospitality on him against his will. He munched coffee biscuits while she explained where her husband was and why.

Macrea's displeasure became steadily more and more obvious as she gave him her husband's message, and Joan's manner became steadily more and more formal. Even in this poky country kitchen feeding her guest biscuits directly from the brown paper bag she could sound like a duchess if she was angry. She wasn't going to explain or excuse Bill to this lump. Finally he thanked her grudgingly for the tea and excused himself, saying he had work to do. She heard him go into the office at the front of the house.

Soon after the children came home for their dinner someone banged on the back door, called, 'Anyone home?' and walked in.

Joan, muttering over a Kookaburra cookery book in the kitchen, looked up to see Matt Franklin grinning in the doorway. Her eyes widened, reading his expression.

'Matt! She's safe!'

Laughing, shaking his head in disbelief, he said, 'And so's our Cordelia.' In two strides he was enfolding her in an enormous bear-hug. 'Can you come over to the pub? They want to see you, but they're a bit worn out and Em's fussing over them.'

'Of course I can. Matt, Matt, I can hardly believe it. Is Bill there too?'

Matt stood back and grabbed her hands. 'Joan, do you want any dragons slain? Castles built? Moons to play with? I'm your man, any time. If it wasn't for you we'd never have found her. I am forever in your debt.'

'It's reward enough that you did find her.'

'And we could have been too late. The man was still hunting her when we got out there.'

'Did you catch him?'

'No. Bowler's gone after him.' Joan's hands jerked; Matt gripped more tightly. 'But he knows what he's doing, Joan, he's all right.'

She studied his face. 'I see. And who is this man he is hunting?'

'We still don't know. Agatha didn't recognise him. He kept his face hidden in a scarf, spoke in whispers, things like that. You go on over, she can tell you all about it. But I saw Macrea in the station as I came in and I'd better pass on a message from Bowler.'

She started tearing off her apron. 'He's not very pleased with Bill just now. Not that Bill will care.'

When Matt Franklin walked into the office and recounted recent events, Macrea realised that, with Mrs Benson found and Brown in hot pursuit of the criminal, he couldn't give the young man the hard time he'd been promising himself. Now he had no need to question him, so he would have no opportunity to give the independent young bugger the right royal dressing down he was asking for, to teach him the dangers of ignoring police instructions.

Thwarted, he leaned back in the chair behind Bowler's desk and regarded the young man on the other side of counter. He said formally, 'You've had a busy day. Successful, too, to find Mrs Benson. Her abductor was our murderer, I suppose.'

Matt shrugged. 'Not much doubt. But Bowler said I'd better tell you what's happened, and he'll fill any gaps when he gets back.'

Kind of him, thought Macrea. Certainly Mounted Constable Brown would furnish him with details of the case; he had no option. He said, 'Who is this man? I assume Mrs Benson could tell you enough to identify him.'

'That's the problem. She couldn't. She didn't recognise him because he was heavily muffled up and he disguised his voice. Spoke in a hissing whisper, she said, even when they were well out of town. He had on overalls so she couldn't recognise his clothes. All she can say is that he was small, not a big bloke anyway, and that he smelled of mothballs. And he wore gloves.'

Matt explained the details of the abduction as Agatha had told the story to him while they were driving back to Kularook. How she had been woken by a torch in her eyes and seen a gloved hand holding a knife to her daughter's throat; seen her daughter, her baby, terrified and struggling, her eyes beseeching over the other hand that gagged her mouth. And when Agatha had hesitated, trying to buy time while she thought of some way to escape, he had slashed her arm with his knife. A big knife that in her shocked vision had appeared large as a machete. Without question she had obeyed the man's instructions to get dressed, to pack up her case, and write a note. That had been her only hope, to write it as her captor dictated yet in such a way that her friends would know something was wrong.

'And we did, of course,' Matt said. 'That's what set us off looking for a break-in at the pub. Once we found that, we started the search.

You weren't here and we couldn't wait. The lucky break was when Joan galloped in to tell us where she'd seen Agatha's clothes buried.'

'So where is Brown now?'

Matt shrugged. 'God knows. Out in the scrub somewhere north of the Government Reserve well. You'd never find him now it's dark. In fact it would be bloody dangerous to try. He'd probably shoot you by mistake.'

Macrea relaxed back into his chair. Then he straightened again, and hoped that Franklin hadn't noticed his relief on hearing that he didn't have to drive out and stride round the landscape with a trigger-happy constable trying to re-live the World War.

He said, 'I'd better get a statement from Mrs Benson.'

'She's exhausted. Can't it wait until morning? I can tell you everything she told me.'

Macrea considered. These people already regarded him as a bloody-minded outsider; he'd only antagonise them further if he started harassing this woman they all felt protective about. So he nodded, picked up a pencil, and pulled a jotter in front of him.

'All right. There's nothing I can do about it until morning anyway, whenever Brown gets back. What about the car? Did she see anything about that to identify it?.'

'She didn't recognise it. Pretty old, she says, but not a T model, like Bensons', or a Dodge. Her father had one of those. But those are the only cars she knows well.'

Macrea said, 'If it's a local car, perhaps she can recognise it again.'

'She's not sure about that, because of the dark. He had it parked under the pines by the oval, so there were no houses anywhere close to hear it start up. And then she drove where he told her, for miles, with no chances to escape while he held Cordelia. But when this faceless bastard told her to stop the car, out there at the well, she flicked off the lights, spun the wheel, and then slammed on the brakes fast, so he was thrown against the door away from her when the car slewed. That gave her seconds to grab her baby and get away from him in the dark, before he could put the lights on again. He had his rifle too, because then he fired a few shots at random. In the dark she couldn't find the track out, and at dawn she saw him again and had to hide, so she crawled in under a clump of banksias, where nobody could see her unless they pushed in and nearly trod on her, as Bowler did.' Matt paused. The irony of that was that Bowler wouldn't have pushed in either, if he hadn't been keeping under cover from the marksman on the ridge. 'Anyway, she watched all day through the leaves and saw him somewhere around, with his rifle, whenever she thought she might move out of hiding. Until we got there, and he cleared out.'

Macrea drummed his fingers on the desk. 'Brown took you with him.'

'I showed him a short cut. And he said to tell you he couldn't see your car anywhere this morning when we left.'

'No, I drove out to see Benson.'

'He isn't home, he went to town yesterday.'

'I know that now. The large publican told me. Eventually. After I got back.'

'What did you want with Rupe?'

'That,' Macrea said, annoyed, 'is none of your business.' His drumming fingers changed rhythm, slowed to a stop. He pushed his chair back from the desk. 'So, all we can do now is wait for our gallant war hero to get in touch.'

Matt gave him a suspicious glance. 'That's it,' he said. 'For what it's worth, this character's got a twenty-two and he fired on us once. I'm glad it's not me trying to stalk him in the dark. And now I've got to go.'

61

The rain began before Bowler reached the crest of the low hill, a fine driving rain that chilled the wind and reduced visibility. He had no overcoat, only a jacket over a thin knitted jumper.

He hadn't worried about the other man's rifle until now, when he was looking down on the flats behind the hill. There wasn't much cover for a man walking, but if he was hiding, he could be anywhere. He'd only have to drop into the unbroken sea of scrub and he'd be invisible, like a swimmer ducking below the surface. And from such a hidden position he could be taking aim at that very moment. Bowler folded to a squat.

Frustration gripped him. His prey was close, somewhere out there, and he couldn't see him, couldn't drag him out of hiding to face the measured justice of the Law.

Darkness was coming on fast and, by the look of the clouds, more and heavier rain was approaching. What did he do now? Give up for the night, walk out to Bruce's and get someone to drive him home? Or stay camped unprotected in the wet scrub, in the hope that he could pick up his murderer again at first light? Darkness always favoured the hunted: he could keep moving towards some known destination, whereas the hunter could only flounder about in the dark, hoping to make contact by chance. He scrutinised the land in front of him, segment by segment, as thoroughly as if a Turkish patrol was in the area.

From a long way off the sound of his car starting up and driving away came fitfully on the wind. That was good. The knowledge that Agatha and Tuppence would soon be warm, and dry, and well fed, cheered him in his comfortless position. Matt would drive them safely, Joan and Em would welcome them.

His eyes were sore from straining into the dusk. He might as well give up. He screwed his eyes shut, to relieve the tension.

He opened them in time to see a dim figure stand up from the hip-high bushes two hundred yards away on his left front. The hunted also had heard the car leave and believed they had all gone. Bowler eased himself to his feet and thumbed off the safety catch on his rifle.

This was a stroke of gorgeous, lovely luck. He was going to get the bastard at last.

The figure appeared to be setting off back the way they had come, towards the reserve. Bowler moved cautiously to intercept it.

He couldn't identify the man, could see no revealing idiosyncrasies of shape or walk or carriage to show who he was. He seemed to be wearing a long overcoat that flapped almost to his heels. Bowler hurried, eager now to close with his quarry.

The wind was cold on his face, his ears were full of the rattle and sigh of bushes. A careful stride, another. He was gaining, he'd —

His foot hit an obstruction and he crashed down on top of a resting kangaroo.

He didn't fire his rifle accidentally, but that was the only bright spot in the debacle. Shocked awake, the roo kicked itself upright, catching him on the chest and half winding him, before it smashed through the mallees in a series of huge terrified leaps away from him. Bowler was left with the musky smell of its fur on his clothes and a fleeting glimpse of the man he hunted running for a stand of thick mallees.

He yelled, 'Stop! Police!' Violent words jolted through his brain like spits of electricity.

The man disappeared into the darkness. Probably he hadn't heard. Then came the snap of the twenty-two so perhaps he had. Bowler started wondering where the bullet had gone when he realised that the tug on his jacket hadn't been because it was caught on a twig. He fingered the hole, and swore aloud. That was closer than he liked. The gunman must have eyes like a cat.

Now what?

If he didn't grab him before dark he might as well give up. Not only would Bowler be unable to find the man, in the darkness the superior range of his rifle would be nullified since if he did accidentally stumble across his quarry he'd be well within range of that bloody twenty-two before he could see the bastard. Bowler decided he didn't feel suicidal, not that evening.

He'd have to wait for daylight before he searched further. So did he wait overnight here, in the wind and the drizzling showers, or did he walk to Bruce Wilson's for shelter?

Castigating himself for a fool — he was certain nothing was going to happen overnight except that the gunman would get miles away — he found a hollow more or less out of the wind, where a banksia kept some of the rain from him, and settled down to wait for dawn.

An hour and seven minutes by his pocket watch from the time he first settled into his not-so-cosy hollow the wind had dropped to a gentle but still cold breeze and the showers had cleared. He was wet, shivering with cold, damn nearly hungry enough to eat the leather sling on his rifle, and beset by memories of other wakeful nights he'd spent with only his rifle for comfort. Then, in the distance, he heard a car engine start up.

The sound came from roughly south, somewhere near the reserve where he had left his own car. But Matt had driven off in that; Bowler had heard him go. What car was this? It was leaving, so it wasn't Matt returning.

It must be the gunman getting away — the hunted, the murderer, the man with the twenty-two — in a car he had hidden before he went after Agatha. Now he was driving off again, and there was not a thing in the world Bowler could do to stop him.

He swore again. That settled that. If the man had gone, Bowler had not the slightest idea which direction he'd taken, and so he had no idea where he should resume his search once this interminable night was over.

He stood up and stretched. Well, it saved him the rest of the night in the open.

Wilsons' place was a fair step. Bensons' was closer, but a longer distance before he came to the cleared paddocks. Anyway, Bruce was a mate of sorts, he'd rather knock him up in the middle of the night if he had to. He picked his direction and set out, stumbling through the tussocky scrub.

It was slow going. The bushes were so wet from the showers that he might as well have been wading in water and, although clouds covered less than a quarter of the heavens, the star-shine wasn't bright enough to show more than the largest bushy obstacles.

He disturbed more roos. A pair and then a trio went thudding away from him through the scrub. A pair of mopokes called to each other in a stand of stringy-barks to the north.

He tramped along, one foot before the other. Where did he look now for his murderer? As he walked he turned over in his mind all his information on the crime, piece by piece. Over and over, as if by twisting and untwisting the strands in his memory, picking at the threads as though they were a tangle of yarn in his hands, he could make the knots unravel.

He reached the first of Bruce's sown pastures, climbed through a five-wire fence, and strode out along one of the farm tracks. And then, as though this easy movement also brought ease to his thinking, the knots did start to unravel.

He stopped in his tracks. He had remembered something Matt had said. He tested it against the other facts he knew, the other things he had been told. He wondered why, and if it wasn't for this, was it for that . . .

He examined his new find from every possible angle.

And when he'd finished Bowler knew who the murderer was. Had to be. He let out a yell of triumph and, despite his weary muscles, did a little war dance to celebrate. There wasn't even a sheep to see him.

The best of it was, now he knew exactly where he had to go to arrest the rotten bastard in the morning.

62

In a calm, overcast morning, just before sunrise, Bowler drove a borrowed car into Kularook. He had his rifle on the seat beside him and a prisoner in the back seat, handcuffed to a folded-down strut for the missing fabric hood.

A rooster crowed in Durwin's back yard and was answered competitively from four other chook yards around the town. In the trees surrounding the oval a wattle bird barked. Rabbits scuttled across the road, bolting away from the kids' vegetable patch in the school yard.

Bowler switched off the headlights. The long night was over.

He pulled up at the side of his house beside his own car, pleased to see that Matt had brought it back in one piece. He got out and stretched in the cold morning air. Then he unlocked the handcuffs and pushed his prisoner straight into the lockup. Paperwork could wait until he'd seen Joan. He knew she would be waiting, knew she found sleep difficult if he was out on a job at night.

Joan lay propped against the headboard of the bed, a lighted lamp on the bedside cupboard beside her, a book upside down on the quilt. Her shoulders were swathed in a woollen plaid; she had some family connection that entitled her to wear that tartan but she had never bothered to explain it to him.

When she saw him, she was transfigured. Her long, rather bony face had never looked more beautiful.

He bent and gathered her into a hard embrace. She gripped his ribs and kissed his throat, his ear, his cheek.

'Oh, Bill!' she said. 'Bill.'

He kissed her lips, but when that started getting out of hand he held her off. 'I can't come to bed yet. I've got a murderer in the lockup.'

'You've caught him! Tell me,' she said. So he did.

When he had finished she said, 'You must be feeling relieved now it's all over, Bill.'

'Yes I am.'

'You did well to work all that out.'

'I was lucky. Give Macrea his due, even though I'd given him my notes he didn't have all the information. I'd written down everything I thought was relevant but I hadn't bothered to write that one revealing detail. That had nothing to do with the case. So he didn't hear about it.' He leaned forward, tucked her plaid more firmly round her, and kissed her nose. 'Just because I don't like him doesn't mean he isn't a good detective.'

'You're a fair man, Bill.'

'I try to be.'

'And an arrogant sod. Don't tell me you're not pleased as punch with your clever self.'

He grinned. 'Of course I am.' He wasn't — he was aghast when he remembered how his mistakes had very nearly led to more deaths — but he would let Joan think he was. 'All the same, that's not why I do my job.'

'No,' she said. 'I know why you do your job.' She leaned and kissed his cheek.

'Now I'd better go and wake Macrea. I reckon he'll want to be part of it when I start asking this bastard questions.'

At the pub nobody was stirring except Durwin, lighting the kitchen stove, and Em, cutting rashers from a flitch of bacon on the table. Bowler nodded to them and went up the passage to knock on the detective's door.

When they stopped their interrogation for breakfast, the two policemen walked over to the pub, Macrea to the dining room, Bowler to the kitchen in search of Em. He wanted to check that Agatha and Cordelia had come through their ordeal unscathed.

He found Cordelia sitting in her high chair in the kitchen. She greeted him with cheerful chirrups and a beaming smile, happy to welcome another of her admirers come to entertain her. Sitting beside her, elbows on the table, Matt cradled a teacup in both hands.

Em turned from the sink. 'Bowler, what's going on? Can't you tell us?'

'You're early, Matt,' Bowler said. 'Couldn't you sleep?'

'Agatha can, she's still asleep, that's his problem. He's driving me nuts.' Em pulled out a chair and sat down. 'Come on, Bowler. Spill the beans.'

'I got him,' Bowler said.

Matt choked on his tea. 'You —? Who is the bastard?'

Bowler paused, strangely reluctant to play his trump card, his ace. He said, 'Turns out it was Figgy Higgins.'

Both his listeners appeared struck dumb with astonishment. Then Matt found his voice.

'Higgins?' he said incredulously. '*Higgins*? He's a fool, an ineffectual sort of coot. A bit smarmy, maybe, but harmless, surely. Are you sure?'

'Oh yes.'

'I wouldn't have thought he had the guts to shoot anyone.'

'I wouldn't have either, until I started putting things together.' Bowler was possessed by an icy rage, a deep, cold fury that this man whom he had so underrated had hoodwinked him for so long. Fury was easier than guilt to live with. Unfortunately, some fury was directed against himself.

Bowler himself had alerted Higgins to the fact that Agatha's evidence posed a threat to him. Bowler himself had explained that he had come to doubt the murder-suicide theory only after she had told him the order of the shots. He had pitied the man, so recently widowed and had taken him into his confidence. And the bastard had acted a part to perfection, feigning grief for his dead wife while all the time planning to eliminate the one witness who could upset the verdict of murder-suicide. Without her, the order of the shots was merely hearsay, the possible delusions of a semiconscious girl.

Higgins had played Bowler for a fool.

Em said, 'But why on earth would he want to shoot all those people? For what possible reason?'

'We don't know yet. Perhaps Lew had upset him. Anyway, make no mistake, we'll find out. In the meantime, don't spread this too widely.'

'But how do you know?' Matt asked. 'I mean, why are you sure it's Higgins?'

'I'll explain later, when we've finished with him. Incidentally, it's partly something you told me. Now I need my breakfast. I'll see you afterwards.'

63

Agatha was awake but still in bed when Matt leant in the doorway. She'd been aware for some time of the morning sounds all around her, of the clatter from the kitchen across the passage, of Trotter rolling casks about in the cellars, of the drone of the separator as Durwin turned the handle to take the cream from the morning's milking. She was waiting for Em, who had promised to find her something to wear, since every garment she owned was wet and most of them muddy from their time underground.

Matt said, 'I came round earlier but you were still sleeping. Do you feel better?'

'Marvellous, thanks.' She smiled, and stretched her arms luxuriously. She saw him looking at the bandage on her right forearm and said, 'Em cleaned it up. It's not too deep. I'll live.'

He shook his head, as though he couldn't bear to think about her past dangers. 'At least Cordelia seems none the worse for wear.'

'No, bright as a button.'

'She's holding court in the kitchen. Em hovers over her smirking like an idiot.' He smiled. 'Well, I did a bit of it myself. But I wanted to see you.'

'Yes.' She owed Snow several explanations. She patted the bed but instead he reversed the single chair and sat astride it, an elbow propped on the back, his chin on his fist.

He regarded her gravely. 'Couple of things I need to tell you.' He dragged his teeth across his bottom lip, began again. 'While I was out in the desert I realised that I had a bit of growing up to do. I saw that I had to back off, because whatever I feel about you doesn't give me any rights. I'm just a kid from your past that you had forgotten all about, someone who's been in Grade Two for the last umpteen years. So I decided when I got back I wouldn't push you. I would give you time.' He half smiled. 'Time to find out what a splendid fellow I've grown into, probably. But then Aubrey moved in on you, and if I'd thought you could possibly take him seriously I'd have said something then. Problem is, I'm never at my most rational when I'm around you.'

'Look, Snow, I —'

'For God's sake, leave Snow in Grade Two where he belongs,' he interrupted. 'I'm Matt.'

'So you are,' she said, surprised. She hadn't been seeing him as a skinny kid for a long time, but she hadn't before taken time to see clearly the mature and self-reliant man he undoubtedly was.

'Anyway, I was rude to you about Aubrey and I'm sorry. Particularly now it seems you had already broken off with him. What made you change your mind?'

'Dear Snow — I mean Matt — you did.'

'Me? But at that stage I hadn't said my persuasive little piece that made you so angry.'

'I know. But I was going to marry Aubrey for a number of reasons that seemed good to me at the time, but ever since you came back I've known every one of them was the wrong reason. I should never have let it go so far.'

She held out her hand, and this time he did get up and did sit on the bed.

Holding her hand, playing with her fingers, but not looking at her, he said, 'Although I have never asked you, does this mean that you would marry me? If I did?'

'You deserve better than me,' she said. 'But yes of course.'

He raised his eyes and stared into hers. Slowly a broad grin spread across his face.

'Crikey!' He shook his head in wonder. 'In that case I'd better get cracking. I haven't even begun to court you yet. Got a lot of catching up to do.' He leaned forward, one hand on each side of her head. 'It's been a long drought. Do you know I've never even kissed you?'

'Of course I know. What's been holding you?'

64

In the middle of the morning Bowler, true to his promise, returned to the pub and took Joan with him. He said he might as well make all the explanations at once.

Trotter left the empty bar to take care of itself and came to join them. They were seated round the table in the pub kitchen when Matt and Agatha emerged. She was wearing an enormous checked woollen dressing-gown of Trotter's that he'd lent her the night before; it wrapped round her twice. Matt was wearing a broad smile.

Bowler looked from one to the other. 'That's settled, then?'

'Not yet,' Matt said. 'I've had permission to pay my addresses, that's all. Give me time.' He tilted his head in calculation. 'Another half hour should do it.'

Agatha was beaming almost as broadly as he was. The others jumped up and crowded round, offering good wishes, shaking Matt's hand. Bowler was surprised to see Joan whisper in Agatha's ear and kiss her cheek: his Joan was not usually so demonstrative in public. And what *had* she said to make Agatha's ivory skin flush so vividly?

Matt said, 'I'm still not sure I believe it.' He gripped Bowler's hand. 'Yeah, I know how lucky I am, you don't have to tell me.'

Trotter watched benevolently but impatiently. 'That's good then. But come on, Bowler, I've got to get back to the bar. For heaven's sake tell us how you found the mongrel out.'

Bowler said, 'Well now.' He looked at the five of them — at Trotter and Em, Matt and Agatha, and his Joan — and said, 'I'm not supposed to tell you any of this, it's all police business. So don't let on to Macrea how much you know or he'll have my head. You all know by now it's Figgy Higgins we've got locked up over there?'

They all nodded. Agatha said, 'I find it very hard to believe. He was such a mild little man.'

Bowler smiled at her. 'He seemed like that to a lot of us.'

'And it was *Figgy* who threatened me and took me out there in the scrub? That man was so different, so cruel and frightening.'

'I think you were seeing the real Figgy. The one we'd all become used to was an act, it seems to me.'

'But the car. That wasn't the Ford, it was a different one. I'd have recognised the Ford.'

'It belongs to young Kenrick. He's living in the shearers' cottage on that place he inherited from his grandfather and he's gone up to town for a week or so and left the car behind, drove himself to the station in an old lorry he owns. Higgins drove the Ford there and swapped to the Fiat for the night so if anyone did wake up and see him driving around they couldn't possibly associate him with the car. At the same time he helped himself to Kenrick's twenty-two. Car and rifle will both be back in their places now.'

Matt said, 'Get on with it. Tell us how you knew it was him.'

'I'd better begin at the beginning. When I first started asking questions, after I began to think perhaps it wasn't murder-suicide, I tackled Rupe Benson and Higgins. I didn't have any suspicions of them — after all, they'd made a frantic dash in to save Agatha — I just had to get the formalities out of the way before I went any further. And they backed each other up; they said they had started work on the new fence the day of the killings. Rupe had started cutting posts and Higgins began digging the post-holes and, according to Rupe, when he went to pick him up he'd dug a surprising number of them. Figgy must have made sure he counted them, because there were so many he couldn't possibly have had any spare time to walk back to the house and shoot the victims. They both spoke of the blisters he'd raised. I had no reason to doubt them.'

Agatha said quickly, 'Rupe wasn't in it too?'

'No, Higgins just used him to back up his story. But they made it clear there were no holes dug before that day. Then a few days ago Matt mentioned that when he was riding the fence line he had to watch that his horse didn't step in the empty post-holes. I didn't take any notice, because I knew there were holes dug along the fence line. But finally the penny dropped: Matt was riding to his uncle's place just on dawn on the day of the murders, before Higgins was supposed to have started digging. They hadn't been there the day before, both he and Rupe were definite about that. They had to have been dug overnight.'

'I suppose I can vouch for that too,' Matt said. 'I'd ridden that way the afternoon before, after I'd had the run in with bloody Lew and the others, and there were none then. I should have realised there was something odd next morning, but you expect to see post-holes along a new fence line.' He glanced sideways at Agatha. 'And I had a lot of stuff on my mind just then.'

Bowler looked round at his attentive audience. 'So then I started wondering, just how they did get there overnight. This was last night, after I lost the gunman in the dark, and heard him drive away. I thought I'd never be able to find him then so I started walking to Bruce's, and that's when I finally made the connections. And after I'd puzzled over it a bit, and sorted out the times, I realised that the only reason a man would dig post-holes in the dark was to hide what he was up to next day. He'd raised blisters all right, but in the night. Higgins's alibi had whiskers on it.'

'How could he go out at night and nobody know?' Trotter asked. 'You'd think his wife would have missed him.'

'After I arrested him I searched his room. Her things were still in a dressing-table, and I found a bottle of sleeping pills. I'll bet he doped her to the eyeballs before he went digging in the dark.'

Agatha said, 'Vida used to complain of insomnia — I think she liked the rather grand sound of the word — and take a pill now and then. They usually made her scratchy and rather dopey next day.' They all watched her as she searched her memory. 'And yes, I think she was a bit woozy and bad-tempered that morning. I just thought she was extra fed up with me, after the row the night before.'

'He'll tell us in the end,' Bowler said. 'Anyway, however he did it, he had to dig enough holes to cover the time he would take to walk back to the house, shoot three people — he didn't know about Thelma until he got there — and walk back again. If he went through the scrub and not on the track Rupe wouldn't see him.'

'But why did he do it?' Matt demanded. 'What possible grudges could he have against those three? Four people, if you count Agatha. It was a bloody massacre.'

'And a massacre that hadn't been caused by any sudden rush of blood to the head, either, he'd very carefully planned that massacre. Anyway, now I knew how he'd done it although I still didn't know why he'd done it. I was floundering around in the dark heading for Bruce Wilson's at this point, so I about-turned, slogged across to Bensons', and woke Higgins up before daylight.' He smiled grimly, remembering the satisfaction he'd felt, lighting a candle, and then silently dragging a shocked and disbelieving Higgins from his bed and clipping on handcuffs while he told him he was under arrest. 'So I brought him in, in Rupe's car. Since then we've interviewed him. And it's a pretty unpleasant story. He only wanted to kill his wife.'

'Kill Vida!' Agatha exclaimed. 'He was fond of her, always dancing attention on her. In fact I thought he was rather sweet, the way he treated her with such old-fashioned courtesy.'

'All the same, he shot two innocent people so that he could get away with killing her. The rest of you were camouflage. If you hadn't survived, Agatha, nobody would ever have doubted that Lew had shot the lot of you. You were supposed to die with the others — if you had, he'd be walking around free now. But you told me the order of the shots, and I got suspicious.'

'What order of shots?' Trotter said. 'Nobody ever tells me anything.'

Bowler explained his reasons for believing that either there was a fifth shot, or the deaths were murder. He said to Agatha, 'You were right, the first shot killed Lew. Higgins had to get rid of him first but he had to shoot him from close range, to fake the suicide. So he clobbered him over the head to stun him before he shot him. That brought the women outside, and although he hadn't expected Thelma he didn't let that slow him down. He thought you were dead, incidentally, but he wasn't much fussed when Rupe rushed you in to Em, to save your life. He was pretty sure you hadn't seen enough to identify him. You hadn't, had you?'

Agatha shook her head.

'Once the police had accepted the murder-suicide scenario, Higgins thought he could relax. Then, after Agatha got back and I started sniffing around about a fifth bullet, he began to suspect I was getting too close to the truth, so he broke into my office one night — Rupe had dropped him off to catch the express at three am — and found an assessment I'd been writing, about all the information I had. This confirmed his worst fears, so he nicked it and hid it — and my fountain pen, by accident — just to slow me down a bit, while he hatched a plan to get rid of the one serious witness against him.'

'Yes, but why did he want to kill poor Vida?' Agatha shook her head. 'I know she was a pain, but she didn't deserve that death. None of them did.'

'I'm coming to that. It seems that Vida's second husband, a man called Alf Birch, had been an old friend of Higgins's. After Birch died, he chased her to the country and married her, believing they would then return to live in suburban Adelaide in the house Birch had left her, and swank around like kings on the pot of money he had also left her. So he married her expecting to lead a life of luxury in congenial surroundings, and instead he was stuck in a primitive house miles from anywhere, with a couple of large stepsons who disliked him, without any of his usual entertainments — he liked a flutter on the neddies and a few jars with the boys, he told us — and with a miserly wife who not only kept him extremely short of pocket money but also adamantly refused his pleas to return to the city. He thought he had a grievance.'

'You mean he shot us all because he wanted Vida's money?' Agatha sounded aghast. 'And I always thought her money was a myth.'

'Far from it. Your mother-in-law was quite a wealthy woman, and Higgins knew it. We think he'd been trying to work out a safe way to get rid of her for some time. But then he had a revelation when he read in the paper about a man in England or somewhere running amuck with a rifle and shooting four or five members of his family indiscriminately, because his wife had enraged him. Higgins did a bit of research, and found this wasn't an isolated case, it had happened before. So, with Lew's suspicions of Agatha sprouting up like weeds, he saw a way that he could shoot his wife and fasten the crime on Lew. He would inherit her house in town, and her money. He would have it made.'

'Who gets her money now? Surely he can't,' Em said.

'No, under the law he gets nothing now. I expect it will go to Rupe Benson and Thelma's kids. Incidentally, Agatha, Higgins says he's had a wire from Rupe in town, saying he's been to a lawyer and Lew did leave a will. Half the farm is yours.'

Distressed, Agatha said, 'I don't want it. He must have made the will when we were first married, and so much has happened — Morally, it should be Rupe's. Or Thelma's, perhaps.'

Matt took her hand. 'You can make him a present of it if you want to. You don't need it now. Anyway, there's plenty of time to sort it all out.'

Bowler said, 'He's due back on the train this afternoon. I have to see him, to give him back his car and get him to make a statement, but after that I'll send him over to you.'

'Thanks,' Matt said. 'I need a word with him too.'

'I'll need statements from you two as well, of course. And that will about wrap it up. Macrea has notified Adelaide and they're sending someone to take Higgins up to town tomorrow on the train seeing Macrea can't because he's driving.' Bowler wriggled his stiff shoulders. 'Higgins doesn't appear at all remorseful that two other innocent people, her son and her daughter, died with his wife. Or over his two attempts to kill Agatha. He's a very cold and calculating man. He planned to murder four people, for no better motive than greed. And when he found he hadn't quite succeeded, he was cold-blooded enough to include a baby among his intended victims next time. He was prepared to kill and go on killing, to save his own precious skin.'

'That's terrible,' Em said. 'What a horrifying man.'

'Don't slander the rest of us,' Matt said. 'I wouldn't call him a man.'

Suppressing a yawn, Bowler got up and stretched.

'He told you all this voluntarily?' Trotter sounded disbelieving.

'We persuaded him.' Bowler caught Matt's eye. 'We didn't lay a finger on him, dammit. In the end I think he was telling us to prove how clever he'd been in planning it so carefully.'

Cordelia had been engrossed with a stack of Nallyware beakers, putting one inside another and taking it out again. Now she became bored with them, and swiped the lot to the floor. None of her fans was waiting to entertain her; she yelled a protest, and then smiled happily on them when she was once more the centre of attention.

Matt stood up, snatched her up out of her high chair, and tossed her in the air. She squealed with pleasure.

He told her, 'You're getting a new Dad, did you know that?' He laughed, astounded and delighted. 'Crikey, me a Dad!'

He lowered her to sit on his shoulders astride his neck, steadying her by an ankle. She took a firm grip on his ears.

Bowler said, 'Well, I'd better get on with it. I have work to do even if you lot don't.'

The others pushed back their chairs as well. Em went to the stove, Trotter departed up the passage.

Matt said, 'Hang on, Bowler, before you go, I've got a message from Spog. He said to tell you that he's transferring the town oval to the Council and they should have the papers to sign by now. We fixed it all up when we were in town.'

'I wondered if that was why you went. It's very generous of him.'

'Just keep the footy boys off his back.'

'They'll behave like lambs after this. You'll see.'

'I won't be around,' Matt said. 'Spog's offered me a job managing a station he owns up north.' He turned his head and smiled down on Agatha, who was once more safe within his arm snuggled against his side. 'We'll be moving north as soon as we're married.'

'I'll miss you all,' she said. 'But this will be a new start for us both.'

Cordelia leaned from her lofty perch and clenched starfish fingers in her mother's hair.

'For all three of us,' Matt corrected. 'Let go, you little pest.'

Bowler had work to do. He left them to it.

ABOUT THE AUTHOR

Alison Manthorpe grew up on a farm with horses. School was correspondence lessons on the end of the kitchen table. She worked as a physiotherapist in Australia and in London, and returned to marry a master mariner, raise a family, and accompany him to sea in yachts. She is also a published poet.

COMING SOON

By

A M Manthorpe

RID OF A PEST

A KULAROOK MYSTERY

Turn the page for a
SNEAK PEAK

1

4.30 pm Saturday 5 September 1931

In the cupboard-sized office of the Kularook Hotel Em Musgrave, frowning over a column of figures in her ledger, heard the rumble of a powerful car engine outside in the street. A second later came a feminine scream, a loud crash, and the screech of metal clawing metal. She slapped shut her ledger. That sounded as though Silas Beadnall had arrived.

After a moment she heard his voice, one of two strong men's voices swearing antiphonally. She didn't recognise the other voice: who had he run into this time? Her curiosity wasn't strong enough to take her outside. She grabbed a couple of room keys from the pigeonholes behind her, lifted the hinged end of the desk, and went into the bar to tell her husband Trotter they were now on the final run-up to Silas's dinner party and he'd better bring in the luggage.

Silas had arranged the dinner by telephone from Adelaide a fortnight before. 'Oysters and lobsters and chickens, things like that, Em. Nothing but the best. And a birthday cake, I'd better have a cake. But don't stick candles on it, I don't want sixty-six damn candles dripping grease everywhere.'

'Yes Silas.' Em hooked her scratch pad from under a drift of bills and scrawled a few notes. 'How many guests?'

'Ten. A slap-up dinner for ten. And get Trotter to order in some decent champagne. We're celebrating more than my birthday.' He added hastily, 'You don't have to tell the boys that, Em. I want to surprise them.'

'I won't say a word.' Ten of them? His two sons and their wives, his unmarried daughter — who else? 'But champagne? What about my policeman friend across the road? He'll do us for trading after hours.'

'I'll take care of a licence.'

'Good. We can manage everything else. What do you want for pudding, Silas? I could make you fruit salad and ice cream, or a trifle, or rum babas. What? Apple pie? Bavarian cream? Plum pudding?'

'Slow down, dammit. Make it a trifle. My grandmother used to make one so full of sherry that all of us small fry got tipsy every Christmas. Make me one like that.'

'All right.'

'And send the bill to Horry; he's paying for this.'

'Does he know that, Silas?'

'Well, not Horry, the farm accounts. It's all right, Em, you'll get your money.'

'Horry is crying poor.'

'Horry is always crying poor. He grudges his poor old dad every penny he has to fork out. But after all, whose farm is it? I could kick the lot of them off tomorrow if I wanted to. And they'd better not forget it. Oh and Em, I need to book a couple of rooms too — we'll be staying with you, not out on the farm. Two rooms.'

'Yes, Silas,' Em said. Though he'd probably only use one, the lecherous old goat: he must be bringing whichever young woman was the current recipient of his volatile affections. And if he was arranging the party for her, she must be something special. Silas didn't usually return to the scenes of his youth to celebrate his birthdays.

Em pencilled two rooms into the guest book and turned to a fresh page of her pad, to begin making lists.

www.ingramcontent.com/pod-product-compliance
Lightning Source LLC
Chambersburg PA
CBHW070530010526
44118CB00012B/1094